How to
Master Skills for the

Second Edition

TOEFL® iBT

LISTENING   Basic

DARAKWON

How to
Master Skills for the

Second Edition

TOEFL® iBT

LISTENING Basic

Publisher Kyudo Chung
Editor Sangik Cho
Authors Monika N. Kushwaha, Jasmine C. Swaney, Christine F. Houck, E2K
Proofreader Michael A. Putlack
Designers Minji Kim, Yeji Kim

First Published in January 2007 By Darakwon, Inc.
Second edition first published in November 2024 by Darakwon, Inc.
Darakwon Bldg., 211, Munbal-ro, Paju-si, Gyeonggi-do 10881
Republic of Korea
Tel: 02-736-2031 (Ext. 250)
Fax: 02-732-2037

ISBN 978-89-277-8086-1 14740
978-89-277-8084-7 14740 (set)

www.darakwon.co.kr

Photo Credits
Shutterstock.com

Components Main Book / Answer Key / Free MP3 Downloads
7 6 5 4 3 2 1   24 25 26 27 28

Table of
Contents

INTRODUCTION

1 Information on the TOEFL® iBT

A The Format of the TOEFL® iBT

Section	Number of Questions or Tasks	Timing	Score

Reading	**20 Questions**
	
	• **2 reading passages**
	  – with 10 questions per passage
	  – approximately 700 words long each
		35 Minutes	30 Points

Listening	**28 Questions**
	
	• **2 conversations**
	  – 5 questions per conversation
	  – 3 minutes each
	
	• **3 lectures**
	  – 6 questions per lecture
	  – 3-5 minutes each
		36 Minutes	30 Points

Speaking	**4 Tasks**
	
	• **1 independent speaking task**
	  – 1 personal choice/opinion/experience
	  – preparation: 15 sec. / response: 45 sec.
	
	• **2 integrated speaking tasks: Read-Listen-Speak**
	  – 1 campus situation topic
	    reading: 75-100 words (45 sec.)
	    conversation: 150-180 words (60-80 sec.)
	  – 1 academic course topic
	    reading: 75-100 words (50 sec.)
	    lecture: 150-220 words (60-120 sec.)
	  – preparation: 30 sec. / response: 60 sec.
	
	• **1 integrated speaking task: Listen-Speak**
	  – 1 academic course topic
	    lecture: 230-280 words (90-120 sec.)
	  – preparation: 20 sec. / response: 60 sec.
		17 Minutes	30 Points

Writing	**2 Tasks**
	
	• **1 integrated writing task: Read-Listen-Write**
	  – reading: 230-300 words (3 min.)
	  – lecture: 230-300 words (2 min.)
	  – a summary of 150-225 words (20 min.)
	
	• **1 academic discussion task**
	  – a minimum 100-word essay (10 min.)
		30 Minutes	30 Points

B What Is New about the TOEFL® iBT?

- The TOEFL® iBT is delivered through the Internet in secure test centers around the world at the same time.

- It tests all four language skills and is taken in the order of Reading, Listening, Speaking, and Writing.

- The test is about 2 hours long, and all of the four test sections will be completed in one day.

- Note taking is allowed throughout the entire test, including the Reading section. At the end of the test, all notes are collected and destroyed at the test center.

- In the Listening section, one lecture may be spoken with a British or Australian accent.

- There are integrated tasks requiring test takers to combine more than one language skill in the Speaking and Writing sections.

- In the Speaking section, test takers wear headphones and speak into a microphone when they respond. The responses are recorded and transmitted to ETS's Online Scoring Network.

- In the Writing section, test takers must type their responses. Handwriting is not possible.

- Test scores will be reported online. Test takers can see their scores online 4-8 business days after the test and can also receive a copy of their score report by mail.

2 Information on the Listening Section

The Listening section of the TOEFL® iBT measures test takers' ability to understand spoken English in English-speaking colleges and universities. This section has 2 conversations that are 12-25 exchanges (about 3 minutes) long and 3 lectures that are 500-800 words (3-5 minutes) long. Each conversation is followed by 5 questions and each lecture by 6 questions. Therefore, test takers have to answer 28 questions in total. The time allotted to the Listening section is 36 minutes, including the time spent listening to the conversations and lectures and answering the questions.

A Types of Listening Conversations and Lectures

- Conversations
  - Between a student and a professor or a teaching assistant during office hours
  - Between a student with a person related to school services such as a librarian, a housing director, or a bookstore employee

- Lectures
  - Monologue lectures delivered by a professor unilaterally
  - Interactive lectures with one or two students asking questions or making comments
    cf. One lecture may be spoken with a British or Australian accent.

B Types of Listening Questions

- Basic Comprehension Questions
  - Listening for Main Ideas Question: This type of question asks you to identify the overall topic or main

idea of a lecture or conversation.

– Listening for Main Purpose Question: This type of question asks you why the speakers are having a conversation or why a lecture is given.

– Listening for Major Details Question: This type of question asks you to understand specific details or facts from a conversation or lecture.

- Pragmatic Understanding Questions

  – Understanding the Function of What Is Said Question: This type of question asks you why a speaker mentions some point in the conversation or lecture. It may involve replaying part of the listening passage.

  – Understanding the Speaker's Attitude Question: This type of question asks you what a speaker's feelings, opinions, or degree of certainty is about some issue, idea, or person. It may involve replaying part of the listening passage.

- Connecting Information Questions

  – Understanding Organization Question: This type of question asks you how the listening passage is organized or how two portions of the listening passage are related to each other.

  – Connecting Content Question: This type of question asks you to classify or sequence information in a different way from the way it was presented in the listening passage.

  – Making Inferences Question: This type of question asks you to draw a conclusion based on information given in the listening passage.

C Question Formats

- There are four question formats in the Listening section: traditional multiple-choice questions with four answer choices and one correct answer, multiple-choice questions with more than one answer, questions that ask test takers to make the order of events or steps in a process, and questions that ask test takers to match objects or text to categories in a chart.

HOW TO USE THIS BOOK

How to Master Skills for the TOEFL® iBT Listening Basic is designed to be used either as a textbook for a TOEFL® iBT listening preparation course or as a tool for individual learners who are preparing for the TOEFL® test on their own. With a total of eight units, this book is organized to prepare you for the test with a comprehensive understanding of the test and thorough analysis of every question type. Each unit consists of seven parts and provides a step-by-step program that provides question-solving strategies and the development of test-taking abilities. At the back of the book is one actual test of the Listening section of the TOEFL® iBT.

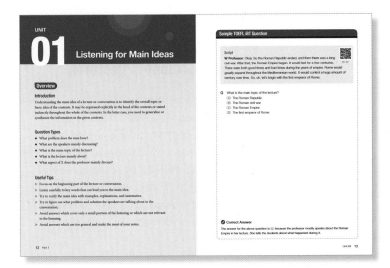

❶ Overview

This part is designed to prepare you for the type of question the unit covers. You will be given a full description of the question type and its application in the passage. You will also be given some useful tips as well as an illustrated introduction and a sample.

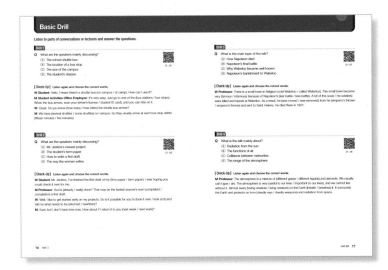

❷ Basic Drill

The purpose of this section is to ensure that you understand the new types of questions that were described in the overview. You will be given a chance to confirm your understanding in brief scripts before starting on the practice exercises. You will listen to some simple conversations or lectures and answer questions of a particular type. This part will help you learn how to deal with each type of question on the Listening section of the TOEFL® iBT.

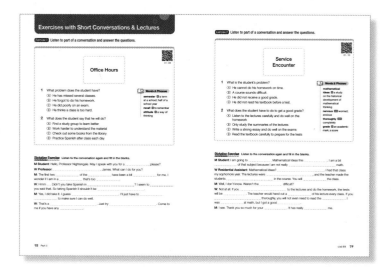

❸ Exercises with Short Conversations & Lectures

This part is the first of the practice exercises in each unit. It is a halfway step before practicing with the mid-length lectures and conversations. A graphic organizer will help you understand the material, and definitions of difficult words are also given to help you solve the questions. You first solve the questions and then fill in the blanks of after listening a second time.

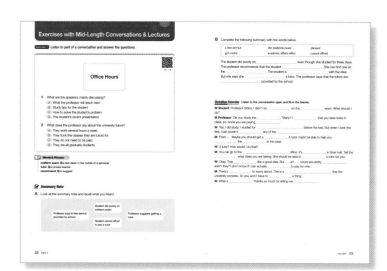

❹ Exercises with Mid-Length Conversations & Lectures

This part is the second of the practice exercises in each unit. As in the previous section, a graphic organizer is offered, and important words are listed to help increase your understanding. You first solve the questions and then fill in the blanks after listening a second time. You can also make sure that you understand everything by using the summary below.

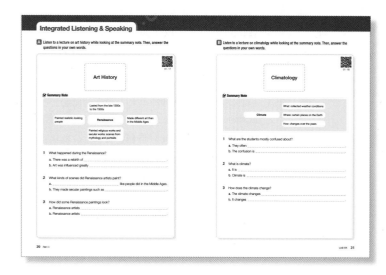

❺ Integrated Listening & Speaking

The TOEFL® iBT is different from previous tests in that it is more integrated than ever. So in this part, you are given the chance to experience the iBT style study by linking your listening skills with your speaking skills. Listen to the different versions of the previous lectures and answer the questions. But remember that this time, you have to say the answers. There is no writing.

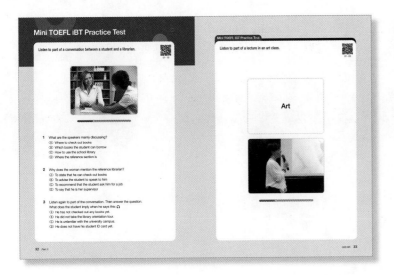

❻ Mini TOEFL iBT Practice Test

This part will give you a chance to experience an actual TOEFL® iBT test. You will be given a conversation with five questions and a lecture with six questions. The topics are similar to those on the actual test, as are the questions.

❼ Vocabulary Check-Up

This part offers you a chance to review some of the words you need to remember after finishing each unit. Vocabulary words for each unit are also provided at the back of the book to help you prepare for each unit.

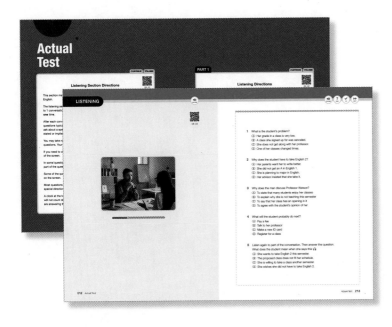

❽ Actual Test

This part offers one full practice test that is modeled on the Listening section of the TOEFL® iBT. This will familiarize you with the actual test format of the TOEFL® iBT.

PART I

Basic Comprehension

Basic comprehension of the listening passage is tested in three ways: listening for the main ideas, listening for the main purpose, and listening for the major details. Listening for the main idea is to identify the overall topic of the contents. Listening for the main purpose is to search for the reason behind the contents. For questions about the major details, you must understand and remember explicit details and facts from a lecture or conversation.

01 Listening for Main Ideas

Overview

Introduction

Understanding the main idea of a lecture or conversation is to identify the overall topic or basic idea of the contents. It may be expressed explicitly in the head of the contents or stated indirectly throughout the whole of the contents. In the latter case, you need to generalize or synthesize the information in the given contents.

Question Types

◆ What problem does the man have?

◆ What are the speakers mainly discussing?

◆ What is the main topic of the lecture?

◆ What is the lecture mainly about?

◆ What aspect of X does the professor mainly discuss?

Useful Tips

➤ Focus on the beginning part of the lecture or conversation.

➤ Listen carefully to key words that can lead you to the main idea.

➤ Try to verify the main idea with examples, explanations, and summaries.

➤ Try to figure out what problem and solution the speakers are talking about in the conversation.

➤ Avoid answers which cover only a small portion of the listening or which are not relevant to the listening.

➤ Avoid answers which are too general and make the most of your notes.

Script

01-01

W Professor: Okay. So the Roman Republic ended, and then there was a long civil war. After that, the Roman Empire began. It would last for a few centuries. There were both good times and bad times during the years of empire. Rome would greatly expand throughout the Mediterranean world. It would control a huge amount of territory over time. So, uh, let's begin with the first emperor of Rome.

Q What is the main topic of the lecture?

Ⓐ The Roman Republic

Ⓑ The Roman civil war

Ⓒ The Roman Empire

Ⓓ The first emperor of Rome

✅ Correct Answer

The answer for the above question is Ⓒ because the professor mostly speaks about the Roman Empire in her lecture. She tells the students about what happened during it.

Introduction to the Skill

Content words are words that have the most information in a sentence. These words include nouns, main verbs, adjectives, adverbs, question words, and demonstratives. In English, content words are usually emphasized. Stressed syllables in content words are longer, louder, and higher in pitch than unstressed ones.

A Kinds of Content Words

1 Nouns: student, professor, topic, biology, etc.
Your **teacher** loves to start off **classes** with **quizzes**.

2 Main verbs: discuss, talk, mean, surround, go, etc.
He **studies** the evolution of communication and the nature of meaning.

3 Adjectives: interesting, amazing, difficult, good, etc.
It was a **difficult** task to complete by Sunday.

4 Adverbs: thoroughly, slowly, consequently, therefore, however, etc.
The situation is **slowly** improving, and people are noticing.

5 Question words: who, what, when, where, why, how, which
Why don't you go to see a doctor?

6 Demonstratives: this, that, these, those
Needless to say, we did not get much sleep **that** night.

B Content Words in Context

1 **University students pay** a **lot** of **money** for their **educations**.

2 Do you **think it** is **harder** to **speak** or to **hear** a new **language**?

3 **There** will be **two written tests** and **one oral test** this **semester**.

4 **Students participate** in an **intern program** during **summer vacation**.

Skill Practice

A Underline the content words in the following sentences. Then, listen to the sentences and check your answers.

01-02

Example

University students pay a lot of money for their educations. (6 words)

1 We went over the course requirements the last time. (5 words)

2 Each place on the Earth has different patterns of weather events. (7 words)

3 She wants to help children by doing a fundraising campaign. (5 words)

4 They can tutor other students who need help for the preparation of the course and the test. (8 words)

B Listen to the following conversation and underline the content words. You must find more than thirty content words.

01-03

W Student: Would you tell me why it is so important to understand Greek mythology in your class? I don't know why I should write a paper about the birth of Aphrodite.

M Professor: Hey, Cindy. Greek myths are not simple and funny old stories. They have tons of characters and events, which have fertilized our lives, culture, and environment for two thousand years. So you can get the essential feeling from that topic for your work just like former great writers did.

C Listen to part of a lecture and fill in the blanks with suitable content words.

01-04

W Professor: As you know, the _____ _____ _____ was _____, especially Florence in the _____ part of Italy. It gradually _____ to many places throughout _____ by the 1600s. However, for many years, or even centuries, Italian opera was thought to be _____, and many non-Italian composers _____ _____ _____ in their works.

Basic Drill

Listen to parts of conversations or lectures and answer the questions.

Drill 1

Q What are the speakers mainly discussing?

Ⓐ The school shuttle bus
Ⓑ The location of a bus stop
Ⓒ The size of the campus
Ⓓ The student's classes

01-05

Check-Up Listen again and choose the correct words.

W Student: Hello. I heard there's a shuttle bus (on campus / at camp). How can I use it?

M Student Activities Office Employee: It's very easy. Just go to one of the (bus stations / bus stops). When the bus arrives, scan your (driver's license / student ID card), and you can ride on it.

W: Great. Do you know (how many / how often) the shuttle bus arrives?

M: We have (several shuttles / some shuttles) on campus. So they usually arrive at each bus stop within (fifteen minutes / five minutes).

Drill 2

Q What are the speakers mainly discussing?

Ⓐ Mr. Jenkins's newest project
Ⓑ The student's term paper
Ⓒ How to write a first draft
Ⓓ The way the woman writes

01-06

Check-Up Listen again and choose the correct words.

W Student: Mr. Jenkins, I've finished the first draft of my (time paper / term paper). I was hoping you could check it over for me.

M Professor: You're (already / really) done? That may be the fastest anyone's ever (completed / completion) a first draft.

W: Well, I like to get started early on my projects. So is it possible for you to (look it over / look at it) and tell me what needs to be (returned / rewritten)?

M: Sure, but I don't have time now. How about if I return it to you (next week / next work)?

Drill 3

Q What is the main topic of the talk?

01-07

    (A) How Napoleon died

    (B) Napoleon's final battle

    (C) Why Waterloo became well known

    (D) Napoleon's banishment to Waterloo

| Check-Up | Listen again and choose the correct words.

W Professor: There is a small town in Belgium (cold Waterloo / called Waterloo). This small town became very (famous / infamous) because of Napoleon's (last battle / less battle). A lot of (his souls / his soldiers) were killed and injured at Waterloo. As a result, he (was moved / was removed) from his (emperor's thrown / emperor's throne) and sent to Saint Helena. He died there in 1821.

Drill 4

Q What is the talk mainly about?

01-08

    (A) Radiation from the sun

    (B) The functions of air

    (C) Collisions between meteorites

    (D) The range of the atmosphere

| Check-Up | Listen again and choose the correct words.

M Professor: The atmosphere is a mixture of (different gases / different liquids) and aerosols. We usually call it (gas / air). The atmosphere is very (useful to our lives / important to our lives), and we cannot live without it. Almost every (loving creature / living creature) on the Earth (breath / breathes) it. It surrounds the Earth and protects us from (deadly rays / deadly weapons) and radiation from space.

Exercises with Short Conversations & Lectures

Exercise 1 Listen to part of a conversation and answer the questions.

01-09

Office Hours

1 What problem does the student have?

    Ⓐ He has missed several classes.

    Ⓑ He forgot to do his homework.

    Ⓒ He did poorly on an exam.

    Ⓓ He thinks a class is too hard.

2 What does the student say that he will do?

    Ⓐ Find a study group to learn better

    Ⓑ Work harder to understand the material

    Ⓒ Check out some books from the library

    Ⓓ Practice Spanish after class each day

Words & Phrases

semester ⓝ a term at a school; half of a school year

recall ⓥ to remember

attitude ⓝ a way of thinking

Dictation Exercise Listen to the conversation again and fill in the blanks.

M Student: Hello, Professor Nightengale. May I speak with you for a _____, please?

W Professor: _____ _____, James. What can I do for you?

M: The first two _____ of the _____ have been a bit _____ for me. I wonder if I am in a _____ that's too _____.

W: Hmm . . . Didn't you take Spanish in _____? I seem to _____ you said that. So taking Spanish II shouldn't be _____ _____.

M: Yes, I did take it. I guess _____. I'll just have to _____ _____ to make sure I can do well.

W: That's a _____. Just try _____. Come to me if you have any _____.

Exercise 2 Listen to part of a conversation and answer the questions.

01-10

Service Encounter

1 What is the student's problem?
- Ⓐ He cannot do his homework on time.
- Ⓑ A course sounds difficult.
- Ⓒ He did not receive a good grade.
- Ⓓ He did not read his textbook before a test.

2 What does the student have to do to get a good grade?
- Ⓐ Listen to the lectures carefully and do well on the homework
- Ⓑ Only study the summaries of the lectures
- Ⓒ Write a strong essay and do well on the exams
- Ⓓ Read the textbook carefully to prepare for the tests

Words & Phrases

mathematical ideas 🄽 a study on the historical development of mathematical thinking

nervous 🄰🄳🄹 worried; anxious

thoroughly 🄰🄳🅅 completely

grade 🄽 an academic mark; a score

Dictation Exercise Listen to the conversation again and fill in the blanks.

M Student: I am going to _____ Mathematical Ideas this _____. I am a bit _____ of that subject because I am not really _____ math.

W Residential Assistant: Mathematical Ideas? _____. I had that class my sophomore year. The lectures were _____, and the teacher made the students _____ in the course. You will _____ the class.

M: Well, I don't know. Weren't the _____ difficult?

W: Not at all. If you _____ to the lectures and do the homework, the tests will be _____. The teacher would hand out a _____ of his lecture every class. If you _____ thoroughly, you will not even need to read the _____. I was _____ at math, but I got a good _____.

M: I see. Thank you so much for your _____. It has really _____ me.

01 - 11

Geography

1 What is the main topic of the lecture?

Ⓐ Energy

Ⓑ Physical geography

Ⓒ The universe

Ⓓ Climatology

2 What does the professor say about physical geography?

Ⓐ It is the study of the universe.

Ⓑ It uses many other sciences.

Ⓒ Many other sciences use it to combine their ideas.

Ⓓ Energy is the biggest subject covered in it.

Words & Phrases

physical geography Ⓝ the study of the natural features of the Earth's surface

climatology Ⓝ the scientific study of the climate

astronomy Ⓝ the scientific study of outer space

Dictation Exercise Listen to the lecture again and fill in the blanks.

W Professor: Hello. My name is Jenny Smith. I will be your _____ geography _____ this semester. Um . . . Since this is your _____ _____, I want to _____ _____ what physical geography is. What is physical geography? Does _____ have any ideas . . . ? Well, uh, _____, it's a science about _____ _____. But it is _____ because it uses _____ from other sciences profoundly. For example, you will find information from _____, biology, climatology, astronomy, and many _____ _____ in physical geography. Does that _____ scary? Actually, you don't really need to _____ about it. _____, this is a _____ class. So we just will use what we _____ _____ in those areas. We will not go into too _____ _____ about those subjects. Okay . . . now let me _____ you some examples . . . Please _____ _____ page eleven. Chapter one. Energy.

Exercise 4 Listen to part of a lecture and answer the questions.

01-12

Course Introduction

1 What is the teacher mainly talking about?
- Ⓐ Written tests
- Ⓑ Lecture summaries
- Ⓒ Final grades
- Ⓓ Tests and grades

2 What do students have to do to get a good grade?
- Ⓐ They must study handouts and participate in class.
- Ⓑ They must get a good score on the written test.
- Ⓒ They have to write a twenty-page paper.
- Ⓓ They have to make a successful class presentation.

Words & Phrases

semester Ⓝ one of the two periods that make up a school year
hand out Ⓥ to give out; to distribute
participation Ⓝ the act of taking part in an activity or event

---

Dictation Exercise Listen to the lecture again and fill in the blanks.

M Professor: Okay . . . Now let's talk about _____ and _____. There will be two _____ and one oral test this semester. Each written test _____ forty multiple-choice questions. The oral test will have _____. Uh . . . Some of you may think the tests are _____ with too many questions. But that is not so. As a _____ of fact, there will be a _____ every class this semester. And if you _____ them well, then the tests will be very _____. And _____ about grades, the written and oral tests will be just a _____ of your final grade. _____ class participation is the most _____ thing to get a good grade. So please listen to my lectures _____, ask many questions, and _____ the topics with your classmates and me _____ the class. It will be very good for you to _____ for each unit before class, too.

Exercises with Mid-Length Conversations & Lectures

Exercise 1 Listen to part of a conversation and answer the questions.

01-13

Office Hours

1 What are the speakers mainly discussing?
- Ⓐ What the professor will teach next
- Ⓑ Study tips for the student
- Ⓒ How to solve the student's problem
- Ⓓ The student's recent presentation

2 What does the professor say about the university tutors?
- Ⓐ They work several hours a week.
- Ⓑ They took the classes they are tutors for.
- Ⓒ They do not need to be paid.
- Ⓓ They are all graduate students.

Words & Phrases

midterm exam Ⓝ a test taken in the middle of a semester
tutor Ⓝ a private teacher
recommend Ⓥ to suggest

Summary Note

A Look at the summary note and recall what you heard.

Student did poorly on midterm exam

Professor says is free service provided by school

Professor suggests getting a tutor

Student cannot afford to pay a tutor

B Complete the following summary with the words below.

a free service	the midterm exam	pleased
get a tutor	academic affairs office	cannot afford

The student did poorly on _____ even though she studied for three days.
The professor recommends that the student _____. She can find one at
the _____. The student is _____ with the idea.
But she says she _____ a tutor. The professor says that the tutors are
_____ provided by the school.

Dictation Exercise   Listen to the conversation again and fill in the blanks.

W Student: Professor Gibbs, I didn't do _____ on the _____ exam. What should I
do?

M Professor: Did you study the _____, Tiffany? I _____ that you take notes in
class, so I know you are paying _____.

W: Yes, I did study. I studied for _____ before the test. But when I took the
test, I just couldn't _____ any of the _____.

M: Hmm . . . Maybe you should get a _____. A tutor might be able to help you
_____ the _____ in the class.

W: A tutor? How would I do that?

M: You can go to the _____ office. It's _____ in Briar Hall. Tell the
_____ what class you are taking. She should be able to _____ a tutor for you.

W: Okay. That _____ like a good idea. But . . . um . . . tutors are pretty _____,
aren't they? I don't know if I can actually _____ to pay for one.

M: There's _____ to worry about. This is a _____ that the
university provides. So you won't have to _____ a thing.

W: What a _____. Thanks so much for letting me _____.

Exercise 2 Listen to part of a conversation and answer the questions.

01-14

Office Hours

1 What are the speakers mainly discussing?
- Ⓐ A group the student works with
- Ⓑ A class presentation
- Ⓒ Donating money to charity
- Ⓓ A school fundraiser

2 How does Jamie want to help children?
- Ⓐ By playing games with them
- Ⓑ By tutoring them
- Ⓒ By babysitting them
- Ⓓ By having a fundraiser

Words & Phrases

volunteer Ⓝ someone who does work without being paid for it
underprivileged adj deprived; disadvantaged

Summary Note

A Look at the summary note and recall what you heard.

Student	Financial support	Professor
• Is preparing a fundraising	• Clothes • School supplies	• Will help ➡ student might get more volunteers

B Complete the following summary with the words below.

who need help	raise some money	making a banner
talk about the organization	an upcoming fundraiser	

The student is preparing for _____ to help underprivileged children
_____ . He is _____ that will advertise the event. At
the fundraiser, he is planning to _____ to buy children various things that
they need. The professor offers to let the student _____ at the end of the
next class.

Dictation Exercise Listen to the conversation again and fill in the blanks.

M1 Professor: Jamie, you _____ these days. Is _____ all right?

M2 Student: You know I do some _____ work in my free time, don't you? Well, I've been
_____ a lot for a special _____ coming up next week. Right now, I'm making a
_____ for it.

M1: Really? _____ are you talking about?

M2: I do a lot of work with underprivileged _____ . The _____ don't have enough
_____ to buy clothes or school supplies. So my _____ is going to hold a
_____ to try to raise some money for them.

M1: It's so _____ of you to try to help other people who don't have the _____
_____ that others do.

M2: Yes, I just hope it _____ them a bit.

M1: Are there many students at _____ _____ that are members of the
organization?

M2: Not really. _____ _____ there were more of them.

M1: Well, if you want, you can make a short _____ at the end of class _____ .
Maybe some other students in the class will _____ to help.

M2: That would be _____ . Thanks so much, Professor Worthy.

Exercise 3 Listen to part of a lecture and answer the questions.

01-15

Art History

1 What is the main topic of the lecture?
- Ⓐ Religious and secular paintings
- Ⓑ Painting methods in the Middle Ages
- Ⓒ *The Last Supper* by Leonardo da Vinci
- Ⓓ Art in the Renaissance

2 Why does the professor mention *The Last Supper*?
- Ⓐ To show that the people in it look realistic
- Ⓑ To claim it is the best Renaissance painting
- Ⓒ To compare it with a painting from the Middle Ages
- Ⓓ To call it his favorite Renaissance work

Words & Phrases

rebirth Ⓝ the act of being born again
influence Ⓥ to affect, often in a good way
secular adj relating to the world; not religious
mythology Ⓝ a collection of stories that are often about gods, heroes, and monsters
rediscover Ⓥ to find again

Summary Note

A Look at the summary note and recall what you heard.

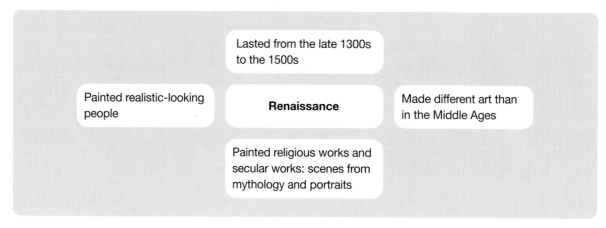

Lasted from the late 1300s to the 1500s

Painted realistic-looking people

Renaissance

Made different art than in the Middle Ages

Painted religious works and secular works: scenes from mythology and portraits

B Complete the following summary with the words below.

| the Middle Ages | Leonardo da Vinci | rebirth of learning |
| scenes from mythology | the Renaissance | looked realistic |

_____ lasted from the late 1300s to the 1500s. It involved a _____ from ancient Greece and Rome. Artists were greatly affected by it. They made paintings different from those in _____. They painted more secular works such as _____ and portraits. They painted people who _____, like the people in *The Last Supper* by _____.

Dictation Exercise Listen to the lecture again and fill in the blanks.

M Professor: The Renaissance _____ in Italy in the late 1300s and _____ until the 1500s. By then, it had _____ around Europe. It was a time when there was a _____ of learning from _____ Greece and Rome. _____ _____ were affected during the Renaissance. Art then was influenced _____ by the ancient Greeks and Romans. As a result, art in the Renaissance was much _____ from art in the Middle Ages. For instance, the _____ changed. Renaissance artists still painted _____ scenes like people did in the Middle Ages. However, they also _____ making more _____ paintings. They painted scenes from _____. They also painted _____, uh, you know, pictures of people. Renaissance artists used a _____ _____ style as well. The main reason was that they _____ certain painting techniques from the past. This _____ them to paint realistic-looking people in paintings. Here, uh, take a _____ at this painting by Leonardo da Vinci. It's _____ *The Last Supper*. Do you see what I'm _____ _____?

Exercise 4 Listen to part of a lecture and answer the questions.

01- 16

Climatology

1 What is the lecture mainly about?
- Ⓐ Weather
- Ⓑ Temperature
- Ⓒ Seasons
- Ⓓ Climate

2 What is the global climate?
- Ⓐ Different kinds of weather
- Ⓑ A combination of worldwide climates
- Ⓒ Places with the same temperature
- Ⓓ A climate which is really cold

Words & Phrases

climate Ⓝ the general weather condition in a certain place
global adj relating to all the world; worldwide
temperature Ⓝ the degree of heat or cold in a place
decade Ⓝ a period of ten years
environment Ⓝ the physical, chemical, and biological factors in an area

Summary Note

A Look at the summary note and recall what you heard.

	What: collected weather conditions
Climate	Where: certain places on the Earth
	How: changes over the years

B Complete the following summary with the words below.

collected weather	one type of	wide variety of
seasonal changes	gradually changes	

The lecturer says that climate is the general pattern of _____ in a certain place on the Earth. There are a _____ climates on the planet, and people live in _____ climate or another. The climate _____ every year in accordance with _____ .

Dictation Exercise Listen to the lecture again and fill in the blanks.

W Professor: Okay, class. Now, before we _____ going into the _____ of climatology, we need to know about _____ . What is climate? What is the _____ of climate? Do you have any _____ ?

M Student: I think it is a _____ of _____ .

W: Yes, that is a correct answer. Actually, climate is the _____ collected weather in a _____ place on the Earth. Let's take some _____ and make it _____ . Hmm . . . Do you know the _____ that happen in the Arctic Circle? Do you think it is a _____ ? No, it is not a climate. It is not even _____ . What about _____ climate? Is there such a thing as a global climate? Yes, there is. It's the _____ of all of the climates on the _____ added up. For example, when the Earth is _____ , we can say, "The global climate is _____ in temperature." So there is a global climate. Hmm . . . Actually, there are _____ of climates on the Earth. And we live in one of them or one that is a _____ of two. As the seasons _____ change, the _____ also changes each year. It can get _____ or _____ . Or there can be more or less _____ . There can even be more or less _____ .

Integrated Listening & Speaking

A Listen to a lecture on art history while looking at the summary note. Then, answer the questions in your own words.

Art History

📝 **Summary Note**

> Lasted from the late 1300s to the 1500s

Painted realistic-looking people

Renaissance

Made different art than in the Middle Ages

Painted religious works and secular works: scenes from mythology and portraits

01-17

1 What happened during the Renaissance?

    a. There was a rebirth of ....

    b. Art was influenced greatly ....

2 What kinds of scenes did Renaissance artists paint?

    a. .... like people did in the Middle Ages.

    b. They made secular paintings such as ....

3 How did some Renaissance paintings look?

    a. Renaissance artists ....

    b. Renaissance artists ....

B Listen to a lecture on climatolgy while looking at the summary note. Then, answer the questions in your own words.

Climatology

📝 **Summary Note**

		What: collected weather conditions
	Climate	Where: certain places on the Earth
		How: changes over the years

1 What are the students mostly confused about?

a. They often _____ .

b. The confusion is _____ .

2 What is climate?

a. It is _____ .

b. Climate is _____ .

3 How does the climate change?

a. The climate changes _____ .

b. It changes _____ .

Mini TOEFL iBT Practice Test

Listen to part of a conversation between a student and a librarian.

01 - 19

1 What are the speakers mainly discussing?
- Ⓐ Where to check out books
- Ⓑ Which books the student can borrow
- Ⓒ How to use the school library
- Ⓓ Where the reference section is

2 Why does the woman mention the reference librarian?
- Ⓐ To state that he can check out books
- Ⓑ To advise the student to speak to him
- Ⓒ To recommend that the student ask him for a job
- Ⓓ To say that he is her supervisor

3 Listen again to part of the conversation. Then answer the question.
What does the student imply when he says this: 🎧
- Ⓐ He has not checked out any books yet.
- Ⓑ He did not take the library orientation tour.
- Ⓒ He is unfamiliar with the university campus.
- Ⓓ He does not have his student ID card yet.

Listen to part of a lecture in an art class.

01-20

Art

4 What is the lecture mainly about?
- Ⓐ Picasso's great masterpiece
- Ⓑ Picasso's great talent
- Ⓒ The Second World War
- Ⓓ The brutality of war

5 According to the professor, what do people say about *Guernica*?
- Ⓐ It is about a bombing in Germany.
- Ⓑ It failed to stop a war from happening.
- Ⓒ It is a great historical painting.
- Ⓓ The symbolism is very simplistic.

6 Listen again to part of the lecture. Then answer the question.
What does the professor imply when she says this: 🎧
- Ⓐ The painting directly expresses the brutality of war.
- Ⓑ The painting shows people during peacetime.
- Ⓒ The painting does not show any bombings.
- Ⓓ The painting contains symbols of the war.

Vocabulary Check-Up

A Choose the correct words that match the definitions.

1 display •
2 midterm exam •
3 secular •
4 mythology •
5 decade •

6 recommend •
7 nervous •
8 bombardment •
9 tutor •
10 opportunity •
11 wrench •
12 borrow •
13 participate •
14 combination •

15 global •

• Ⓐ to suggest
• Ⓑ to pull or twist violently in order to move or remove
• Ⓒ a chance
• Ⓓ a test taken in the middle of a semester
• Ⓔ to check out; to use something for a short time and then to return it
• Ⓕ to take part in or to join in
• Ⓖ relating to all the world; worldwide
• Ⓗ a period of ten years
• Ⓘ to put something in a particular place to be seen
• Ⓙ the act of mixing different elements together
• Ⓚ relating to the world; not religious
• Ⓛ a strong and continuous bombing attack
• Ⓜ a private teacher
• Ⓝ a collection of stories that are often about gods, heroes, and monsters
• Ⓞ sensitive; excitable; timid

B Complete the sentences by choosing the correct words.

Ⓐ fundraiser	Ⓑ author	Ⓒ climate	Ⓓ technique	Ⓔ portrait

1 The _____ of the book is a popular professor at the school.
2 This _____ takes a lot of time for artists to learn.
3 They will attend a charity _____ on the weekend.
4 The _____ in this region is hot and sunny most of the year.
5 She wants to have her _____ painted by the artist.

02 Listening for Main Purpose

Overview

Introduction

Understanding the purpose of a lecture or a conversation is being able to identify the reason behind the contents. This type of question occurs in conversations more often than in lectures. As in the main idea, the purpose may be expressed explicitly in the beginning of the contents or stated indirectly and spread throughout the contents. In the latter, you need to generalize or synthesize information in the given contents.

Question Types

◆ Why does the student visit the professor?

◆ Why does the student visit the Registrar's office?

◆ Why did the professor ask to see the student?

◆ Why does the professor explain X?

Useful Tips

➤ Focus on the reason behind the lecture or conversation.

➤ Listen carefully to the ends of casual talks.

➤ Avoid answers that cover only a small portion of the listening or which are not relevant to the listening.

➤ Avoid answers that are too general and make the most of your notes.

Script

02-01

W Student: Professor Chambers, could I speak with you, please?

M Professor: Sure, Sarah. What's going on?

W: I'm curious about our midterm exam. What exactly do we need to study for it?

M: You should know all of the material up to chapter 11.

W: Does that include today's lecture?

M: It sure does. Good luck studying for the test.

Q   Why does the student visit the professor?

Ⓐ   To request assistance with a project

Ⓑ   To inquire about a test

Ⓒ   To confirm a homework assignment

Ⓓ   To ask about a recent lecture

 **Correct Answer**

The answer to the above question is Ⓑ. The student asks the professor what material she needs to know for the midterm exam. So she visits the professor to inquire about a test.

Skill & Tip   Focusing on Structure Words

Introduction to the Skill

Structure words are not very important words. They are small, simple words that make sentences correct grammatically. They give sentences correct form and structure. These words include pronouns, prepositions, articles, be verbs, conjunctions, and auxiliary verbs. In English, structure words are usually deemphasized. When contents words are emphasized and structure words are deemphasized, the contrast helps the listener hear the important words.

A Kinds of Content Words

1 pronouns: I, you, he, she, it, they…

2 prepositions: of, to, at, for, in, on, with, by…

3 articles: a(n), the

4 be verbs: am, are, is, was, were…

5 conjunctions: and, but, or, for, so, however, therefore…

6 auxiliary verbs: can, have, do, will, shall, would, could, might…

B Auxiliary verbs and contractions

1 *will* and *have*

They will ➡ They'll   They have ➡ They've   It is ➡ It's

2 *would* and *had*

I would ➡ I'd   He had ➡ He'd

3 *not*

She cannot ➡ She can't   He is not ➡ He isn't

C Phrasal verbs

There are a large number of two-word verbs in English. They are phrasal verbs. They are called that because the verb itself is a kind of phrase, verb + particle(s). Some of these verbs consist of as many as three words. It is very important in listening comprehension to listen and to distinguish the particle employed in a phrasal verb. You can become familiar with these kinds of verbs through plenty of practice. Several examples are shown below.

Phrasal Verb	Meaning	Phrasal Verb	Meaning
figure out	to find a solution	hang up	to end a telephone call
fill up	to fill completely with gas, water, coffee, etc.	pick up	to lift
get over	to recover from an illness	put on	to put clothes on one's body
hand in	to give homework, a test, paper, etc. to a teacher	run into	to meet by chance

Skill Practice

A Listen and fill in the blanks with the word in parentheses.

02-02

1 I _____ run in that race. (can / can't)

2 Sorry, but I _____ figure out what the right answer is. (can / can't)

3 You _____ also record the call number of the book. (should / shouldn't)

4 You _____ talk so loudly in the hospital. (should / shouldn't)

B Listen to the following conversation and fill in the blanks with the correct words.

02-03

M1 Student: Professor Kimball, I didn't know you were going to _____ _____ school in summer.

W Professor: Actually, I'm preparing to teach a class. What are you doing here?

M: I'm attending summer school. I want to get some credits out of the way. So I _____ _____ for Economics 23.

W: I have some great news for you. I'm going to be your instructor in that class.

C Listen to part of a lecture and fill in the blanks with the suitable words.

02-04

W Professor: Okay, students. We'll _____ _____ Beethoven's deafness today. It is not known for sure when he began to go deaf. But he kept the fact a secret until 1801, when he wrote a friend about his "miserable life." _____ you imagine how deeply he suffered from that? He was totally deaf by 1818. That means his greatest work, the *Ninth Symphony*, was done without him being able to hear. That symphony was written in 1822. The fact that one of the greatest symphonies in the world was _____ _____ by an old deaf person should be kept in our minds.

Basic Drill

Listen to parts of conversations or lectures and answer the questions.

Drill 1

Q Why does the student visit the professor?

02-05

    Ⓐ To ask her to explain a topic to him
    Ⓑ To say that he cannot find a resource
    Ⓒ To return a book that he borrowed
    Ⓓ To describe the topic of his term paper

Check-Up Listen again and choose the correct words.

M Student: Professor Starling, I'm (holding trouble / having trouble) finding a book for my final paper. The library doesn't have it, and the book is (out of print / out of stock).

W Professor: What's the title of the book? As you can see, I have a (large correction / large collection) here in my office.

M: It's Classical Economic Theory by Theordore Randolph. It was printed in the (early 1800s / early 1900s).

W: Ah, yes, I do have (a coffee / a copy) of that book. You can borrow it, but please make sure (nothing happens / something has it) to it.

Drill 2

Q Why does the student visit the Registrar's office?

02-06

    Ⓐ To submit some addresses
    Ⓑ To ask how to fill out a form
    Ⓒ To get copies of her transcript
    Ⓓ To pay a fee

Check-Up Listen again and choose the correct words.

W Student: Hello. I want to get some copies of (my transcript / my plan script), please. I need to send them to companies I'm (appalling to / applying to).

M Registrar's Office Employee: We can send them directly to (the ferns / the firms) if you want. Just provide us with (the addresses / the add rests).

W: Oh, that's (one for you / wonderful). I had no idea. Is there a form that I should fill out?

M: Here you are . . . In addition, each copy of your transcript will (call five / cost five) dollars.

Drill 3

Q Why does the professor explain why people share food?

    Ⓐ To describe the foods most people eat

    Ⓑ To talk about the importance of neighbors

    Ⓒ To explain some reasons people do it

    Ⓓ To prove that relationships are important

02-07

❚ Check-Up ❚ Listen again and choose the correct words.

W Professor: People of all cultures (sheer food / share food) to create and (maintain friendships / make friendships) with one another. When we invite others into our homes, we (often except / often expect) to have fun eating together. We also go out to have dinner or to (meet for lunch / meat for lunch) for many social reasons. Sharing food (indicates affection / indicated effects), familiarity, and (good willing / good will).

Drill 4

Q Why does the speaker explain body language?

    Ⓐ To compare it with various facial expressions

    Ⓑ To state that it was important in silent films

    Ⓒ To point out its usages in films in the 1920s

    Ⓓ To describe how actors learned to use it

02-08

❚ Check-Up ❚ Listen again and choose the correct words.

M Professor: It would (be bored / be boring) if there were no sound when you watched a movie. But most films were silent before the late 1920s. Films required a (greater emphasis / great emphasize) on body language and (face impressions / facial expressions) so that the (audios / audience) could understand better (what actors / what acts) were feeling and (portraits on screen / portraying on screen).

Exercises with Short Conversations & Lectures

Exercise 1 Listen to part of a conversation and answer the questions.

02-09

Office Hours

1 Why did the professor ask to see the student?

    Ⓐ To return a test to her

    Ⓑ To recommend she take summer school

    Ⓒ To test her on her Greek skills

    Ⓓ To offer her a job

2 What will the student probably do next?

    Ⓐ Respond to the professor's offer

    Ⓑ Read some books for the professor

    Ⓒ Go to her next class

    Ⓓ Sign up for summer school

Words & Phrases

campus n the area occupied by a school and its buildings

translate v to change from one language to another

a bunch of phr a lot of; very much; very many

document n an official paper

Dictation Exercise Listen to the conversation again and fill in the blanks.

W Student: Hello, Professor Ozuna. I heard you want to _____ with me. What can I do _____ you?

M Professor: Good morning, Alanis. I _____ you said you were _____ a job during summer. Have you _____ one yet?

W: Not yet. It _____ that most of the jobs on campus have already been _____.

M: Well, how would you like to be my _____ this summer? I need someone to _____ a bunch of documents from Greek. I know you _____ it very well.

W: That sounds like a lot of _____. It's a _____, right?

M: Yes, it is. You'll _____ fifteen dollars an hour and will _____ for around twenty-five hours a week. How does that _____?

Exercise 2 Listen to part of a conversation and answer the questions.

02-10

Office Hours

1 Why does the student visit the professor?

   Ⓐ To turn in a paper that he wrote

   Ⓑ To ask for help in finding some material

   Ⓒ To discuss a topic for a class assignment

   Ⓓ To ask for some study tips for a test

2 What must the student do for his presentation?

   Ⓐ Write a ten-page paper and read it aloud

   Ⓑ Discuss both sides of an argument

   Ⓒ Answer questions asked by students

   Ⓓ Conduct an experiment and talk about the results

Words & Phrases

sociology n the study and classification of human societies

cloning n the act of making identical copies

ethics n motivation based on ideas of right and wrong

unexpected adj unforeseen

unethical adj amoral; morally wrong

Dictation Exercise Listen to the conversation again and fill in the blanks.

W Professor: Have you _____ your _____ for your sociology presentation yet, Karl?

M Student: Yes, I have. I _____ to discuss _____ ethics.

W: That sounds good. But _____ that you need to discuss _____ of the subject. By that, I mean talk about how people are both _____ and _____ it. How are you going to _____ the topic?

M: Well, I plan to _____ the bad side and the good side. For example, some people say it is good because it will _____ scientists to grow vital body parts for _____. But others say it is unethical to _____ with human body parts. _____, people say it should be stopped because there could be _____.

W: Hmm . . . That sounds interesting. I'm _____ to hearing your presentation.

02-11

History

1 Why does the professor explain Augustus's actions toward doctors?

Ⓐ To show how he improved the medical system

Ⓑ To prove that he had some medical experience

Ⓒ To explain why Roman health care became worse

Ⓓ To compare Roman doctors with modern doctors

2 Why did Roman army doctors attend the army's medical school?

Ⓐ The civil war was important.

Ⓑ They were important to the army.

Ⓒ They had fairly low status.

Ⓓ The Roman army did not have doctors.

Words & Phrases

assassinate Ⓞ to kill someone, often an important or famous person

innovation Ⓞ a creation resulting from study and experimentation

dignified (adj) self-respecting

retirement Ⓞ the state of being retired from one's business or occupation

---

Dictation Exercise Listen to the lecture again and fill in the blanks.

M Professor: Okay, class. Today, I want to talk about _____ at the beginning of the first century. As I noted in our _____ class, there was a fifteen-year-long war after Julius Caesar was _____. The war was _____. Many people were _____. There were so many injured that it became one of the _____ of the new emperor to give _____ care to those in need. It was _____ this time that the new emperor, Augustus, started thinking about _____ the status of doctors. He _____ that medical care was _____ to the empire and especially the _____. In order to improve the _____, he needed better doctors. So he started making the _____ look more enticing. All army doctors were _____ to attend the new army _____. They were given dignified _____, land grants, and special retirement _____. Before that, doctors had a _____ status.

Exercise 4 Listen to part of a lecture and answer the questions.

02-12

Physical Education

1 Why does the professor explain handball violations?
- Ⓐ To talk about referees' jobs
- Ⓑ To argue that they are called incorrectly
- Ⓒ To discuss a rule in soccer
- Ⓓ To state that they happen too much

2 What will the professor probably do next?
- Ⓐ Answer the questions she asked
- Ⓑ Talk about another sport
- Ⓒ Show a video of soccer to the students
- Ⓓ Give the students a short test

Words & Phrases

clarify Ⓥ to make clear
intentionally ⓐdⓥ on purpose

Dictation Exercise Listen to the lecture again and fill in the blanks.

W Professor: Okay, now let's talk about _____ violations. I _____ you all know that you aren't _____ to use your _____ when you play soccer. It is called a _____. You cannot _____ any part of the ball with your _____ unless you are the _____. Only the _____ can touch the ball with his hands. A handball violation _____ using any part of the body from the _____ to the _____. Now, I want to ask you some questions. First, _____ this situation. In the middle of the game, a player _____ the ball, and the ball touches the hand of a player on the _____. But he didn't touch it _____. Now, is that a handball violation? I want you to think about it. Here is _____ question. What if the kicker did that _____? Is that a handball violation?

Exercise 1 Listen to part of a conversation and answer the questions.

02-13

Service Encounter

1 Why does the student visit the student employment office?

Ⓐ To pick up a paycheck

Ⓑ To search for a job

Ⓒ To have an interview

Ⓓ To quit his current job

2 Where does the woman suggest the student work?
Click on 2 answers.

Ⓐ For a professor

Ⓑ For a departmental office

Ⓒ At the sports stadium

Ⓓ At the library

Words & Phrases

binder n a folder; a cover for holding pieces of paper

contact person n an individual who can be asked about something such as a job

shift n the time a person works a job

Summary Note

A Look at the summary note and recall what you heard.

Student
- Looking for jobs
- Asks about hours and payment
- Asks about popular jobs

Woman
- Tells student to look in binders
- Says information is in binders
- Outdoor work ➡ Buildings and Grounds
- Indoor work ➡ library and departmental offices

B Complete the following summary with the words below.

popular jobs	the number of hours	a departmental office
Buildings and Grounds	look in the binders	the contact person

The student visits the office to ask about a job. The woman say he can _____.
He can find jobs he likes and speak with _____. The woman says that
information such as _____ per work and the pay are on the forms. The
student asks about _____. The woman recommends working outdoors for
_____ or indoors at the library or _____.

Dictation Exercise Listen to the conversation again and fill in the blanks.

M Student: Hello. I'm _____ to look for a _____. What do I need to do?

W Student Employment Office Employee: Good afternoon. We have a couple of _____ over there on that _____. They list a lot of the jobs that are _____.

M: Ah, okay. So . . . what _____ do I need to do?

W: The _____ is to look through the binders. Find a couple of jobs you are _____. Then, talk to the _____ _____ listed on the form.

M: Do the forms _____ how many hours a week are needed and the _____?

W: Yes, they do. Is there anything else?

M: One more question . . . What are some of the _____ on campus?

W: Hmm . . . If you're an _____ person, you could work for Buildings and Grounds. You might _____ or do something similar. You'd be _____ most of your _____.

M: That's not something I'm _____ interested in.

W: Ah, you're an _____ then. In that case, try to get a job at the _____. Or look for a job in one of the _____. Good luck.

Exercise 2 Listen to part of a conversation and answer the questions.

02-14

Office Hours

1   Why does the professor explain the kinds of fossils the students will find?
   Ⓐ To respond to the student's question
   Ⓑ To state that they should find large bones
   Ⓒ To say that the student's idea is incorrect
   Ⓓ To note that there are few fossils in the area

2   What will the students do with the fossils?
   Ⓐ Leave them in the fossil beds
   Ⓑ Donate them to the museum
   Ⓒ Attempt to identify them
   Ⓓ Give them to the professor

Words & Phrases

expedition ⓝ a trip, often for the purpose of learning or exploring
fossil ⓝ the petrified remains of a plant or animal
fascinating ⓐdⓙ very interesting
latecomer ⓝ a person who is not on time

Summary Note

A   Look at the summary note and recall what you heard.

Talking about an expedition to the riverside	Always come away with some nice fossils like trilobites, other shells, and small bones	Working in the lab to try to identify the findings

B Complete the following summary with the words below.

fascinating	to identify	find trilobites
the riverside	latecomers	be on time

The student is looking forward to going to _____ to search for fossils. The professor says they usually _____, other shells, and small bones. She adds that they will attempt _____ the fossils in the lab next week. The student thinks that is _____. The professor reminds him to _____ tomorrow because the bus will not wait for _____.

Dictation Exercise Listen to the conversation again and fill in the blanks.

W Professor: Are you _____ to go on tomorrow's _____ to the riverside, Jason?

M Student: I sure am. I've _____ _____ searching for fossils before. It should be an _____ experience.

W: I take my students to the _____ _____ there every year. They always come away with some _____ _____.

M: What are we _____ going to find?

W: Hmm . . . Most of the time, we find trilobites and _____. We also find small _____ from various creatures.

M: I hope I find something _____. Oh, what do we do with the fossils that _____ _____?

W: That's the _____ part. Next week, we'll be working in the _____ to try to _____ them. Some, such as trilobites and ammonites, are _____ to identify. But the pieces of bone are _____ _____.

M: That sounds _____. I can't wait to go.

W: Just _____ you are in front of Matterhorn Hall by six thirty in the morning. That's when the bus _____ _____. And we won't wait for _____.

M: I'll be there. Don't worry.

Listen to part of a lecture and answer the questions.

02-15

Psychology

1 Why does the professor explain reasons for war?

Ⓐ To talk about wars currently going on

Ⓑ To ask the students to give their own answers

Ⓒ To prove that wars can be stopped in the future

Ⓓ To show why people have fought many of them

2 According to the professor, why did hunter-gatherers fight wars in the past?

Ⓐ Because of injustices in the past

Ⓑ Because of borders

Ⓒ Because of access to food and water

Ⓓ Because of human rights

Words & Phrases

complicated adj difficult to analyze or understand

disagreement n a difference of opinion or sentiment

negotiation n a discussion intended to produce an agreement

clear the air phr to make differences or negative emotions go away

Summary Note

A Look at the summary note and recall what you heard.

Disagreements ➡ cannot resolve peacefully

Argue over borders, rights to natural resources, injustices in the past, and human rights

War

Another version of instinctive animal

B Complete the following summary with the words below.

human version	human rights	fight between nations
organized society	hard to list	argue over borders

A war is a _____ when there is a disagreement. It is like a fight between two people. Nations _____, natural resources, injustices in the past, and _____. There are so many issues that it is _____ everything. Animals have instinctive behavior, and war is the _____ of animal behavior. Since humans _____, wars have happened.

Dictation Exercise Listen to the lecture again and fill in the blanks.

W Professor: Why do countries go to _____? That is a _____ question. There have been thousands of wars throughout _____. Each one has its own _____. In general, wars between _____ and _____ start a lot like fights between _____. There is a _____ over something. When people disagree, they usually try to _____ their differences _____ through negotiations; Sometimes they _____ the air; other times they don't. With countries, you cannot just put a _____ between you and your _____ when things _____. Wars happen when nations have disagreements that can't be _____. There are many things that nations argue over: _____, rights to natural resources, _____ in the past, and human rights, among others. The list _____ on and on. War is as old as _____ society. Hunter-gatherer _____ from thousands of years ago _____ one another over access to food and water. Some psychologists believe war is the human _____ of instinctive _____.

02-16

Biology

1 Why does the professor explain some characteristics of mammals?
- Ⓐ To contrast them with amphibians
- Ⓑ To explain why they are warm blooded
- Ⓒ To compare them with those of birds
- Ⓓ To argue that they are superior to other animals

2 What does the professor imply about birds?
- Ⓐ The biggest of them is the ostrich.
- Ⓑ They do not give birth to live young.
- Ⓒ They use their wings for defense.
- Ⓓ Most of them hunt other animals for food.

Words & Phrases

amphibian Ⓝ an animal like a frog that can live on land and in the water
vertebrate Ⓝ a creature with a backbone
feed Ⓥ to give food to
flightless ⓐⓓⓙ being unable to fly

Summary Note

A Look at the summary note and recall what you heard.

Similarities
- Are warm-blooded vertebrates
- Breathe oxygen and take care of their young

Birds
- Wings + can fly + lay eggs
- Feathers

Birds and Mammals

Mammals
- Can't fly + give birth to live young
- Hair or fur

B Complete the following summary with the words below.

some similarities	take care of	lay eggs
wings and feathers	breathe oxygen	hair or fur

The professor says birds and mammals have _____. They are both warm-blooded vertebrates that _____. They also both _____ their young. However, birds have _____ and aside from a few animals, can fly. Mammals have _____ and except for bats, cannot fly. Birds also _____, but mammals give birth to live young.

Dictation Exercise Listen to the lecture again and fill in the blanks.

M Professor: Birds and mammals, _____ being different, have a few _____ with each other. For instance, both of them are _____ animals. This is unlike _____ and amphibians, which are _____ blooded. Birds and mammals can therefore regulate their own _____ _____, primarily through _____ food. They are both _____. This means that they have _____. Like all creatures, they breathe _____. And one more important _____ is this one: They take care of their young by _____ them. Of course, there are many other _____. For instance, birds have _____ on their bodies. Mammals, on the other hand, have _____ or _____ instead. Birds have _____ and are capable of flying. Sure, not all birds can fly. Penguins and ostriches are two _____ birds. But _____, birds can fly. Other than bats, mammals are not able to _____ flight. Birds _____, too, which is different from mammals. Mammals give birth to _____ young.

Integrated Listening & Speaking

A Listen to a lecture on psychology while looking at the summary note. Then, answer the questions in your own words.

02-17

Psychology

📝 **Summary Note**

Disagreements ➡ cannot resolve peacefully

Argue over borders, rights to natural resources, injustices in the past, and human rights

War

Another version of instinctive animal

1 Why do countries go to war?

a. They go to war when they can't _____.

b. They go to war when disagreements between countries

_____.

2 What do countries usually have disagreements over?

a. They argue over _____.

b. There are _____.

3 What does the lecturer say about human nature?

a. War happens because humans have _____.

b. Animals _____, and so do humans.

B Listen to a lecture on biology while looking at the summary note. Then, answer the questions in your own words.

Biology

02-18

📝 **Summary Note**

Similarities
- Are warm-blooded vertebrates
- Breathe oxygen and take care of their young

Birds
- Wings + can fly + lay eggs
- Feathers

Birds and Mammals

Mammals
- Can't fly + give birth to live young
- Hair or fur

1 What is true about birds and mammals but not reptiles and amphibians?

    a. Birds and mammals are _____, unlike reptiles and amphibians.

    b. Reptiles and amphibians are _____, but birds and animals are not.

2 What are some other similarities between birds and mammals?

    a. Both of them are _____.

    b. Both of them have _____.

3 How are birds and mammals different?

    a. Birds _____, but except for bats, mammals cannot.

    b. Birds lay eggs while mammals _____.

Mini TOEFL iBT Practice Test

Listen to part of a conversation between a student and a professor.

02-19

1 Why does the student visit the professor?

   Ⓐ To inquire about taking her next class

   Ⓑ To ask for her help on a research project

   Ⓒ To prepare for an upcoming examination

   Ⓓ To find out her thoughts on his term paper

2 What is the professor's attitude toward the student?

   Ⓐ She thinks his idea is not good.

   Ⓑ She is somewhat critical.

   Ⓒ She praises him a lot.

   Ⓓ She is very helpful to him.

3 What will the student probably do next?

   Ⓐ Check out some library books

   Ⓑ Write a proposal for his thesis

   Ⓒ Speak with a different professor

   Ⓓ Sign up for the professor's class

Listen to part of a lecture in a biology class.

02-20

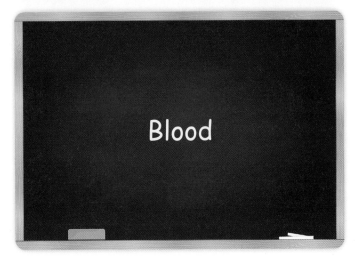

Blood

4   Why does the professor explain blood types?

    Ⓐ To state why people know their blood type

    Ⓑ To name the four different ones

    Ⓒ To claim they are not very important

    Ⓓ To show how all blood is not the same

5   According to the professor, what is the main reason that some people donate their own blood?

    Ⓐ To keep their bodies healthy

    Ⓑ To make new blood in their bones

    Ⓒ To have a perfect blood match for transfusions

    Ⓓ To donate blood to other people

6   Listen again to part of the lecture. Then answer the question.

    What does the professor imply when she says this: 🎧

    Ⓐ Humans have a lot of blood in their bodies.

    Ⓑ The blood delivers essential elements and removes harmful waste.

    Ⓒ Blood has a life cycle like all living organisms do.

    Ⓓ The human body would stop working without blood.

Vocabulary Check-Up

A Choose the correct words that match the definitions.

1 wound • • Ⓐ a source of materials to nourish the body

2 argue • • Ⓑ a creature with a backbone

3 nourishment • • Ⓒ a close or warm friendship

4 instinctive • • Ⓓ on purpose

5 vertebrate • • Ⓔ the ability to take in or absorb through one's body

6 fascinating • • Ⓕ to make clear

7 familiarity • • Ⓖ to present or contribute in an effort to help

8 vital • • Ⓗ to debate or discuss

9 intentionally • • Ⓘ acting or produced without reasoning

10 feed • • Ⓙ to give food to

11 digestion • • Ⓚ a feeling of liking someone or something

12 defend • • Ⓛ any break in the skin or an organ

13 affection • • Ⓜ very interesting

14 clarify • • Ⓝ to act in order to protect something

15 donate • • Ⓞ very necessary; highly important; essential

B Complete the sentences by choosing the correct words.

Ⓐ latecomers   Ⓑ complicated   Ⓒ expedition   Ⓓ flightless   Ⓔ regulate

1 Due to its big size, the ostrich is a(n) _____ bird.

2 The heater can _____ itself so that it does not get too hot.

3 _____ to class are likely to lose points.

4 They are going on a(n) _____ into the rainforest.

5 This machine is _____ because of its many parts.

03 Listening for Major Details

Overview

Introduction

In detail questions, you must understand and remember explicit details or facts from a lecture or conversation. These details are typically related to the main idea of the text by giving examples and elaborating on a topic or many other supporting statements. Questions are mostly asked about major details from the conversation or lecture, not minor ones.

Question Types

◆ According to the professor, what is one way that X can affect Y?

◆ What is X?

◆ What resulted from the invention of X?

◆ According to the professor, what is the main problem with the X theory?

Useful Tips

➤ No question type needs note taking more than detail questions. Make most of your notes about details.

➤ Listen carefully to the major details of the conversation or lecture, not the minor ones.

➤ The answers to detail questions are mostly written in paraphrased form from the text.

➤ If you are not sure of the correct response, decide which one of the choices is the most consistent with the main idea of the conversation or lecture.

Script

03-01

M Student: Professor Watson, I have a question about today's lecture. It concerns plant adaptations.

W Professor: Sure. What's your question?

M: Well, uh, you said that cacti have adapted to live in the desert. But I'm not sure how they do that.

W: Okay, first, they are able to survive on small amounts of water. They can also store water when it rains. That helps them during dry times.

M: I see. And what about other trees that live in deserts?

W: Let's take the mesquite tree as an example. Its roots can grow around fourteen or fifteen meters beneath the surface.

M: Ah, so that lets the tree get access to water underground, right?

Q According to the professor, how has the mesquite tree adapted to the desert?

- (A) It needs little water to grow.
- (B) It grows deep roots.
- (C) It thrives in strong sunlight.
- (D) It can store lots of water.

✅ **Correct Answer**

The correct response to the above question is (B). The professor says that mesquite tree roots "can grow around fourteen or fifteen meters beneath the surface."

Skill & Tip　Linking

Introduction to the Skill

In a dictionary, words are given in isolation. In natural connected speech, however, words within the same phrase or sentence are often connected into sound groups. Connecting groups of words is referred to as linking. Linking is a way of joining the pronunciation of two words so that they are easy to speak and flow together smoothly. If you recognize and use linking, two things will happen: (1) You will understand what you are told. (2) People will understand what you say more easily. There are basically five types of linking:

A Consonant to Vowel

Link words ending with a consonant sound to words beginning with a vowel sound. The consonant seems to become part of the following word.

live in　　　with it　　　pull out　　　push out　　　back up

B Consonant to Consonant

When a word that ends with a stop consonant is followed by a word that begins with a consonant, the stop consonant at the end of the first word is usually kept unreleased, and there seems to be a pause or a sudden stoppage of breath in between. This is known as open juncture.

lap dog　　　get by　　　light glass　　　bad case　　　old man

C Identical Consonants

Two identical and adjacent consonants are pronounced as one long consonant. This is another case of open juncture.

hit two　　　tough fight　　　some money　　　black cat　　　big girl

D Vowel to Vowel

When one word ends with a vowel sound such as /iy/, /ey/, /uw/, or /ow/ and the next word begins with a vowel, another sound, a /w/ or /j/, can be added depending on the particular sounds in order to make a smooth transition.

be on　　　pay up　　　blue ocean　　　grow up

E Vowel to Semi-Vowel

When one word ends with a vowel sound such as /iy/, /ey/, /uw/, or /ow/ and the next word begins with the same semi-vowel, they will be linked like identical consonants.

free union　　　say yes　　　who would　　　go west

Skill Practice

A Read the following sentences loudly and underline the linking parts. Then, listen to the sentences and check your answers.

03-02

   1 A man cannot be said to have succeeded in this life if he does not satisfy one friend.

   2 He has been a potter, and he's not bad as a sculptor.

   3 Money is merely a convenient medium of exchange.

   4 Better be wise by the misfortunes of others than by your own.

   5 Due to the kindness of friends, we have an apartment to stay in here and can easily reach the hospital.

B Listen to the following conversation and underline the linking parts.

   W Student: Professor Boyle, can I ask a favor of you?

   M Professor: Of course. What can I do for you?

03-03

   W: Actually, I was so sick that I couldn't attend your class yesterday. Can I have yesterday's material?

   M: Why not? Here you are.

C Listen to part of a lecture and fill in the blanks with suitable words.

   W Professor: Okay, so if you have no further questions on this, let's _____ _____ the makeup of the atom. An atom _____ _____ an extremely small _____ _____ surrounded by a _____ negatively charged electrons. Although the nucleus is typically less than one _____ _____ of the atom, the nucleus contains more than 99.9 percent of the atom's mass. The nuclei consist of positively _____ _____ and electrically neutral neutrons _____ _____ by the so-called strong, or nuclear, force.

03-04

Basic Drill

Listen to parts of conversations or lectures and answer the questions.

Drill 1

Q What will the librarian do?
- (A) Find the student's card
- (B) Fill out an application
- (C) Check out a book for the student
- (D) Cancel the student's card

03-05

Check-Up Listen again and choose the correct words.

W1 Student: Hi. I need to (cheek out / check out) some books today, but I lost my library card. Did anyone (return / review) it by any chance?

W2 Librarian: Let me check the lost and found. What's your name?

W1: Kelly Hamm.

W2: Give me a second . . . Sorry. Nobody turned it in. I think we have to cancel your (preview card / previous card) and issue you a new one.

W1: Oh, thanks. Please do whatever it takes. Oh . . . By the way, can you check if anyone has checked out a book with my card?

W2: (Certainly / Contain). I'll do that. Meanwhile, just (fill out / feel our) this (appliance / application).

Drill 2

Q What is a problem with the student's writing?
- (A) There were many spelling mistakes.
- (B) The information did not support the theme.
- (C) The student wrote a poor introduction.
- (D) There was no conclusion in the paper.

03-06

Check-Up Listen again and choose the correct words.

W Professor: Speaking about your writing, you had a (strong introduction / strong introduce) and (conduction / conclusion), but the body did not strongly support the theme.

M Student: Can you (explaining tale / explain in more detail)?

W: Sure. You need to explain and support your theme in the body. Some of the information didn't support the theme, and some parts were (confusing / puzzling).

M: I see. Could you underline the parts that were confusing and (miss lead / misleading)?

W: I already did. I wrote down some (comments in the margin / commend in the margin).

M: Thank you, Mrs. Larson. I'll redo it correctly this time.

Drill 3

Q What were the people protesting?

ⓐ Racism in the country

ⓑ A recent election

ⓒ The fighting of a war

ⓓ Illegal actions by police officers

03-07

❚ Check-Up ❚ Listen again and choose the correct words.

M Professor: In 1963, Martin Luther King, Jr. led a massive (demonstration / presentation) in Birmingham, Alabama. The protest was (about racial / against racism) in the United States. People, including children and teenagers, took to the streets to fight for their rights. However, (tremendously / tragically), police officers and firefighters tried to stop them with dogs and high-pressure water hoses. The protesters were (vitally attacked / brutally attacked) by dogs and torrents of water from fire hoses. These scenes were shown in newspapers and on televisions around the world. Of course, these scenes (touched person's hurt / touched people's hearts). So the demonstrators gained support against (sensation / segregation).

Drill 4

Q About how long does the moon take to orbit Earth?

ⓐ One week

ⓑ Two weeks

ⓒ One month

ⓓ Two months

03-08

❚ Check-Up ❚ Listen again and choose the correct words.

W Professor: Both the rotation of the moon and its (revolution / evolution) around Earth take twenty-seven days, seven hours, and forty-three minutes to be exact. That's a bit less than a month. Because of its (motion / emotion), the moon appears to move about thirteen degrees against the stars each day. That's around half a (agree per our / degree per hour). If you watch the moon over the course of several hours one night, you will notice that its position among the stars changes by a few degrees. The (alter location / changing position) of the moon with (respect to the sun / expect to the son) leads to (longer face / lunar phases).

Exercises with Short Conversations & Lectures

Exercise 1 Listen to part of a conversation and answer the questions.

03-09

Office Hours

1 What subject is the woman concerned about?

Ⓐ Economics

Ⓑ Political science

Ⓒ American history

Ⓓ International relations

2 What does the professor recommend the student do?

Ⓐ Try harder to learn

Ⓑ Join a study group

Ⓒ Read the book every night

Ⓓ Find a tutor

Words & Phrases

political science ⓝ the study of the principles and structure of government and of political institutions

regret ⓥ to be distressed about

constitution ⓝ the system of fundamental laws and principles

Dictation Exercise Listen to the conversation again and fill in the blanks.

W Student: I have a problem with my _____ _____ class. I don't _____ what you're talking about and regret taking it. I should _____ _____ the class.

M Professor: Calm down, Jane. Students take classes to _____.

W: I know. But I am so _____. I am just not into politics, the Constitution, and _____. And again, the words are so _____ to me.

M: Jane, let me tell you something. Based on my _____, you just need to try. You know, the words may sound _____, but they are not really that hard. Once you become _____ with the vocabulary, the basic laws, and the events, political science is a very _____ and _____ subject. On top of that, you have me to _____ you.

W: Do you really think so?

M: Yes, I'm sure. Everything's _____ you. If you think _____ and put effort into it, everything will become _____.

Exercise 2 Listen to part of a conversation and answer the questions.

03-10

Office Hours

1 What does the student tell the professor about?
- Ⓐ The courses she will take next semester
- Ⓑ Some classes she is taking now
- Ⓒ Some classes she already completed
- Ⓓ The classes she will take in summer school

2 According to the professor, what does Professor McCloud teach?
- Ⓐ Archaeology
- Ⓑ Art history
- Ⓒ Math
- Ⓓ History

📖 **Words & Phrases**

decide on phr to choose; to select
archaeology n the study of past cultures and civilizations
enroll in phr to register for; to sign up for
requirement n something that is needed or must be done

Dictation Exercise Listen to the conversation again and fill in the blanks.

W Student: I've finally _____ on my classes for next semester. Would you care to take a look?

M Professor: Sure, Caroline. What are you taking?

W: I'm _____ in your archaeology class. I'll also _____ Roman Archaeology with Professor Hern.

M: You'll really _____ his class. _____ are you taking?

W: I'm enrolling in a class on Byzantine history _____ Math 202. I need to _____ my math requirement.

M: Those look _____. Will you take _____ classes?

W: One more. It's an _____ _____ class on Renaissance art. It looks _____.

M: I believe that Professor McCloud teaches it. You're really going to _____ it. I _____ your schedule a lot.

Exercise 3 **Listen to part of a lecture and answer the questions.**

03-11

Biology

1 According to the professor, what is true about the leaves of deciduous trees?
   Ⓐ They stay on the trees all year long.
   Ⓑ They may change colors at times.
   Ⓒ They are thin like needles.
   Ⓓ They may have waxy coatings.

2 Where are the seeds of coniferous trees produced?
   Ⓐ In nuts
   Ⓑ In seeds
   Ⓒ In flowers
   Ⓓ In cones

Words & Phrases

concern Ⓥ to be about

replace Ⓥ to put something new in place of another thing

dormant (adj) inactive

needle (n) a sharp, thin, pointed object

coating (n) an outer covering

Dictation Exercise **Listen to the lecture again and fill in the blanks.**

M Professor: It's _____ to break down trees into two types: coniferous trees and deciduous trees. The main _____ between them concerns their leaves. You see, uh, coniferous trees have leaves during _____ _____. They _____ lose some, but then new ones grow to _____ them. Deciduous trees are _____. They are broad-leafed trees that _____ their leaves during _____ of the year. For the most part, that season is _____. Then, deciduous trees go _____. Their leaves don't grow again until _____ comes. As a _____ rule, the leaves of coniferous trees are _____ like needles or have a waxlike coating. Deciduous trees, on the other hand, have _____ leaves that change colors in _____. Coniferous trees have _____ produced in cones whereas deciduous trees produce _____. These flowers then produce _____ fruits that _____ seeds.

Exercise 4 Listen to part of a lecture and answer the questions.

03-12

American History

1 According to the professor, what was Pocahontas?
- Ⓐ She was a spy.
- Ⓑ She was a chieftain.
- Ⓒ She was a merchant.
- Ⓓ She was a colonist.

2 What happened after Pocahontas got married?
- Ⓐ She and her husband lived with a Native American tribe.
- Ⓑ Many colonists left Jamestown and lived elsewhere.
- Ⓒ She and her husband sailed to England to live there.
- Ⓓ A war between colonists and Native Americans ended.

Words & Phrases

native adj being such by birth or origin
mediator n a person who solves disputes between people
capture v to seize
diplomatic adj relating to the act of negotiations

Dictation Exercise Listen to the lecture again and fill in the blanks.

M Professor: In my opinion, Pocahontas was a _____ for the colonists. Yes, she _____ as a mediator between the British colonists and the Native Americans, but she was _____ of a spy. As you know, she even provided _____ food supplies to the colonists. However, she didn't think of _____ as a spy. In addition, the colonists didn't _____ her much despite her help. In a way, we could say she was a _____ spy. _____, a war broke out _____ the Powhatans and the colonists. The colonists _____ her and brought her to Jamestown. While she was in Jamestown as a _____, she freely converted to Christianity and _____ John Rolfe. As we all know, this _____ brought the war to its _____. What do you think? Was she a mediator or a spy? I believe she was a spy, a spy who _____ a role as a mediator.

Exercises with Mid-Length Conversations & Lectures

Exercise 1 Listen to part of a conversation and answer the questions.

03-13

Service Encounter

1 What kind of club does the student want to start?

   Ⓐ A photography club

   Ⓑ A hiking club

   Ⓒ A chess club

   Ⓓ A math club

2 What does the man give the student?

   Ⓐ A form

   Ⓑ A book

   Ⓒ A pamphlet

   Ⓓ A poster

Words & Phrases

student center n a building for students to do various activities in

hiking n the act of walking outdoors

trail n a path, often in a forest or in the mountains

definitely adv surely; for sure

put down phr to sign; to write, as in one's name

📝 Summary Note

A Look at the summary note and recall what you heard.

Student	Man	Student
• Wants to start a hiking club	• Tells student to get ten students to sign up	• Says that she can do that by next week

B Complete the following summary with the words below.

have ten members	to start	about clubs
many good trails	a form	hiking club

The student visits the office to ask _____. She says that she wants _____ her own club. She is interested in a _____ because there are _____ in the mountains nearby. The man tells her that she needs to _____. He gives her _____ to have students sign up by next week.

Dictation Exercise Listen to the conversation again and fill in the blanks.

W Student: Hello. Is this the _____ I should go to for _____?

M Student Activities Office Employee: That's right. However, we already had our _____ last week. All the school clubs were at the student center in order to _____ themselves to interested students.

W: Actually, I _____ it, but there weren't any clubs I was interested in _____.

M: Ah, so you would like to _____ your own club?

W: Yes, I would. But I don't _____ what to do.

M: First, what _____ of club would you like to start?

W: I'd like to have a _____ _____. There are so many good _____ in the mountains near here. I think it might be _____.

M: Hmm . . . You could be right. Okay, you can _____ start that club.

W: Great. What do I _____ to do?

M: Every club is _____ to have ten members. You need to have ten students _____ this sheet here . . . Have them put down _____ _____ and student ID numbers. Do that _____ next week, and you can _____ your club.

W: Thanks so much for _____. See you next week.

M: Bye.

03- 14

Office Hours

1 Why is the student grateful?

ⓐ She got an A on her midterm exam.

ⓑ Her presentation went very well.

ⓒ The professor checked her essay for her.

ⓓ The professor helped her in the class.

2 What does the professor believe teachers should do?

ⓐ Help students learn and succeed

ⓑ Help students enjoy their lives

ⓒ Help students improve their writing

ⓓ Help students get good grades

Words & Phrases

completely adv wholly; totally

effort n the use of energy to do something

amazing adj causing great wonder; incredible; impressive

tremendously adv extremely large in amount, extent, or degree

📝 Summary Note

A Look at the summary note and recall what you heard.

Student	Professor
• Thanks the professor • Professor helped her; she can pass the class	• Says the student will meet talented and helpful teachers

B Complete the following summary with the words below.

on the other hand	economics professor	encouragement
make an effort	is grateful to	could not have completed

The fall semester is over, and the student _____ her _____ for his help and _____ throughout the semester. The student believes that without his help, she _____ the class. _____, the professor insists that he doesn't help students who don't _____.

Dictation Exercise Listen to the conversation again and fill in the blanks.

W Student: Finally, the semester is _____.

M Professor: Are you happy that you don't have to come to my class _____?

W: Yes . . . I'm just _____.

M: I'm sure that you are.

W: I actually want to say _____ you. As you know, I was _____ when this class started. I thought I wouldn't be able to _____ this class, and look what I got.

M: _____.

W: Thank you. _____ your help, I probably would have _____ this class. You made economics so _____ and _____ for me.

M: Well, you are the one who _____ _____ and put in the time and effort. If you weren't _____ any effort, I _____ wouldn't have helped you.

W: You _____ me to put in the effort and try my best.

M: It's my job to help students learn and _____ in the future.

W: You are an _____ teacher. _____ _____ you could teach all my classes.

M: I'm sure you are going to meet _____ talented and helpful teachers throughout your _____. Come by _____ you need help.

W: I will. Thank you so much.

M: Enjoy your _____ _____.

03- 15

Botany

1 Where do plants get water from for photosynthesis?

   (A) Their roots

   (B) Their leaves

   (C) Their flowers

   (D) Their stems

2 What do plants produce when they do photosynthesis?
Click on 2 answers.

   (A) Glucose

   (B) Water

   (C) Carbon dioxide

   (D) Oxygen

Words & Phrases

humidity (n) dampness

respiration (n) the movement of gases in and out of an organism

dissolve (v) to cause to pass into a solution

substance (n) something that has mass and occupies space

Summary Note

A Look at the summary note and recall what you heard.

Plants and Water

Water plays an important part in lives of plants

Water carries nutrient and minerals ➡ photosynthesis

B Complete the following summary with the words below.

oxygen and glucose	the roots	respiration processes
complete photosynthesis	with these nutrients	survive

Plants cannot _____ without water. One of the major
_____ that requires water is called photosynthesis. During
photosynthesis, water moves from _____ to leaves while carrying
dissolved nutrient and minerals. Then, _____, carbon dioxide, water, and
sunlight _____. They form _____.

Dictation Exercise   Listen to the lecture again and fill in the blanks.

W Professor: Today's topic is on _____ and water. As you all know, water is very
_____ for all the living things on the Earth. We can't live _____ water.
_____ can plants. Water plays a very _____ _____ in the lives of plants.
Too much water _____ root damage, and too little may _____
them _____. Depending on the species, some plants have the _____ to store water
for short periods of time while others can store water for _____ periods of time. In addition,
_____ and humidity play important _____ in the respiration
process of plants. Now, I want to talk about a _____ called photosynthesis.

M1 Student: I _____ learning about it in junior high. Isn't it a process which _____
water and sunlight?

W: Yes, _____. Let's see _____ _____ you remember what you were
taught in junior high. Who can tell me about photosynthesis _____ _____?

M2 Student: Water moves _____ from the roots to the leaves. In doing that, it
_____ dissolved nutrients and minerals.

W: Anyone else?

M1: These nutrients, _____ carbon dioxide, water, and sunlight, allow
photosynthesis to _____ _____. It produces both oxygen and a kind of
_____ called glucose.

W: Very good!

Exercise 4 Listen to part of a lecture and answer the questions.

03-16

Art

1 Why did Abbé Breuil think people made cave paintings in the past?
- Ⓐ They were used to teach people about animals.
- Ⓑ They were primitive symbols of early languages.
- Ⓒ They were meant to increase the number of animals.
- Ⓓ They were used to show people how to hunt.

2 What does the professor say about cave paintings of humans?
- Ⓐ They are colorful.
- Ⓑ They are naturalistic.
- Ⓒ They are rare.
- Ⓓ They are detailed.

Words & Phrases

bison Ⓝ a buffalo
interpret Ⓝ to explain the meaning of
schematic 🔲 of, relating to, or in the form of a diagram
tribe Ⓝ a group of people with the same race, language, and customs

📝 Summary Note

A Look at the summary note and recall what you heard.

Cave Paintings			
Period	**Artist**	**Theme**	**Color**
• Paleolithic, 40,000 years ago	• Elders and shamans	• Bison, horses, aurochs, and deer	• Yellow, brown, charcoal, and red

B   Complete the following summary with the words below.

were believed	approximately	in contrast to
schematic	mainly of animals	were mostly limited

Cave paintings started _____ 40,000 years ago during the upper
Paleolithic Period. The pictures are _____ such as bison, horses,
aurochs, and deer. The colors _____ to yellow, brown, charcoal, and red.
_____ naturalistic animal paintings, drawings of humans are
_____ and rare. The artists _____ to be respected
elders and shamans.

Dictation Exercise   Listen to the lecture again and fill in the blanks.

M1 Professor: We are going to _____ chapter three today. It's on _____
_____. Who can tell me about cave paintings?

M2 Student: The _____ are mostly of animals.

M1: Correct. The animals are _____ bison, horses, and deer. The most common
_____ in cave paintings are large _____ _____ such as bison, horses,
aurochs, and deer. Anthropologist Abbé Breuil interpreted the paintings as being _____
_____. That is to say, they were _____ to _____ the number of animals.
Drawings of humans are _____ and are usually schematic rather than the more naturalistic
_____ subjects. Who can _____ when cave painting started?

W1 Student: Prehistoric times . . .

M1: Yes . . . the first paintings _____ during the upper Paleolithic Period
about 40,000 years ago. Let me ask you _____ _____. Who drew the paintings?

W1: Artists . . .

M1: Good answer, but who were the artists? What were their _____?

W2 Student: Tribal _____?

M1: Close but _____. The artists were believed to be _____ elders or shamans.
The _____ _____ of the paintings were yellow, brown, charcoal, and red.

Integrated Listening & Speaking

A Listen to a lecture on botany while looking at the summary note. Then, answer the questions in your own words.

03-17

Botany

📝 Summary Note

Plants and Water

Water plays an important part in lives of plants

Water carries nutrient and minerals ➡ photosynthesis

1 What relationship do plants and water have?

    a. Too much water can ....

    b. .... play important roles in the plant
    respiration process.

2 How does water move in plants?

    a. Water moves from ....

    b. Water carries .... as it goes up.

3 What happens during photosynthesis?

    a. Nutrients, ...
    let photosynthesis happen.

    b. The photosynthesis process produces ....

B Listen to a lecture on art while looking at the summary note. Then, answer the questions in your own words.

03-18

Art

📝 **Summary Note**

Cave Paintings

Period	Artist	Theme	Color
• Paleolithic, 40,000 years ago	• Elders and shamans	• Bison, horses, aurochs, and deer	• Yellow, brown, charcoal, and red

1 How did anthropologist Abbé Breuil interpret cave paintings?

   a. She interpreted the paintings as _____.

   b. She interpreted the paintings as _____.

2 What do most paintings show?

   a. The paintings are mostly of _____.

   b. The paintings are mostly of _____.

3 How are the drawings of human and animal paintings in comparison to one another?

   a. The animal paintings are _____
     than the drawings of humans.

   b. The drawings of humans are _____
     compared to the animal paintings.

Listen to part of a conversation between a student and a professor.

03-19

1 Why did the professor ask to see the student?

Ⓐ To ask him about his test performance

Ⓑ To show him his grade on an assignment

Ⓒ To encourage him to work harder in class

Ⓓ To give him a new writing project

2 What is the topic of the student's paper?

Ⓐ Political science

Ⓑ English literature

Ⓒ History

Ⓓ Chemistry

3 What will the professor probably do next?

Ⓐ Ask the student to explain his ideas in more detail

Ⓑ Go to her next class with the student

Ⓒ Show the student one of her books

Ⓓ Provide the student with more information

Listen to part of a lecture in a literature class.

03-20

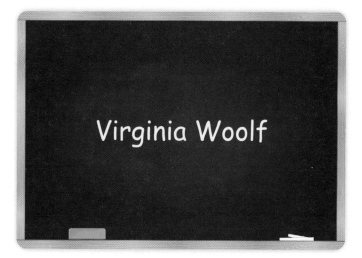

Literature

Virginia Woolf

4 What aspect of Virginia Woolf does the professor mainly discuss?

    Ⓐ The popularity of her books

    Ⓑ The themes of her works

    Ⓒ Her writing influences

    Ⓓ Her early life

5 What is the main subject of *A Room of One's Own*?

    Ⓐ Pride that helped women writers

    Ⓑ Obstacles and prejudices that hindered women writers

    Ⓒ Women's achievements in literacy

    Ⓓ The importance of a culture just for women

6 Why does the professor discuss *Three Guineas*?

    Ⓐ To focus on the theme of the book

    Ⓑ To compare it with *The Lighthouse*

    Ⓒ To call it her favorite book

    Ⓓ To note how popular the book was

Vocabulary Check-Up

A Choose the correct words that match the definitions.

1 convert	•	• Ⓐ	a suggestion; an offer
2 semester	•	• Ⓑ	something that has mass and occupies space
3 mediator	•	• Ⓒ	to make something difficult to progress
4 proposal	•	• Ⓓ	to explain the meaning of
5 interpret	•	• Ⓔ	to be distressed about
6 effort	•	• Ⓕ	the act of keeping things apart from one another
7 identical	•	• Ⓖ	a person who solves disputes between people
8 completely	•	• Ⓗ	one of two divisions in an academic year
9 limitation	•	• Ⓘ	to persuade or induce to adopt a particular religion, faith, or belief
10 substance	•	• Ⓙ	wholly; totally
11 dissolve	•	• Ⓚ	a limiting condition
12 hinder	•	• Ⓛ	a path, often in a forest or in the mountains
13 segregation	•	• Ⓜ	the use of energy to do something
14 regret	•	• Ⓝ	being the same
15 trail	•	• Ⓞ	to be mixed with liquid and disappear or to melt

B Complete the sentences by choosing the correct words.

> Ⓐ humidity   Ⓑ establish   Ⓒ survive   Ⓓ adaptation   Ⓔ impressed

1 The _____ level in a rainforest is almost always very high.

2 One common plant _____ is requiring little water to grow.

3 The student _____ the teacher with her hard work.

4 It can be hard for some animals to _____ in very cold places.

5 He hopes to _____ a new restaurant later this year.

PART II

Pragmatic Understanding

Pragmatic Understanding questions test understanding of certain features that go beyond basic comprehension. Generally, two question types test pragmatic understanding: Function of What Is Said and Speaker's Attitude. Function of What Is Said questions test whether you can understand the underlying intentions of what is said. Speaker's Attitude questions test whether you can understand a speaker's attitude or opinion that has not been directly expressed. Pragmatic Understanding questions typically involve a replay of a small portion of the listening passage.

04 Understanding the Function of What Is Said

Overview

Introduction

Function of What Is Said questions test whether you can understand the underlying intentions of what is said. The underlying intentions are typically hidden in the context surrounding the text of the question. Frequently, the intentions are acquired by focusing on the entire text. This question type often involves replaying a portion of the listening passage.

Question Types

◆ What does the professor imply when he says this: (replay)

◆ What can be inferred from the professor's response to the student? (replay)

◆ What is the purpose of the woman's response? (replay)

◆ Why does the student say this: (replay)

Useful Tips

➤ Practice reading between the lines.

➤ Try to take notes of the context of the lecture or conversation.

➤ Refer to the tones the speakers are using in the lecture or conversation.

Script

M Student: Good afternoon, Professor Anderson. I wonder if you can give me any hints about the midterm exam tomorrow.

W Professor: Now, that wouldn't be fair to the other students, Kevin.

M: Yeah, you're right. I am just worried about how I will do on the test.

W: Don't worry too much. I know you take good notes and pay attention in class. Just study your notes and the book, and you'll do fine.

M: Thanks for believing in me. I appreciate that.

04-01

Q   Listen again to part of the conversation. Then answer the question.
What does the professor imply when she says this: 🎧
  Ⓐ She thinks the student is doing very well.
  Ⓑ She cannot tell the student about the test.
  Ⓒ She is not worried about the student's performance.
  Ⓓ She thinks the test will be very difficult.

✅ **Correct Answer**

The answer to the above question is Ⓑ. When the professor says, "Now, that wouldn't be fair to the other students," she is implying that she cannot tell the student anything about the test.

Skill & Tip   Chunking

Introduction to the Skill

As we listen to words, we assign meanings by chunking the words into thought groups and storing them as meaningful units and phrases in our short-term memory. From these chunks of meaning, or memory markers, we get the gist of the message. Usually, listeners focus on what they understand. Listeners pass over unknown or unintelligible vocabulary words and concentrate instead upon identifying the main idea and following its course of development. Chunking is a way of sorting and organizing information. There are two kinds of signals to mark the end of a thought group: pause and falling pitch. A pause gives listeners time to understand what was said.

A Chunk Developing

The number of chunks increases as a sentence becomes longer.

1 I saw Jane.

I saw Jane / with Tom.

I saw Jane / with Tom / in the movie theater.

I saw Jane / with Tom / in the movie theater / last night.

2 I heard a strange sound.

I heard a strange sound / downstairs.

I heard a strange sound / downstairs, / Dad.

B Chunking Units in Context

1 You have a very nice site / with great information.

2 Will you show me a shortcut / to the library?

3 All he did / was study / and play basketball.

4 Call today / to schedule a session / with our personal tutor!

5 Robert wants to finish / his lunch / as quickly as possible.

6 They're taking tests, / which is why I'm home / from school.

Skill Practice

A Read the following sentences loudly, and put a / mark between the words where you want to chunk. Then, listen to each sentence and check your answers.

04-02

1 I never managed to discuss this with my father while he lived.

2 I don't remember when I got home last night.

3 Which color do you like more, black or yellow?

4 When you're young, there's almost no place you can go at night.

5 There's nothing I can do for them except what I can do in the future.

6 Next month, we are both supposed to go to Chicago to visit my uncle.

B Listen to the following conversation and put a / mark between the words where you want to chunk.

04-03

W Resident Assistant: Hi, Jamie! How was your presentation in psychology class?

M Student: Oh, it was not so bad. I got the right answers on every single question, even from Professor Graham.

W: That sounds great. Actually, Professor Graham is very strict about students' presentations. I knew you were so worried about it. Good job!

C Listen to part of a lecture and fill in the blanks with suitable words. Then, put a / mark between the words where you want to chunk.

04-04

W Professor: Using _____ household materials, you can make a pinhole _____ like this. It can _____ real pictures, and it will provide an inexpensive and _____ way to take pictures. To make a pinhole camera, you only need a can or _____. If you take a picture with the camera you build, you'll be very _____ of it.

Basic Drill

Listen to parts of conversations or lectures and answer the questions.

Drill 1

Q What can be inferred from the woman's response to the student: 🎧

   Ⓐ She will call the professor for the student.

   Ⓑ She should be able to help the student.

   Ⓒ She can give the student a key.

   Ⓓ She thinks the professor is gone for the day.

04-05

❙ Check-Up ❙ Listen again and choose the correct words.

M Student: Hello. I wonder if you can give me (a band / a hand).

W Math Department Office Employee: I'll do (the rest / my best). What do you need?

M: I was up at Professor Oaktown's office a moment ago. But (the light / the right) was off, and the door (was blocked / was locked).

W: He just finished his office hours about (half an hour / has an hour) ago.

M: Oh, I see. Will he be at school tomorrow?

W: Yes, he will. He has an (early class / early mass), so why don't you come here around nine in the morning?

Drill 2

Q Why does the professor say this: 🎧

   Ⓐ She wants the student to drop her class.

   Ⓑ She wants the student to concentrate on sports.

   Ⓒ She wants the student to get help with football.

   Ⓓ She wants the student to study.

04-06

❙ Check-Up ❙ Listen again and choose the correct words.

M Student: Professor Dean, did you want to see me?

W Professor: Yes, Joseph. I just want to talk to you about your (class participation / glass participation).

M: I know. It has been pretty (rough for me / tough for me) because of football practice.

W: I see. I hope you get (plenty of rest / a lot of rest) every day. It is great that you are playing sports, but don't let it (get in the way / get out of the way) of your studying.

M: Yes, ma'am. I know that education is more important. I will (pace myself / space myself).

Drill 3

Q What does the professor imply when he says this: 🎧

04-07

    Ⓐ Pollution is a natural phenomenon.

    Ⓑ Humans cannot get rid of pollution.

    Ⓒ Pollution is manmade.

    Ⓓ The environment shows no signs of damage.

┃Check-Up┃ Listen again and choose the correct words.

M Professor: Are we doing enough to protect the environment from pollution? The environment is (suffering from / buffering from) various kinds of pollution. These negatively (affect / effect) the nature and well-being of all living organisms. Major (pollutants / solutions) include water, air, and noise pollution and soil (contamination / containment). Unfortunately, all this pollution is manmade, and there is no sign of slowing down. We, as (humans / mankind), must work together to reverse the damage we have done to the (environment / nature).

Drill 4

Q Why does the professor say this: 🎧

04-08

    Ⓐ To point out some dangers of bullying

    Ⓑ To suggest a way to reduce bullying

    Ⓒ To claim most students are not bullied

    Ⓓ To say bullying can have positive effects

┃Check-Up┃ Listen again and choose the correct words.

W Professor: In the past, (bullying / cooling) was considered a part of (growing up / glowing up). However, there is an increasing (awareness / knowledge) of the harmful effects of bullying. It causes not only long-term (social behavior / social attitude) problems but also leads to other types of (violence / aggression). Therefore, schools need to run active (programs to prevent / programs to select) or stop bullying.

Exercises with Short Conversations & Lectures

Exercise 1 Listen to part of a conversation and answer the questions.

04-09

Service Encounter

1 Listen again to part of the conversation. Then answer the question.

Why does the woman say this: 🎧
- Ⓐ To give the student a class schedule
- Ⓑ To show the student how to pay for a class
- Ⓒ To tell the student he cannot take classes
- Ⓓ To determine the student's status

2 Why does the student visit the Registrar's office?
- Ⓐ To find the schedule for a class
- Ⓑ To ask for help paying his tuition
- Ⓒ To get directions to an office
- Ⓓ To learn how to register for summer school

Words & Phrases

inquire Ⓥ to ask; to question
provide Ⓥ to furnish; to supply
tuition Ⓝ a fee to attend a school

Dictation Exercise Listen to the conversation again and fill in the blanks.

W Registrar's Office Employee: Hi. Can I help you?

M Student: I would like to _____ how to register for _____ _____.

W: Are you currently _____ in this school?

M: Yes, I am.

W: Okay, if not, I would have to ask you to _____. Since you are _____ enrolled, look through this _____ of classes and decide _____ you would like to take. Then, either go to the _____ or call the number on the schedule to enroll.

M: Great. How do I pay my _____?

W: It's the _____ as in normal semesters. You can pay _____ online while enrolling, mail your payment, or _____ in person right in this office.

M: Thank you very much.

Exercise 2 Listen to part of a conversation and answer the questions.

04-10

Office Hours

1 Listen again to part of the conversation. Then answer the question.

What can be inferred from the student's response to the professor?

- Ⓐ She is too busy to do more work.
- Ⓑ She does not want to do an assignment.
- Ⓒ She agrees with the professor's opinion.
- Ⓓ She is surprised by his comment.

2 What must the student do by Friday?

- Ⓐ Study for a test
- Ⓑ Submit an idea for a thesis
- Ⓒ Rewrite her paper
- Ⓓ Read a chapter in the textbook

📖 **Words & Phrases**

submit Ⓥ to turn in
regret Ⓥ to feel bad about something
proper adj correct

Dictation Exercise Listen to the conversation again and fill in the blanks.

M Professor: Melissa, do you know _____ I _____ to see you today?

W Student: No, sir. I'm afraid that I don't.

M: It's about the _____ you submitted. I _____ to say that it isn't _____ .

W: Are you sure? What's _____ with it?

M: You didn't _____ the proper format. For instance, you were _____ to include an introduction and a _____ . But the paper didn't have _____ .

W: Oh, I see.

M: In addition, you didn't properly _____ the arguments you made in the essay. You're going to need to _____ the paper.

W: Okay. I _____ . _____ do you need me to return it by?

M: I'd like to _____ by this Friday. So you have three _____ .

W: Okay, Professor Mellon. Thanks for giving me a _____ . I appreciate that.

Exercise 3 Listen to part of a lecture and answer the questions.

04-11

Communication

1 Listen again to part of the lecture. Then answer the question. Why does the professor say this: 🎧

   (A) To speak about herself

   (B) To talk about her lecture

   (C) To respond to a question

   (D) To describe an assignment

2 According to the professor, when must the students give their speeches?

   (A) Today

   (B) In the next class

   (C) Next week

   (D) In two weeks

> **📖 Words & Phrases**
>
> **narrative** adj telling a story
> **history** n past events
> **personal** adj of a person; individual

Dictation Exercise Listen to the lecture again and fill in the blanks.

W Professor: Hello, class. Welcome to Communications 101. Today, I will _____ narrative speech. Each of you needs to _____. The _____ is "Who Am I?" You will _____ this class with a _____ idea of who you are. First, begin with _____, what it means, why your parents chose this name, and how you _____ about it. Next, tell us _____. Where you were born, when you were born, where you _____, and, if you like, how _____ met. Then, give us more _____ about yourself. Items should _____ your hobbies, talents, things you like, dislikes, your passion, goals, _____, and so forth. Please turn in your _____ by next week. The speeches _____ the week after you turn in your outline.

Exercise 4 Listen to part of a lecture and answer the questions.

04-12

Geometry

1 Listen again to part of the lecture. Then answer the question. What does the professor imply when he says this: 🎧
   Ⓐ The golden ratio is used in designs.
   Ⓑ Few people know about the golden ratio.
   Ⓒ The golden ratio is taught in math class.
   Ⓓ People in the past knew about the golden ratio.

2 According to the professor, when did people first learn the golden ratio?
   Ⓐ Since the invention of the TV
   Ⓑ Since the early Greeks
   Ⓒ Since the last decade
   Ⓓ Since the year 1618

Words & Phrases

ratio 🅝 one value divided by another
geometry 🅝 the mathematics of points, lines, curves, and surfaces
approximately 🅐🅓🅥 around; about
appealing 🅐🅓🅙 attractive; inviting

Dictation Exercise Listen to the lecture again and fill in the blanks.

M Professor: Let's say that you are a designer that needs to _____ a rectangular TV or a _____ _____. Would you randomly _____ any ratio, or would you _____ a certain rule? If you know geometry, you will _____ the golden ratio. This ratio has a length-to-width ratio of _____ 1.618. Since the _____ _____, it has been known as the most visually _____ ratio to the eye. Therefore, we can _____ many things around us that _____ this ratio. The Greek Parthenon and wide-screen TVs are two _____. The golden ratio _____ in art, architecture, and even in natural structures. Why don't you find an example _____ _____?

Exercises with Mid-Length Conversations & Lectures

Exercise 1 Listen to part of a conversation and answer the questions.

04-13

Office Hours

1 Listen again to part of the conversation. Then answer the question.

What can be inferred from the professor's response to the student?

- Ⓐ He has been waiting for the student.
- Ⓑ He needs to leave his office soon.
- Ⓒ He has a busy schedule today.
- Ⓓ He has time to speak with her.

2 What can be inferred about Professor Anderson?

- Ⓐ The student does not know him well.
- Ⓑ He teaches in the Archaeology Department.
- Ⓒ He knows the professor very well.
- Ⓓ The student has taken a class with him before.

 Words & Phrases

algebra Ⓝ a branch of math
elective Ⓝ a class that is not required to graduate

fascinating adj extremely interesting
lecturer Ⓝ a teacher; a professor

📝 Summary Note

A Look at the summary note and recall what you heard.

Student
- Needs another class
- Trying to decide between Egyptian archaeology and international relations

Professor
- Praises Professor Anderson
- Recommends taking his class

Student
- Decides to take archaeology class

B Complete the following summary with the words below.

Professor Anderson	four of the classes	Egyptian archaeology
archaeology class	an elective	her schedule

The student asks to speak with the professor about _____ for next semester. She already knows _____ she will take. She wants to take _____ for her fifth class. She is trying to decide between _____ and an international relations class. The professor recommends _____, so the student decides to take the _____.

Dictation Exercise Listen to the conversation again and fill in the blanks.

W Student: Professor Monroe, how are you? Do you have time to speak about _____ for next semester now?

M Professor: I don't have anything _____ for the rest of the day.

W: That's great _____. Thanks.

M: So what's _____ _____ with your schedule?

W: I _____ one more class to take. I have _____ chosen four. They are an American history course, an algebra course, _____ to psychology, and organic chemistry.

M: Do you want to take an _____ or a class in your _____?

W: I'd prefer to take an _____.

M: Okay. What are your _____?

W: I'm _____ a class on Egyptian archaeology as well as an _____ _____ class.

M: Professor Anderson is a fascinating _____. I _____ _____ his course.

W: Great. Then I guess I'll be _____ about ancient Egypt next semester. Thanks.

Exercise 2 Listen to part of a conversation and answer the questions.

04-14

Service Encounter

1   Listen again to part of the conversation. Then answer the question.
    What does the student imply when she says this: 🎧
    Ⓐ She lived in Germany as a child.
    Ⓑ She is unable to speak Italian.
    Ⓒ She is studying Spanish now.
    Ⓓ She has never been abroad before.

2   What will the student probably do next?
    Ⓐ Inquire about studying in Japan
    Ⓑ Ask the man some questions
    Ⓒ Sign up for a program
    Ⓓ Read some information

Words & Phrases

abroad adv relating to another country
particular adj certain; specific
attitude n a way of thinking
brochure n a booklet; a pamphlet

📝 Summary Note

A   Look at the summary note and recall what you heard.

Student	Man
• Wants to study abroad in Italy but doesn't speak Italian • Wants to improve language skills	• Says student can study in Spain or Germany; no language requirement there • Gives student pamphlet about programs to look through

B Complete the following summary with the words below.

| her junior year | some brochures | study abroad |
| Spain and Germany | interested in Italy | her language skills |

The student wants to _____ for one semester during
_____. She is _____ but cannot speak Italian.
Programs in _____ are for students that speak those languages and for
English speakers. She wants to study abroad to improve _____. The man
gives her _____ so that she can look through them.

Dictation Exercise Listen to the conversation again and fill in the blanks.

M Study Abroad Office Employee: Welcome to the _____ office. What
can I do for you?

W Student: Hello. I'm going to be a _____ next year. I'm thinking of studying _____
for one semester.

M: Do you have a _____ in mind?

W: Well, I'd love to _____ Italy and study there.

M: Do you speak Italian? That's a _____ if you want to study there.

W: _____ _____ Spain or Germany then? Those countries have _____
_____ to me.

M: Sure. There are programs for students that _____ those languages. But there are also
programs for _____ speakers.

W: I'm not _____ at any foreign languages. That's _____
_____ I'd like to study abroad. I want to _____ my skills.

M: That's a good _____. Let me give you a couple of _____. Why don't
you _____ _____ them? I'll be right here if you have _____
_____.

W: Thanks a lot.

Exercise 3 **Listen to part of a lecture and answer the questions.**

04-15

Music

1 Listen again to part of the lecture. Then answer the question.

What can be inferred from the student's response to the professor?

Ⓐ Turkish music uses different musical instruments.

Ⓑ Turkish music was different in the past.

Ⓒ Turkish music is not popular today.

Ⓓ Turkish music can be heard in many places.

2 What does the professor say about the music?

Ⓐ Only a few musicians are able to play it.

Ⓑ Musicians should not play it too fast.

Ⓒ There are few bands that perform it today.

Ⓓ It must be played very loudly.

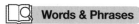 **Words & Phrases**

sonata Ⓝ a classical composition for solo instruments

movement Ⓝ a major self-contained part of a symphony or sonata

andante adv at a moderately slow tempo

variation Ⓝ a repetition of a musical theme with modifications or embellishments

Summary Note

A Look at the summary note and recall what you heard.

Mozart's *Sonata Number 11*

Movement 1
- Andante grazioso
- One theme, six variations
  ➡ famous melody

Movement 2
- Menuetto
- Minuet and trio ➡ delicate

Movement 3
- Rondo alla turca
- Allegretto ➡ varying intensity, accuracy

B Complete the following summary with the words below.

followed by	Turkish	resembles
be played delicately	distinct sounds	consistent pace

Sonata Number 11 by Mozart is a very famous piano piece. This piece has three movements that have very _____. The first movement starts with a well-known theme, and it is _____ six variations. The second movement is a minuet that should _____. The third movement is known as the _____ Rondo because it _____ the sounds of Turkish bands. This piece requires varying intensity, accuracy, and a _____.

Dictation Exercise Listen to the lecture again and fill in the blanks.

W1 Professor: We will start on a new _____ by Mozart today. Let's _____ to page six for *Sonata Number 11*. This piece has three _____: andante grazioso, menuetto, and rondo alla turca.

W2 Student: Is the third movement from the _____ Turkish Rondo?

W1: Yes, it is. Very good. Do you know _____ it is called Turkish Rondo?

W2: It's supposed to _____ the sound of Turkish bands.

W1: That's correct. The bands were called Janissary bands, and they were very _____.

W2: I did not know that the Turkish music was that popular _____. Things were sure _____ from now.

W1: Yes . . . _____. Now going back to the piece . . . The Andante grazioso is _____ of a theme with six variations. Menuetto has a minuet and trio, and rondo alla turca is allegretto. Andante grazioso is _____ its main melody. Menuetto should be played _____. And the rondo alla turca should be _____ with fluctuating intensity but with _____. Since it is very _____, you have to be careful to play every note _____. In addition, try not to get _____ as you play. You need to keep a consistent _____.

Exercise 4 Listen to part of a lecture and answer the questions.

04-16

History

1 Listen again to part of the lecture. Then answer the question.
   What does the professor imply when she says this: 🎧

   Ⓐ People of many different ages fought in the Civil War.
   Ⓑ The United States fought the Civil War in the 1800s.
   Ⓒ The Civil War was different from wars in the past.
   Ⓓ Many people died during the Civil War.

2 How did the Civil War involve the public?

   Ⓐ The public started fighting with soldiers.
   Ⓑ The public helped many soldiers.
   Ⓒ The public saw the war through photographs.
   Ⓓ The public often went to see battles be fought.

Words & Phrases

objective Ⓝ an aim; a goal
preserve Ⓥ to continue, keep, or maintain
advancement Ⓝ a forward step; a development
suffer Ⓥ to feel pain or distress
ego Ⓝ an inflated feeling of pride

📝 Summary Note

A Look at the summary note and recall what you heard.

> **Civil War**
>
> | **Objective** | **Characteristics: New Type of War** | **Results** |
> |---|---|---|
> | • To preserve the Union
• To free slaves | • Advancement of technology
• Photography | • Suffering of the Confederacy
• Ego boost to the Union |

B Complete the following summary with the words below.

advancing social conditions	terrible aspects	its victory
freeing the slaves	realities of war	economic downfall

The Civil War began to keep the Union together, but later _____ in the South became an important reason. The war was the first to introduce many modern technological features, thereby _____. It also involved the public in the _____ for the first time. The _____ of the war hit home thanks to the photographs. As the Union won the war, the Confederates went through an _____ while the Union boasted about _____.

Dictation Exercise Listen to the lecture again and fill in the blanks.

W Professor: The American Civil War _____ from 1861 to 1865 and was _____ between the Union and the Confederacy. Although many people think that the Civil War's main _____ was to free the slaves, the war began to _____ the authority and unity of the Union. The Civil War also _____ the beginning of a new generation of modern wars. The Civil War _____ brand-new war plans, weapons, communications, and _____.

M Student: I once heard that the war brought changes to the _____ as well.

W: That's correct. The war advanced hygiene, _____, and social services. The war was modern not only because it involved a wide variety of _____ but the public as well. The people _____ the war front received much more _____ information and learned about the _____ of the war.

M: Why was that?

W: Photography had been recently _____. Therefore, for the first time in history, many aspects of the war, such as dead bodies and tensions, were _____ by the general public. As the war came close to an _____, the Confederacy suffered a great deal of economic _____, and those were chronicled by _____ as well.

M: How was the Union's condition?

W: The Union _____ many of its people, but since they won the war, their ego and _____ were sometimes viewed as conceited.

Integrated Listening & Speaking

A Listen to a lecture on music while looking at the summary note. Then, answer the questions in your own words.

04-17

Music

📝 Summary Note

Mozart's *Sonata Number 11*

Movement 1
- Andante grazioso
- One theme, six variations
  → famous melody

Movement 2
- Menuetto
- Minuet and trio → delicate

Movement 3
- Rondo alla turca
- Allegretto → varying intensity, accuracy

1 Describe the music piece.

a. The piece is called *Sonata Number 11* by Mozart, and

_____ .

b. _____ , and it was composed by Mozart.

2 What is the characteristic of the first movement?

a. It has a well-known theme that _____ .

b. There are _____ in the movement.

3 How should a musician play the third movement?

a. It should be played with _____ .

b. The third movement requires _____ .

B Listen to a lecture on history while looking at the summary note. Then, answer the questions in your own words.

04-18

History

📝 **Summary Note**

Civil War

Objective	Characteristics: New Type of War	Results
• To preserve the Union • To free slaves	• Advancement of technology • Photography	• Suffering of the Confederacy • Ego boost to the Union

1 What were the main objectives of the Civil War?

    a. The objectives of the Civil War were to

    .... and to free the slaves.

    b. .... and freeing the slaves were the

    main objectives of the Civil War.

2 Why was the Civil War the first modern war?

    a. The Civil War introduced many ....

    b. The Civil War was the first war in the modern era to use

    ....

3 What were the effects on the Union and the Confederacy?

    a. The Union .... to its ego, but

    the Confederacy ....

    b. The Confederacy .... , but the

    Union's ego ....

Mini TOEFL iBT Practice Test

Listen to part of a conversation between a student and a student activities office employee.

04-19

1 According to the woman, how does the camp bring attendees together?

    Ⓐ Attendees compete against the others.

    Ⓑ Attendees are asked to bring their friends.

    Ⓒ Attendees are placed onto teams.

    Ⓓ Attendees are introduced to one another.

2 What does the woman say about the camp?

    Ⓐ It is free for students to attend.

    Ⓑ It requires students to go cycling.

    Ⓒ It has several elective activities.

    Ⓓ It will be challenging for the student.

3 Listen again to part of the conversation. Then answer the question.

What is the purpose of the woman's response?

    Ⓐ To see if the student likes camping

    Ⓑ To see if the camp level fits the student

    Ⓒ To find out which activities the student is interested in

    Ⓓ To persuade the student to attend the camp

Listen to part of a lecture in an ecology class.

04-20

4 According to the professor, what is in an ecosystem?
Click on 2 answers.

Ⓐ Rocks

Ⓑ Clouds

Ⓒ Sunlight

Ⓓ Bacteria

5 Why does the professor discuss microecosystems?

Ⓐ To say that they are everywhere

Ⓑ To compare them with ocean ecosystems

Ⓒ To ask the students to think of some

Ⓓ To give an example of them

6 Listen again to part of the lecture. Then answer the question.
What is the purpose of the professor's response?

Ⓐ To ask the student to try again

Ⓑ To tell the student she got the right answer

Ⓒ To make the student think harder

Ⓓ To indicate that the student is wrong

Vocabulary Check-Up

A Choose the correct words that match the definitions.

1	enormous	A	to save or protect something from damage or decay
2	suffer	B	certain; specific
3	damage	C	attractive; inviting
4	preserve	D	of a person
5	puddle	E	a booklet; a pamphlet
6	approximately	F	to endure; to feel pain
7	contamination	G	a small pool of water
8	particular	H	well liked; admired
9	appealing	I	harm or injury
10	prevent	J	a purpose; a goal
11	individual	K	sporty, healthy, and strong
12	objective	L	huge; very large
13	popular	M	around; about
14	athletic	N	to stop; to avoid
15	brochure	O	the act of making something dirty or harmful

B Complete the sentences by choosing the correct words.

Ⓐ fascinating	Ⓑ elective	Ⓒ registration	Ⓓ abroad	Ⓔ submit

1 _____ for the program begins on the nineteenth of October.

2 Students should _____ their homework before class starts.

3 Many students like to study _____ during their junior year.

4 The students found the teacher's lectures to be _____.

5 A(n) _____ is a course a student does not need to take to graduate.

05 Understanding the Speaker's Attitude

Overview

Introduction

Speaker's Attitude questions test whether you can understand a speaker's attitude or opinion. This question asks you about the speaker's feelings, likes and dislikes, or reason behind various emotions. You are also often asked about a speaker's degree of certainty. This question type often involves replaying a portion of the listening passage.

Question Types

◆ What can be inferred about the student?

◆ What is the professor's attitude toward X?

◆ What is the professor's opinion of X?

◆ What can be inferred about the student when she says this: (replay)

◆ What does the woman mean when she says this: (replay)

Useful Tips

➤ Focus on the tone of voice, the intonation, and the sentence stress the speakers use in the conversation or lecture.

➤ Practice distinguishing between referencing and giving personal opinions.

➤ Avoid answers that are too far from the general tone of the conversation or lecture.

➤ Try to take notes on the context of the conversation or lecture.

➤ Pay attention to adjectives and verbs of feeling.

Script

M Student: Hello, Professor Charles. You are looking for me?

W Professor: Good afternoon, Kenny. Yes, I have been looking for you. I'd like to be the first person to congratulate you.

05-01

M: Congratulate me for what?

W: For winning first prize in the art contest. The painting you submitted was selected as the winner. Congratulations. You made an incredible work.

M: Wow. I . . . I don't know what to say.

Q What can be inferred about the student?

    Ⓐ He often enters art contests.

    Ⓑ He has never met the professor before.

    Ⓒ He is majoring in art.

    Ⓓ He is surprised by the award.

✔ Correct Answer

The correct answer to the above question is Ⓓ. The student acts surprised by the professor's comments, so he clearly did not expect to win the award.

Introduction to the Skill

At the beginning of a conversation, the last content word is usually the focus of the meaning. Focus means to see clearly. The focus word in a sentence has the most emphasis so that the listener can hear it clearly. The focus word is marked by a rise and then a fall. The fall in pitch helps listeners recognize the end of a thought group. However, a question may end with a rising or a falling pitch.

Put this in the drawer.   Do you want some coffee?

Where are you going?

A Changing Focus

After a conversation, the focus changes as each person speaks, so any word can be the focus. The focus changes because the speaker wants to call attention to new information. Old information is already understood and does not need to be emphasized.

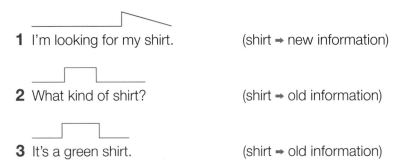

1 I'm looking for my shirt.   (shirt ➡ new information)

2 What kind of shirt?   (shirt ➡ old information)

3 It's a green shirt.   (shirt ➡ old information)

B Exception

Usually, the normal emphasis pattern reduces structure words. However, when a speaker feels strongly or wants to disagree with something said before, any word may be emphasized, including structure words.

A: I bought a book at the library.

B: No, you borrowed a book from the library.

Skill Practice

A Read the following sentences out loud, and underline the most emphasized or pitched words. Then, listen to each sentence and check your answers.

05-02

1 Why is the door locked?

2 Do you want coffee or tea?

3 It will look really nice when it is sitting on the table.

4 Now, when you read, don't just consider what the author thinks.

5 **W**: Which is more important, health or wealth?

   M: You need health and wealth together.

B Listen to the following conversation and underline the high-pitched words.

05-03

W Student: What are those workmen doing on the roof of the dorm?

M Resident Assistant: I was told that they're fitting some solar panels.

W: What are they for?

M: They're for heating water using just the heat of the sun. They can provide from thirty to seventy percent of an ordinary home's needs for hot water each year.

W: And for free! That's really worth having.

C Listen to part of a lecture and underline the high-pitched words.

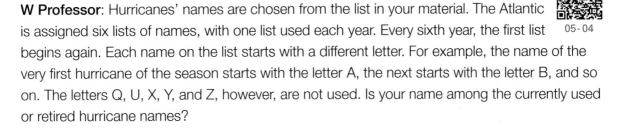
05-04

W Professor: Hurricanes' names are chosen from the list in your material. The Atlantic is assigned six lists of names, with one list used each year. Every sixth year, the first list begins again. Each name on the list starts with a different letter. For example, the name of the very first hurricane of the season starts with the letter A, the next starts with the letter B, and so on. The letters Q, U, X, Y, and Z, however, are not used. Is your name among the currently used or retired hurricane names?

Basic Drill

Listen to part of a conversation and answer the question.

Drill 1

Q What can be inferred about the professor?

05-05

    Ⓐ He wants the student to retake a test.

    Ⓑ He is the student's academic advisor.

    Ⓒ He teaches in the History Department.

    Ⓓ He prefers the more challenging topic.

|Check-Up| Listen again and choose the correct words.

W Student: I thought of two possible topics for the project. The first one is on how soil (affects the pH of water / effects the pH of eater), and the second one is on how soil (challenges with deep / changes with depth).

M Professor: They are both okay. Which one do you feel more (relaxed / comfortable) with?

W: I like the second one, but it is more challenging.

M: Will you go with something that is easy or something that you can learn and (accomplish more / accommodate more) through putting in more of an (afford / effort)?

W: It sounds like you are telling me to do the second one.

M: Well, it is up to you. I was just giving you a (suggestion / submission).

Drill 2

Q What is the woman's attitude toward the student?

05-06

    Ⓐ She does not want to speak to him.

    Ⓑ She is interested in his opinion.

    Ⓒ She is unconcerned about him.

    Ⓓ She is helpful to him.

|Check-Up| Listen again and choose the correct words.

M Student: It's my first time here.

W Computer Lab Assistant: Okay. Just (fill out this application / feel out those complications), and you are registered.

M: Thank you. One more thing . . . Can you tell me how to (us / use) the lab?

W: You can just go to any computer or come to the help desk to (reserve a computer / keep computation). The time limit is two hours. If you want to (pin an argument / print a document), it costs five cents per page. No food or drinks are (allowed / permitted).

M: Thank you. It's pretty much the same as the old one I (used for / used to) go to before.

Drill 3

Q What is the professor's opinion of vitamin A?

05-07

- (A) It is the best way to improve one's eyesight.
- (B) It is not very useful.
- (C) Everyone needs to take more vitamin A.
- (D) It is important to the eyes.

|Check-Up| Listen again and choose the correct words.

W Professor: Vitamin A (plays a vital role / pays a vital roll) in your eyes. It helps your eyes (administer to night charges / adjust to light changes) so that you can see during the day and night. Plus, it helps your eyes stay (oyster / moist). Therefore, if you feel uncomfortable (seeing at night / sing at night) or your eyes (dehydrate / feel dry), your eyes need vitamin A. Of course, there can be other reasons, but studies show that vitamin A prevents those (illnesses/ eel less) from happening.

Drill 4

Q What is the professor's opinion of the qualifications to be a U.S. presidential candidate?

05-08

- (A) They are easy.
- (B) They are difficult to understand.
- (C) There are too many of them.
- (D) There are problems with them.

|Check-Up| Listen again and choose the correct words.

W Professor: The U.S. president is (elected every four years / ejected every for yards). Everyone probably thinks that the qualifications for the (candidates / applicants) are very high. But once you find out the (cry out / criteria), you will have a different idea. First, the candidate has to be a (natural-born / neutral-bone) citizen of the U.S. Second, the person should be at least thirty-five years of age and a (legend of the U.S. / resident of the U.S.). for at least fourteen years. Since gender and race are not (told / mentioned), anyone here who is a natural-born citizen can dream of being the president.

Exercises with Short Conversations & Lectures

Exercise 1 Listen to part of a conversation and answer the questions.

05-09

Service Encounter

1 Listen again to part of the conversation. Then answer the question.

What does the woman mean when she says this: 🎧
- Ⓐ The student should invest in the stock market.
- Ⓑ The student should buy a suit.
- Ⓒ The student should make a résumé.
- Ⓓ The student should save his money.

2 What are the speakers mainly discussing?
- Ⓐ The student's appearance
- Ⓑ A coming job fair
- Ⓒ Making a résumé
- Ⓓ Finding employment

📖 **Words & Phrases**

advice Ⓝ a recommendation or suggestion on what to do

suit Ⓝ a formal type of men's clothes

worthwhile adj being worth the time or effort

impress Ⓥ to make someone have positive thoughts about something

Dictation Exercise
Listen to the conversation again and fill in the blanks.

M Student: Hello. I _____ if you can help me.

W Student Activities Office Employee: I'll do my _____. What do you need?

M: I heard there is a _____ coming up soon. Can you tell me about it?

W: Sure. It's going to _____ this Saturday. Around 200 companies will be in _____. They will be from all kinds of _____. So no matter what your _____ is, there should be something there for you.

M: That's great to hear. Do you have any _____ for me?

W: Please bring some _____ of your résumé to hand out. And be sure to wear a _____.

M: I don't actually _____ one.

W: It's a worthwhile _____. It will _____ recruiters if you wear one.

M: _____. I guess I need to go shopping soon.

Exercise 2 Listen to part of a conversation and answer the questions.

05-10

Service Encounter

1 Listen again to part of the conversation. Then answer the question.

What does the librarian mean when she says this: 🎧

- Ⓐ She does not have much time to read.
- Ⓑ She wants the student to read more books.
- Ⓒ She likes the books the student is borrowing.
- Ⓓ She likes nonfiction more than fiction.

2 What does the student enjoy doing?

- Ⓐ Reading nonfiction books
- Ⓑ Writing essays about books
- Ⓒ Talking about books with others
- Ⓓ Spending time at the library

📖 **Words & Phrases**

borrow v to obtain or receive something on loan

creativity n the ability or power to create

favorite adj best liked

nonfiction n prose works other than fiction

Dictation Exercise Listen to the conversation again and fill in the blanks.

W1 Librarian: Hi, Jennifer. What are you _____ today? Wow! Are you sure you can _____ all these in time?

W2 Student: Yes. I'm so into _____ these days. I _____ them all night long. It is so _____ to imagine and guess where the story is _____.

W1: Yes, it enhances your creativity and _____. Do you have a _____?

W2: I kind of have one, but I'm trying to read one book by _____ _____. I'll definitely have one _____. What are you reading these days?

W1: I like mysteries, but I'm more into _____ that deals with politics and _____.

W2: That _____ interesting.

W1: Yes, it is. Well, you know your interests and thoughts _____ over time. I might get _____ in mysteries like you _____. We will talk about _____ when I do.

W2: That is a wonderful idea. I _____ talking about books with people.

Exercise 3 Listen to part of a lecture and answer the questions.

05-11

Nutrition

1 Listen again to part of the lecture. Then answer the question. What does the professor mean when he says this: 🎧
- Ⓐ The students know the material the professor will discuss.
- Ⓑ He wants to tell the students some new information now.
- Ⓒ The students need to take good notes during his lecture.
- Ⓓ He thinks the students should ask questions during class.

2 What does the professor say about fiber?
- Ⓐ It should be consumed regularly.
- Ⓑ It is found in meats and grains.
- Ⓒ Most people do not get enough of it.
- Ⓓ Some people can be harmed by it.

📖 **Words & Phrases**

nutrition Ⓝ a source of nourishment
essential adj necessary
source Ⓝ a basis
relation Ⓝ a logical or natural association between two or more things
consume Ⓥ to eat

Dictation Exercise Listen to the lecture again and fill in the blanks.

M Professor: Last week, we talked about food and its _____ to health in general. Starting today, we will go into more _____. We are going to spend six weeks studying food and _____. We are going to _____ _____ fiber. I'm sure you have heard a lot about fiber _____. I'm also sure you have heard the _____ I'm going to talk about now. First of all, fiber is good for the _____ system, and it _____ the body's cholesterol level. Foods with fiber are good _____ of essential nutrients. This means that foods with fiber are good for our _____. In addition, fiber should be _____ frequently and regularly to be _____.

Exercise 4 **Listen to part of a lecture and answer the questions.**

05-12

Literature

1 Listen again to part of the lecture. Then answer the question. What can be inferred about the professor when she says this: 🎧
   Ⓐ She wants the students to read more poetry.
   Ⓑ She considers poetry to be more important than novels.
   Ⓒ She thinks that poetry is not particularly important.
   Ⓓ She believes poetry is a common topic of discussion.

2 Why does the professor mention the origin of the word poetry?
   Ⓐ To compare it with the origin of fiction
   Ⓑ To answer a student's question
   Ⓒ To point out it comes from Latin
   Ⓓ To explain its meaning

Words & Phrases

create Ⓥ to produce
express Ⓥ to make one's feelings or opinions known
intense adj extreme in degree

Dictation Exercise **Listen to the lecture again and fill in the blanks.**

W Professor: Let me ask you a question before I start. Do you love _____ or have a favorite _____? Some of you may answer yes, and some of you may answer no. You might not have _____, but we talk about poems and poetry a lot in our _____ _____. What is written in poetry is a _____ of our daily lives. However, we don't have a clear _____ of what poetry is. How would you _____ poetry? I believe most of you are not _____ with the meaning. Therefore, what I am going to do is _____ the word poetry for you. First of all, the word is of Greek _____ and means to make or to _____.

Exercises with Mid-Length Conversations & Lectures

Exercise 1 Listen to part of a conversation and answer the questions.

05-13

Service Encounter

1 What is the student's opinion of his schedule?

  Ⓐ He wants to take even more classes.

  Ⓑ He likes he has no Monday classes.

  Ⓒ He believes it will be very difficult.

  Ⓓ He thinks he has the wrong class.

2 What is the woman's attitude toward the student?

  Ⓐ She is unhappy with the student's manners.

  Ⓑ She thinks the student has a bad personality.

  Ⓒ She believes the student is very smart.

  Ⓓ She finds the student easy to deal with.

Words & Phrases

enroll Ⓥ to enter or register in a roll

request Ⓥ to ask for

flexible adj accommodating

personality Ⓝ character

📝 Summary Note

A Look at the summary note and recall what you heard.

Mistake in class schedule	Student just wants to switch chemistry to biology	Fix the mistake without other changes

B Complete the following summary with the words below.

luckily	fix his schedule	switched chemistry
a pleasure	found a mistake	doesn't mind changes

The student _____ in his schedule. He went to see the employee
to _____. Many students don't like their schedules being switched.
However, the student _____ in his schedule. The employee believes the
student is _____ to deal with. Luckily, the student can keep his other
classes in the same periods and _____ to biology.

Dictation Exercise   Listen to the conversation again and fill in the blanks.

M Student: Hello. I got my schedule and _____ that I was enrolled in the _____
class.

W Registrar's Office Employee: Let me see your schedule _____ I can find out what
_____ _____.

M: Here you are.

W: Thank you. What are the classes you _____, Jake?

M: I _____ biology, English, algebra, tennis, art, and American history.

W: Hmm, you have chemistry _____ _____ biology. I'll _____ that now.
Give me a second.

M: Am I going to have the _____ schedule and just _____ chemistry to biology? Or
are you going to change the _____ schedule?

W: Let me check. _____ I have to switch classes around, but _____, that won't be
the _____ for you.

M: It wouldn't be a _____ _____ even if you changed my classes around.

W: Good. Some students _____ _____ making changes.

M: I'm _____. I'm _____ as long as I get to take all the classes I chose.

W: You are an _____ person with a great personality. I'm _____ done here.
Fortunately, there's a biology class during third period, so you get to _____ your schedule as is.

M: Great!

Exercise 2 Listen to part of a conversation and answer the questions.

05-14

Office Hours

1 What is the professor's opinion of the student?

Ⓐ He believes she is trying her best.

Ⓑ He thinks she can do better in his class.

Ⓒ He considers her a good student.

Ⓓ He wants her to take the class again.

2 Listen again to part of the conversation. Then answer the question.
What can be inferred about the professor when he says this: 🎧

Ⓐ He believes the student will get an A in his class.

Ⓑ He wants the student to come to every class.

Ⓒ He believes the student is making a mistake.

Ⓓ He thinks the student should study more.

Words & Phrases

material 🅝 information
habit 🅝 an action a person does often or repeatedly
poorly 🅐🅓🅥 badly
review 🅥 to look over again
definitely 🅐🅓🅥 for sure

Summary Note

A Look at the summary note and recall what you heard.

Professor says student got a C+ and a C- on two tests; asks about her study habits	Student says she studies two days before the test	Professor tells her to review her notes after class and to do the reading	Student says she is busy but will try

B Complete the following summary with the words below.

not good enough	her study habits	two days
she is busy	two low grades	review her notes

The professor tells the student she got _____ on her tests. He asks about
_____. The student studies _____ before the exam.
The professor tells her that is _____ and that she needs to
_____ daily and do the reading. The student says
_____ but will try.

Dictation Exercise Listen to the conversation again and fill in the blanks.

M Professor: Brenda, you aren't doing _____ _____ in this class. You got a C+ on
the first test and a C- on the _____ _____.

W Student: I'm _____ my best, sir. This is just _____ material for me.

M: What are your _____ _____ like?

W: Well, I usually study about two days _____ the exam.

M: Is that all?

W: My other classes keep me _____, so I don't have _____ time to study biology.

M: That's not _____ enough. That _____ why you're doing so poorly.

W: What should I do then?

M: _____ your notes after every class. In addition, be _____ to do the reading for
each lecture. If you do those two things, you should _____ your grade.

W: I'll try, but I am _____ _____ this semester. But I want to _____
_____ in this class.

M: Please spend _____ _____ on the material. It will _____ help your
grade.

Listen to part of a lecture and answer the questions.

05-15

Sociology

1 What is the professor's opinion of Native Alaskans?
- Ⓐ Their living conditions are not good.
- Ⓑ They do not work hard enough.
- Ⓒ They are treated unfairly these days.
- Ⓓ They live better than they used to.

2 What is the professor's attitude toward native Alaskans?
- Ⓐ They need to rely on the government more.
- Ⓑ They should start looking for better jobs.
- Ⓒ They are not dealing with their problems well.
- Ⓓ They do not care at all about education.

Words & Phrases

virtually ad almost but not quite; practically
abuse n improper use or handling
neglect v to pay little or no attention to

identity n characteristics
emotional adj of or relating to emotion

Summary Note

A Look at the summary note and recall what you heard.

Alcohol abuse, domestic violence, homicides, and suicides

Many children are abused and not educated properly

Lack of mental and emotional well-being among native Alaskans

Losing hold of their communities, cultural identities, and their childhoods

B Complete the following summary with the words below.

lose control	alcohol abuse	a lack of education
taken care of	unprivileged	their economy

Native Alaskans' lives are _____. They lack mental and emotional well-being. _____, domestic violence, homicides, and suicides are some results. In addition, children are not properly _____ by their parents. _____ leads to alcohol and other chemicals abuse. As native Alaskans _____ of themselves, they also lose control of _____ and governing institutions.

Dictation Exercise Listen to the lecture again and fill in the blanks.

M Professor: One social issue _____ by the state of Alaska is the _____ of mental and emotional well-being among native Alaskans. It is _____ that many Native Americans live in _____ conditions throughout the country. In the cases of native Alaskans, virtually entire villages _____ from a lack of mental and emotional well-being, which _____ poor physical and mental health. Alcohol abuse, domestic violence, homicides, and _____ are frequent in them, which, of course, lead to families _____. It is _____ to see that many children are abused and not educated _____. As a matter of fact, children themselves are abusing alcohol and other _____, and the rate is increasing over time. Since parents are _____ mental illnesses and alcohol abuse, they can't take care of their children, so many _____ being taken care of by others or are simply neglected. Therefore, we can _____ that Alaskan natives are losing hold of their _____, cultural identities, and, most importantly, their childhoods. So you can see how _____ the issue is. Plus, rather than making a living for themselves, many _____ public services and subsidies. They have lost _____ of their economy and governing institutions.

Listen to part of a lecture and answer the questions.

05- 16

Literature

1 What is the professor's attitude toward the student?

Ⓐ She is happy with his question.

Ⓑ She believes he is a good writer.

Ⓒ She dislikes his distractions.

Ⓓ She wants him to pay more attention.

2 What can be inferred about the professor?

Ⓐ She prefers to read fiction instead of nonfiction.

Ⓑ She will give the students a fiction writing assignment.

Ⓒ She thinks nonfiction is not always completely true.

Ⓓ She has published some nonfiction books in the past.

Words & Phrases

fact Ⓝ knowledge or information based on real occurrences

content Ⓝ something contained

imaginary ⒶⒹⒿ having existence only in the imagination; not real

afterward ⒶⒹⓋ at a later time

biography Ⓝ a person's life story written by another individual

📝 Summary Note

A Look at the summary note and recall what you heard.

Fiction & Nonfiction

Fiction
• Storytelling of imagined events
• Stir people's emotions
• Novels, fables, comics, movies

Nonfiction
• Fact or reality
• Essays, journals, biographies

B Complete the following summary with the words below.

emotions	created stories	novels
laugh and cry	true or false	essays

The difference between fiction and nonfiction is that fiction is based on
_____ while nonfiction is based on facts. Fiction includes
_____, fables, cartoons, comics, and movies that can touch people's
_____ and which make people _____. Contrasted
with fiction, nonfiction includes _____, journals, documentaries, and
biographies and can be either _____ depending on the information the
author has.

Dictation Exercise   Listen to the lecture again and fill in the blanks.

W Professor: Class, we are going to distinguish the _____ between fiction and nonfiction.
Basically, fiction is storytelling of _____ events, and nonfiction is fact or _____.
Specifically, fiction is imagined stories such as _____, fables, fairy tales, cartoons, and
_____. These can _____ some factual events that are _____ with
imaginary contents.

M Student: What about _____?

W: Excellent question. I'm pleased you asked that. What do you think?

M: Fiction.

W: Very good! Movies and video games—the ones you guys always _____ after school—are
fiction. Most of them are made-up _____. Some are _____ on true stories, but they
have _____ imaginary stories to grab people's attention. Fiction has the _____ to
stir people's _____. It can give us hope and make us _____ or _____.
I'm sure you have cried, laughed hard, or felt _____ for characters in fiction works you have
read or seen. Finally, _____ with fiction, nonfiction _____ facts.
However, the facts could contain _____ information.

M: How?

W: Well, the author believes that what he or she has written is _____, but that information
could be _____ false afterward. _____ examples of nonfiction works are
_____, journals, documentaries, photographs, and biographies.

Integrated Listening & Speaking

A Listen to a lecture on sociology while looking at the summary note. Then, answer the questions in your own words.

05-17

Sociology

📝 **Summary Note**

Alcohol abuse, domestic violence, homicides, and suicides	Many children are abused and not educated properly

Lack of mental and emotional well-being among native Alaskans

Losing hold of their communities, cultural identities, and their childhoods

1 Why does the professor say it is unfortunate to learn about native Alaskans?

    a. Alaskan natives lack _____.

    b. Alcohol abuse, domestic violence, child abuse, homicide, and suicide are the
       results that _____.

2 What does the professor say is tragic for the children?

    a. Many children are _____ or neglected.

    b. Parents cannot _____ sometimes.

3 What are the causes of the destruction of native Alaskans?

    a. The causes are _____ and spiritual wounds.

    b. The causes are unsettled cultural _____.

B Listen to a lecture on literature while looking at the summary note. Then, answer the questions in your own words.

05-18

Literature

📝 **Summary Note**

Fiction & Nonfiction

Fiction
- Storytelling of imagined events
- Stir people's emotions
- Novels, fables, comics, movies

Nonfiction
- Fact or reality
- Essays, journals, biographies

1 What is fiction?

a. _____, and comics are fiction.

b. Some fiction is based on factual events, but it is

_____.

2 What does fiction do to people?

a. Fiction stirs _____.

b. Fiction makes people _____.

3 How can nonfiction contain false information?

a. _____ could contribute to false information in a book.

b. _____ at a later time in the future.

Mini TOEFL iBT Practice Test

Listen to part of a conversation between a student and an Economics Department office employee.

05-19

1 Why did the student visit the man?
- Ⓐ To submit some paperwork
- Ⓑ To find out where a professor is
- Ⓒ To ask for help
- Ⓓ To start her new job

2 What is the man's attitude toward the student?
- Ⓐ He tells her to behave herself.
- Ⓑ He is helpful to her.
- Ⓒ He warns her to be careful.
- Ⓓ He gives her some advice.

3 What is the student's opinion of her job?
- Ⓐ It will be educational.
- Ⓑ It will be boring.
- Ⓒ It will be difficult.
- Ⓓ It will be entertaining.

Listen to part of a lecture in a history class.

History

4 What are the students going to do during their next class?

Ⓐ Watch a movie

Ⓑ Visit a museum

Ⓒ Take a test

Ⓓ Submit their papers

5 Why does the student mention the *Mayflower*?

Ⓐ To call it the name of an early colony

Ⓑ To claim it was a book a colonist wrote

Ⓒ To name a ship some colonists sailed on

Ⓓ To point out that it was a warship

6 Listen again to part of the lecture. Then answer the question. What does the professor mean when she says this: 🎧

Ⓐ The question she asked is very difficult.

Ⓑ It is important that the student try.

Ⓒ She is not worried about the problem.

Ⓓ The student should know the right answer.

Vocabulary Check-Up

A Choose the correct words that match the definitions.

1 flexible • • Ⓐ for sure

2 consume • • Ⓑ to fail to look after something properly

3 definitely • • Ⓒ almost but not quite; practically

4 assist • • Ⓓ at a later time

5 neglect • • Ⓔ to eat

6 imaginary • • Ⓕ a recommendation or suggestion on what to do

7 virtually • • Ⓖ badly

8 habit • • Ⓗ not real; existing only in the mind

9 favorite • • Ⓘ a formal type of men's clothes

10 afterward • • Ⓙ accommodating

11 fact • • Ⓚ to cause something to happen or exist

12 poorly • • Ⓛ best liked

13 advice • • Ⓜ to help another person

14 suit • • Ⓝ knowledge or information based on real occurrences

15 create • • Ⓞ an action a person does often or repeatedly

B Complete the sentences by choosing the correct words.

Ⓐ pleasure　　Ⓑ file　　Ⓒ impress　　Ⓓ colonies　　Ⓔ motivation

1 Please _____ these documents in the cabinet over there.

2 Many countries founded _____ in Africa in the past.

3 He gained a lot of _____ from traveling around the world.

4 His _____ for doing the project is to get an A.

5 He tried to _____ his boss by arriving early every day.

PART III

Connecting
Information

Connecting Information questions test your ability to integrate
information from different parts of the listening passage to make
inferences, to draw conclusions, to form generalizations, and to make
predictions. To choose the right answer, these question types require you
to make connections between or among pieces of information in the text
and to identify the relationships between the ideas and the details.

06 Understanding Organization

Overview

Introduction

Organization questions require you to identify the overall organization of the listening passage or the relationship between different portions of the listening passage. In organization questions, you are also asked to recognize the role of specific information such as topic changes, exemplifying, digressing, and inducing introductory and concluding remarks. This is to see whether you know how the specific part of the sentence is related to the entire content. This question type usually appears after lectures rather than conversations and sometimes requires you to choose more than one answer.

Question Types

◆ How does the professor organize the information about X that he presents to the class?

◆ How is the discussion organized?

◆ Why does the professor discuss X?

◆ Why does the professor mention X?

Useful Tips

▶ Typical types of organizations include the following patterns: giving examples, contrasting, comparing, classifying, categorizing, describing causes and effects, and explaining in chronological order

▶ Listen carefully for the transitions that indicate the sequence.

▶ Focus on the relationship between the contents led by the transitional words.

Script

06-01

M Professor: It's possible for rocks and minerals to be broken down over time. One process that can do this is weathering. Weathering can be caused by, well, let's see . . . water, ice, temperature changes, salt, acid, plants, and even animals. The process of weathering can take a very long time to occur. Yet it can also happen quickly in some cases. Because of weathering, the surface of the Earth is constantly changing. For instance, imagine that you have a time machine. If you go 500 years into the future, the campus the school is on will look much different than today. The reason is weathering.

Q Why does the professor mention the surface of the Earth?

Ⓐ To prove that it changes slowly

Ⓑ To note that it has many features

Ⓒ To argue that it can remain the same

Ⓓ To say it is affected by weathering

✅ Correct Answer

The correct answer to the above question is Ⓓ. The professor points out that the surface of the Earth changes due to weathering.

Introduction to the Skill

Signal words are those words that provide clues as to where information in a chapter or lecture is going. Their purpose is to help you organize information, recognize key ideas, and notice shifts in focus in the lecture as follows.

Key Signal Words and Phrases

Initiating Topics	The first thing is . . . Now, I'd like to give you . . .	Let's begin with . . . Today, I would like to . . .	Let me talk about . . . What I'd like to do is . . .
Main Idea	Okay, so . . . To sum up . . . There are two reasons why . . .	The main point is . . . In other words . . .	And most importantly . . . To tie this up . . .
Topic Shifting	The next point is . . . Let's turn to . . .	Let me go to . . . This leads to . . .	Okay, now . . . The other thing is . . .
Supporting Ideas	On the other hand . . . For example . . . Similarly . . . Furthermore . . . In order to . . .	On the contrary . . . As an example . . . Additionally . . . Likewise . . . Because . . .	In contrast . . . For instance . . . Further . . . In addition to . . .
Conclusion or Summary	Therefore . . . As a result . . . From this we see . . .	Okay, so . . . Finally . . . The main point is . . .	In conclusion . . . In summary . . . In short . . .
Emphasizing	important to note / most of all / a significant factor / a primary concern / a key feature / the main value / especially valuable / most noteworthy / remember that / a major event / the chief outcome / the principal item / pay particular attention to / the chief factor / a vital force / above all / a central issue / a distinctive quality / especially relevant / should be noted / the most substantial issue		

Skill Practice

06-02

A Fill in the blanks with the appropriate signal words in the boxes. Then, listen to the sentences and check your answers.

therefore	on the contrary	for example
because	the first thing	

1 As I said in the previous lecture, this is a sophisticated problem. _____, it needs a profound study.

2 To the surprise of all the people in the scientific community, the laboratory was closed _____ it was contaminated by radiation.

3 Lots of questions are asked in the field of historical linguistics. _____, what was English like when it was first used?

4 Arteries carry blood with oxygen away from the heart. _____, veins carry blood without oxygen back to the heart.

5 Among all the theories about the infection, _____ I want to talk about is through human remains.

B Listen to the following conversation and underline the signal words.

06-03

W Professor: Okay, class. Let's turn to chapter four. Chapter four is on organic chemistry.

M Student: Is it different from what we have dealt with so far?

W: Sure. There is a huge difference. Remember that organic means "coming from vitality." Let's start with carbon-carbon bonding.

C Listen to part of a lecture and fill in the blanks with the correct words.

06-04

W Professor: Now _____ _____ tell you the origin of waves. Most waves are formed as a result of wind passing over water. Wind speed and direction _____ the sizes of waves. Steady winds blowing over water for a long period produce _____. _____, waves can be formed by moving something _____, such as a boat or by underwater earthquakes that can create very large, long waves called tsunamis. These can reach heights of up to _____.

Basic Drill

Listen to parts of conversations or lectures and answer the questions.

Drill 1

Q Why does the women mention a form?

    Ⓐ To ask the student to sign it

    Ⓑ To tell the student to save it

    Ⓒ To have the student fill it out

    Ⓓ To request that the student copy it

06-05

| Check-Up | Listen again and choose the correct words.

M Student: Hello. I lost my ID card. What do I do to (display it / replace it)?

W Registrar's Office Employee: Fill out your name and social security number on this form and stand (behind that line / beyond that line). I will (take your pick / take your picture) here.

M: I am ready.

W: Okay. You are all set. I will print your new ID (in about a minute / in a while).

M: Great. Thank you.

W: You'll have to (play for free / pay a fee) of ten dollars.

M: That's (a big problem / not a problem) at all.

Drill 2

Q Why does the man mention the hard drive?

    Ⓐ To advise the student to buy a new one

    Ⓑ To point out that it has no more space on it

    Ⓒ To note that it is possible to repair

    Ⓓ To tell the student it is no longer working

06-06

| Check-Up | Listen again and choose the correct words.

W Student: Hello. My laptop computer died on me. Can you (fix it / repair it)?

M Computer Lab Assistant: Let me (take a peek / take a look). When did this happen?

W: This morning while I was working on my homework. I didn't even get to save it.

M: Oh . . . That's not good. Let me see if I can (recover your file / discover your file).

W: Do you know (why it cashed / why it crashed)?

M: It looks like the hard drive (just went up / just gave up). But your file has been stored in the backup.

W: Oh, thank you so much. You have (saved my day / saved my date)!

Drill 3

Q Why does the professor discuss the hypocenter?

   Ⓐ To say it is very dangerous

   Ⓑ To define what it means

   Ⓒ To claim that it causes earthquakes

   Ⓓ To compare it with an earthquake

06-07

❙Check-Up❙ Listen again and choose the correct words.

W Professor: An earthquake happens when two (adjusting blocks / adjacent blocks) of earth suddenly move. The surface of the movement is called the fault or (fault plane / faulty lane). There are several enormous faults in the state of California alone. The (hypocenter / hypothermia), the location where the earthquake starts, (located below / sits below) the Earth's surface whereas the epicenter sits on the (Earth's surface / Earth's face) (right above / directly above) the hypocenter.

Drill 4

Q How is the discussion organized?

   Ⓐ By comparing DNA and nucleotides

   Ⓑ In chronological order

   Ⓒ By defining the terms

   Ⓓ From the largest to the smallest components

06-08

❙Check-Up❙ Listen again and choose the correct words.

M Professor: The genetic information of a(n) (higher organism / upper organism) is contained in large molecules called (chronicle / chromosomes). These chromosomes are a package of a very long, continuous, (double helix / double match) DNA. (One stand / One strand) of the helix is a long chain of molecules called nucleotides, and the other helix has the (pairing nucleotides / paring nucleotides) of the opposite helix. There are four types of nucleotides. Each nucleotide has only one (possible game / possible match).

Exercise 1 Listen to part of a conversation and answer the questions.

06-09

Office Hours

1 Why does the professor mention Professor Morrisson?
- Ⓐ To say that he is retiring
- Ⓑ To recommend his class
- Ⓒ To give the student his room number
- Ⓓ To tell the student to speak with him

2 Why did the student visit the professor?
- Ⓐ To request some advice
- Ⓑ To drop the professor's class
- Ⓒ To ask about her last lecture
- Ⓓ To turn in his homework

Words & Phrases

extra adj bonus; more than necessary
popular adj liked by many people
register v to sign up for something like a class

Dictation Exercise Listen to the conversation again and fill in the blanks.

M Student: Professor Campbell, I'm trying to _____ if I should attend _____ _____ or not.

W Professor: Do you need to _____ _____ some extra credits?

M: No, I don't. But I have a summer job on _____. So I thought I might _____ a class or two as well.

W: Hmm . . . In that case, why don't you take an _____? Did you know Professor Morrisson is _____ a class this summer?

M: He's really _____, isn't he? I _____ to get in his English literature class last year, but it was _____.

W: That's right. He's teaching a _____ on English literature about King Arthur. You might try _____ for it.

M: That's a _____ _____. I think I'll do that.

06-10

Office Hours

1 Why does the professor mention the Revolution of 1848?
   - Ⓐ To correct a mistake he made about it
   - Ⓑ To say it will not be on an exam
   - Ⓒ To advise the student to study it
   - Ⓓ To assign it as the student's paper topic

2 What are the speakers mainly discussing?
   - Ⓐ The topic of a recent lecture
   - Ⓑ A presentation the student must give
   - Ⓒ A report that the student wrote
   - Ⓓ Information that will be on an exam

Words & Phrases

assign v to give as work to do

notes n information about a lecture that students write down

quite adv very

Dictation Exercise Listen to the conversation again and fill in the blanks.

W Student: Professor Robinson, I have a _____ of questions about the _____.

M Professor: Sure, Penelope. What do you want to know?

W: Um . . . What _____ do I need to _____ for the test?

M: Just study all of the _____ I assigned in the textbook. Be sure to read _____ _____ as well.

W: What about the _____ we just had today? Will that be on the test?

M: You should definitely know about the _____ that _____ in the Revolution of 1848.

W: Ah, okay. I wasn't _____ about that.

M: Study those things, and I'm sure you'll do _____.

06-11

Biology

1 How does the professor organize the information about bacteria that she presents to the class?

Ⓐ By using a descriptive method
Ⓑ By using a comparative method
Ⓒ By using a chronological method
Ⓓ By using a visual method

2 According to the professor, what are bacteria walls made of?

Ⓐ DNA
Ⓑ Fiber
Ⓒ Protein
Ⓓ Fungus

📖🔍 **Words & Phrases**

distinct adj clearly different
habitat n a home; a territory
extremely adv very; tremendously
reproduction n the act of breeding; procreation

Dictation Exercise Listen to the lecture again and fill in the blanks.

W Professor: Bacteria are a _____ of living organisms. The term "bacteria" is _____ to such a wide variety of single-cell _____ that it is difficult to define. However, bacteria have many _____ that set them apart from other organisms. Bacteria are found nearly _____ in soil, water, and other organisms with symbiotic relationships. Most are _____, being only about 0.5 to 5.0 μm in _____. They usually have cell walls like _____ and fungus, but bacteria walls are made of _____. On the other hand, plants have fiber-based cell walls, and fungus has cell walls _____ insects' bodies. Many bacteria _____ by simply dividing; thus, their colonies _____ explosively under the right _____.

Exercise 4 Listen to part of a lecture and answer the questions.

06-12

Geology

1 Why does the professor discuss pillow lava?
   - (A) To name volcanoes that created it
   - (B) To say how hot it can become
   - (C) To explain how it is formed
   - (D) To point out where it can be found

2 Which type of lava rock formed Hawaii?
   - (A) Pillow
   - (B) Pole
   - (C) Pillar
   - (D) Cushion

Words & Phrases

submarine adj underwater; pertaining to the ocean

common adj widespread; frequent; general

pillar n a column; a post

pillow n a cushion; a headrest

Dictation Exercise Listen to the lecture again and fill in the blanks.

W Professor: Submarine volcanoes are _____ on the ocean floor. In _____ water, some produce the same _____ as land volcanoes. However, many will not show any _____ above water due to their _____. Submarine volcanoes produce _____ lava rocks than land volcanoes. One type of rock is pillar rock. These pillars can be so _____ that they could become islands. One _____ example is Hawaii. Lava can also _____ rocks called pillow lava. These rocks are called pillow lava because they _____ round blobs or pillows. They are _____ as hot lava oozes out of a solidified lava crust. These pillow types are the _____ type of lava rocks.

Unit **06**   **145**

Exercises with Mid-Length Conversations & Lectures

Exercise 1 Listen to part of a conversation and answer the questions.

06-13

Office Hours

1 Why does the student mention pond ecosystems?
- Ⓐ To note a topic that he enjoyed
- Ⓑ To name the topic of his project
- Ⓒ To ask a question about them
- Ⓓ To request information about them

2 What does the professor give the student?
- Ⓐ A study sheet for an exam
- Ⓑ A list of books to read
- Ⓒ The name of the class's teaching assistant
- Ⓓ Some descriptions of past projects

Words & Phrases

marine adj relating to the sea
pond n a small body of water surrounded by land on all sides; a small lake
folder n a folded cover used to hold paper
content n information found in written work
appreciate v to be pleased about someone's kindness

Summary Note

A Look at the summary note and recall what you heard.

Student	Professor	Student
• Needs help with class project topic	• Gives student folder with previous project descriptions	• Will read contents and return tomorrow to talk to professor

B Complete the following summary with the words below.

past projects	marine creatures	lectures
the contents	a class project	experiment

The student visits the professor to talk about _____. The professor asks
what _____ interested him. He enjoyed the ones on
_____ and pond ecosystems. The student says he does not know
what kind of _____ to do since he has never taken a biology class. The
professor gives him a folder with descriptions of _____. She tells the
student to read _____ and to come back later to discuss them.

Dictation Exercise   Listen to the conversation again and fill in the blanks.

W Professor: What are you _____ to do for your _____, Jason?

M Student: I'm not really sure, Professor Campbell. _____ I came here to
see you.

W: Well, tell me something . . . What about this class _____ you?

M: Let me think for a moment . . . Hmm . . . I really _____ the lectures you gave on
_____. The talk you gave about _____ was
particularly interesting.

W: Okay. Perhaps you could do some kind of experiment _____ one of
those topics.

M: That _____ great. But, uh, my problem is . . . I just don't know _____
_____ of experiments to do. I mean, uh, I have _____ a biology
class before. So I'm a bit _____.

W: Ah, I _____ your problem now. Here, uh, take this _____.

M: What is it?

W: It has _____ of _____ that students have done for this class.
It _____ about ten years.

M: Wow. I should be able to get some _____ by reading everything then.

W: That's right. Why don't you _____ the folder with you and read the _____
tonight? Then, come back tomorrow, and we can _____ what you can do.

M: I really appreciate your _____. I'll see you tomorrow around three.

06-14

Service Encounter

1 Why does the woman mention workshops?
- Ⓐ To convince the student to take them
- Ⓑ To see if the student wants to lead any
- Ⓒ To compare them with tutoring
- Ⓓ To encourage the student to tutor

2 What does the student decide to do?
- Ⓐ Only tutor
- Ⓑ Only lead workshops
- Ⓒ Tutor and lead workshops
- Ⓓ Neither tutor nor lead workshops

Words & Phrases

counselor ⓝ an advisor
requirement ⓝ a necessity; a condition
pass ⓥ to move on; to finish a class successfully
agree ⓥ to consent; to be in accord
lead ⓥ to guide or direct

📝 Summary Note

A Look at the summary note and recall what you heard.

Student wants to be a tutor

Requirements: Classes passed with A- or better

Workshops ➡ teach effective ways to study and provide reviews on science classes

Student decides to lead workshops

B Complete the following summary with the words below.

lead the workshops	will provide training	passed with
study efficiently	the requirements	register as a tutor

A student goes to the school student services office to _____. He talks to a counselor to find out _____ to join. He wants to tutor three classes that he _____ A's. The employee asks the student if he would like to lead the workshops that teach students how to _____ and also review science classes. After learning that the center _____, the student decides to tutor and to _____.

Dictation Exercise Listen to the conversation again and fill in the blanks.

M Student: Hi. I would like to find out how to be a _____ here. Can you tell me what the _____ are?

W Student Services Office Employee: Sure. You can only tutor classes you _____ already _____, and you must have passed them with an A- or _____. Which classes are you _____ in tutoring?

M: I _____ _____ tutor Biology 1A, Calculus 1B, and Organic Chemistry 1A. I _____ all these classes with A's.

W: Okay. We _____ tutors for those classes. We also offer _____ in science and study sessions. Would you be interested in _____ these workshops, too?

M: Can you give me more _____ on them?

W: These workshops teach students _____ _____ to study and provide reviews on certain _____. You, as a leader, will be given topics and _____ before the workshop.

M: Will leaders _____ _____ to study the material before the workshops?

W: Yes. You will be _____ _____ before the workshop.

M: In that case, I will give it a _____.

W: Great! Here is an _____ form.

06-15

Music

1 How is the lecture organized?
   Ⓐ The professor compares and contrasts two different operas.
   Ⓑ The professor talks about the main characters in an opera.
   Ⓒ The professor focuses on the similarities between Verdi and Dumas.
   Ⓓ The professor stresses the importance of opera in the past.

2 Who are the main characters in the opera?
   Click on 2 answers.
   Ⓐ Alfredo
   Ⓑ Dumas
   Ⓒ Violetta
   Ⓓ Verdi

Words & Phrases

courtesan ⓝ a woman who lives with an important man; a prostitute
elite ⓝ a group of people with high social and intellectual status
relationship ⓝ a bond; a connection between people or bodies
shady adj being of questionable taste or morality

Summary Note

A Look at the summary note and recall what you heard.

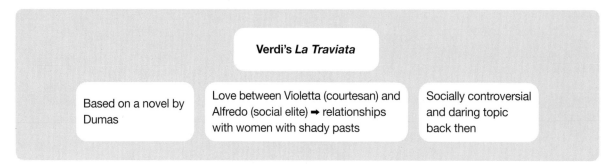

Verdi's *La Traviata*

Based on a novel by Dumas

Love between Violetta (courtesan) and Alfredo (social elite) ➡ relationships with women with shady pasts

Socially controversial and daring topic back then

B Complete the following summary with the words below.

based on	used art	fairly common practices
bold thing to do	heartbreaking ending	falls in love

The opera *La Traviata* was written by Verdi and was _____ a novel by Dumas. The main character, Violetta, is a Paris courtesan that _____ with a man named Alfredo. However, their romance meets a _____. Verdi and Dumas had similar relationships with women just like in the novel and the opera they wrote, respectively. Even though this story was based on _____, publicly writing about it was a _____. They _____ to express social issues.

Dictation Exercise Listen to the lecture again and fill in the blanks.

M Professor: We will _____ on opera today. The first opera we will _____ is *La Traviata*. The opera was _____ by Verdi and was _____ on a novel by Dumas called *La Dame Aux Camélias*. Alfredo, the _____, falls in love with a famous Paris courtesan _____ Violetta. Their whirlwind _____ is not welcomed by Alfredo's father. The romance ends, and Violetta becomes _____, which leads to her tragic death. Both Verdi and Dumas lived in the same _____ and shared similar _____. Dumas wrote the novel based on his _____ _____ with a notorious courtesan. Verdi lived with an _____ who had a history like Violetta. Both Verdi and Dumas had _____ with women who lived fast and died _____. Although the story does not seem scandalous in _____, it was a socially controversial and _____ topic back then. These men _____ the dark, troublesome side of their era and _____ it in art.

Listen to part of a lecture and answer the questions.

06-16

Zoology

1 How is the lecture organized?
  Ⓐ In chronological order
  Ⓑ By comparing the hippo and tortoise
  Ⓒ By comparing Owen and Mzee
  Ⓓ By size

2 How did the tortoise react to the hippo's friendship?
  Ⓐ He ran away.
  Ⓑ He returned the friendship.
  Ⓒ He disliked the hippo.
  Ⓓ He ignored the hippo.

Words & Phrases

stranded adj cut off or left behind
rescue v to set free from harm
friendship n the state of being friends
blossom v to develop, grow, or flourish
inseparable adj impossible to part

Summary Note

A Look at the summary note and recall what you heard.

Animal Friendship

Baby hippo stranded ➡ rescued by people in Kenya	Hippo came to animal park and was named Owen	Owen met Mzee, a giant tortoise ➡ their friendship blossomed

B Complete the following summary with the words below.

have overcome	for safety	terrified
soon befriended	lost his family	an incredible friendship

When a tsunami hit Kenya, a baby hippo _____ and was rescued by people. The hippo was brought to an animal park, and the park named him Owen. _____, Owen ran to a giant tortoise named Mzee _____. Owen's action caught Mzee by surprise, but he _____ Owen. They spend most of their time together now. They _____ the age and species difference and have developed _____.

Dictation Exercise Listen to the lecture again and fill in the blanks.

W Professor: There was an _____ animal friendship story a few years ago. You all remember the tsunami _____ in Indonesia, right? Well, the same tsunami stranded a _____ of hippos near Kenya. Unfortunately, only a baby hippo _____, and people _____ the hippo.

M Student: What _____ to the hippo after it was rescued?

W: It was brought to an _____ _____. They named him Owen for the _____ who rescued him.

M: How did Owen _____ his new home?

W: Well, he was really _____, obviously. But when he saw a _____ named Mzee, Owen ran behind him and _____ there. Mzee was really _____, but he accepted the _____ and became friends with Owen. Their _____ has grown ever since, and now they eat, sleep, and _____ all the time. Mzee, the tortoise, is more than 140 years old, and he was _____ than Owen in the beginning.

M: What a _____ story of friendship.

Integrated Listening & Speaking

A Listen to a lecture on music while looking at the summary note. Then, answer the questions in your own words.

Music

06-17

📝 Summary Note

Verdi's _La Traviata_

Based on a novel by Dumas	Love between Violetta (courtesan) and Alfredo (social elite) ➡ relationships with women with shady pasts	Socially controversial and daring topic back then

1 Describe the two main characters in _La Traviata_.

    a. Violetta is a courtesan who _____ .

    b. The main characters are Violetta and Alfredo, who _____ _____ despite their difference in status.

2 Who wrote the opera, and what was it based on?

    a. Verdi wrote the opera _La Traviata_ _____ by Dumas.

    b. The composer Verdi _____ _La Traviata_ on Dumas's novel.

3 What did Verdi and Dumas share in common?

    a. They both had relationships with women like Violetta, and they _____ .

    b. They shared similar experiences with women with shady pasts, and they _____ .

B Listen to a lecture on zoology while looking at the summary note. Then, answer the questions in your own words.

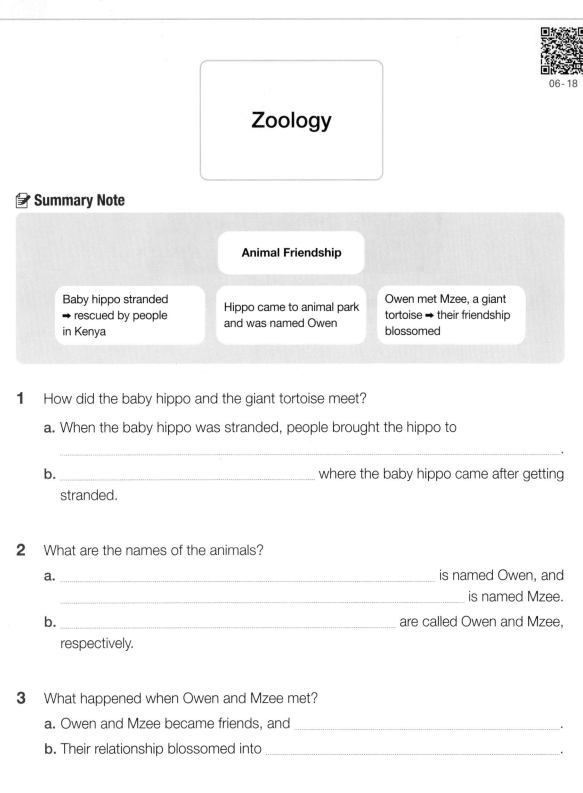

Zoology

06-18

📝 **Summary Note**

Animal Friendship

Baby hippo stranded
➡ rescued by people
in Kenya

Hippo came to animal park
and was named Owen

Owen met Mzee, a giant
tortoise ➡ their friendship
blossomed

1 How did the baby hippo and the giant tortoise meet?

a. When the baby hippo was stranded, people brought the hippo to

....

b. .... where the baby hippo came after getting

stranded.

2 What are the names of the animals?

a. .... is named Owen, and

.... is named Mzee.

b. .... are called Owen and Mzee,

respectively.

3 What happened when Owen and Mzee met?

a. Owen and Mzee became friends, and ....

b. Their relationship blossomed into ....

Listen to part of a conversation between a student and a professor.

06-19

1   What are the speakers mainly discussing?
   Ⓐ   An internship opportunity
   Ⓑ   A part-time job
   Ⓒ   The student's post-graduation interests
   Ⓓ   The professor's favorite student

2   Why does the professor mention one of her old students?
   Ⓐ   To compare him with the student
   Ⓑ   To let the student know his name
   Ⓒ   To advise the student to call him soon
   Ⓓ   To say that he called her with some news

3   What will the professor probably do next?
   Ⓐ   Give the student a phone number
   Ⓑ   Send an email to the student
   Ⓒ   Hand the student a pamphlet
   Ⓓ   Let the student borrow a book

Listen to part of a lecture in a biology class.

06-20

Adaptations

4 How is the lecture organized?

    Ⓐ The professor compares the effectiveness of different adaptations.

    Ⓑ The professor discusses both water and heat adaptations.

    Ⓒ The professor describes daily life in the desert for some animals.

    Ⓓ The professor covers different parts of the desert to explain different adaptations.

5 How do kangaroo rats survive the dry desert?

    Ⓐ By using water from their metabolism

    Ⓑ By reducing water loss through their skin

    Ⓒ By producing concentrated urine

    Ⓓ By breathing less

6 According to the lecture, why do desert rabbits have big ears?

    Ⓐ To avoid the sun

    Ⓑ To store water

    Ⓒ To remove body heat

    Ⓓ To remove water

Vocabulary Check-Up

A Choose the correct words that match the definitions.

1 alumnus • • Ⓐ sad; disastrous

2 adjacent • • Ⓑ a bond; a connection between people or bodies

3 organism • • Ⓒ the act of changing from a liquid state to a gas

4 tolerate • • Ⓓ astonishing; remarkable

5 relationship • • Ⓔ to accept something or someone although it is not acceptable

6 tragic • • Ⓕ to develop, grow, or flourish

7 pillar • • Ⓖ to adjust to a different situation or condition

8 blossom • • Ⓗ a life form; a living being

9 surface • • Ⓘ an opening in the Earth's surface where lava is expelled

10 evaporation • • Ⓙ an exterior; an outer layer

11 volcano • • Ⓚ a graduate of a school

12 amazing • • Ⓛ relating to the sea

13 adapt • • Ⓜ next to; neighboring

14 marine • • Ⓝ to make something increase greatly in number or amount

15 multiply • • Ⓞ a column; a post

B Complete the sentences by choosing the correct words.

Ⓐ assigned	Ⓑ earthquake	Ⓒ extra	Ⓓ friendship	Ⓔ popular

1 The teacher _____ the students some reading to do.

2 The Italian restaurant has become very _____ with local residents.

3 Many buildings collapsed due to the _____.

4 The professor let her do a report for _____ credit.

5 They have a(n) _____ that started forty years ago.

07 Connecting Content

Overview

Introduction

Connecting Content questions require you to identify the relationships among ideas in a lecture or conversation. These relationships may be explicitly stated, or you may have to infer them from the words you hear. For example, you may be asked to classify items in categories, identify a sequence of events or steps in a process, or specify relationships among ideas in a manner different from the way they were presented in the listening passage. In other Connecting Content questions, you may be required to make inferences about things mentioned in the listening passage and predict an outcome, draw a logical conclusion, or extrapolate some additional information.

Question Types

◆ What is the likely outcome of doing procedure X before procedure Y?
◆ What can be inferred about X?
◆ What does the professor imply about X?

Useful Tips

➤ Pay attention to the way you format your notes.
➤ Focus on the category words, their characteristics, and examples.

Script

M Professor: When Europeans first discovered the Magdalenian paintings in Altamira Cave, Spain, in 1879, they were considered hoaxes by academics and ignored. Recent reappraisals and the increasing numbers of discoveries, however, have illustrated their authenticity and have indicated high levels of artistry by Upper Paleolithic humans who used only basic tools. The ages of the paintings at many sites remain a contentious issue since methods like radiocarbon dating can lead to faulty data by contaminated samples of older or newer material, and caves and rocky overhangs are typically littered with debris from many time periods.

07-01

Q What does the professor imply about radiocarbon dating?

- Ⓐ It is a new method.
- Ⓑ It is not very accurate.
- Ⓒ It can be expensive.
- Ⓓ It is done by academics.

✅ Correct Answer

The right answer to the above question is Ⓑ. The professor talks about radiocarbon dating because that system is not accurate at telling an exact period of time.

Introduction to the Skill

When numbers are said in addresses, telephone numbers, and other instances, a pause must come at the right time. Pauses could be accompanied with a space or punctuation such as a hyphen, a comma, or parentheses. A unit of measurement is a fixed standard quantity, length, or weight that is used for measuring things. They usually come right after the number. You should be familiar with various unit systems.

A Kinds of Content Words

1 Room number: 108, 180A, 118B

My dorm room number is **118**. Please drop in on me any time.

2 Price: 1 dollar, 4,920 dollars, 25 cents (quarter), 10 cents (dime), 5 cents (nickel), 1 cent (penny)

You should pay **1,990 dollars** for this refrigerator.

3 Phone number: 999–1121, 232–0083, 487–3465

Your new phone number is **778-897**. Thank you.

4 Year: 1860, 240 A.D., 460 B.C.

In **1680**, this famous artist was born.

5 Date: Dec. 2, Nov. 21, Saturday, March 31

You have to submit this paper by **December 12**.

B Units

1 Weight: pound

The overall weight of the box is 1,000 **pounds**.

2 Temperature: Fahrenheit & Celsius

The surface temperature varies widely from -250 degrees **Fahrenheit** to 270 degrees **Fahrenheit**.

3 Magnitude of an earthquake: Richter scale

The earthquakes measured from 7.6 to 7.9 on **the Richter scale**.

4 Distance in the universe: light year

Polaris is 780 **light years** away.

5 Light intensity: lux

A 50-watt halogen light source outputs light intensity up to 46,000 **lux**.

6 Distance: mile

The speed limit for motor vehicles is 30 **miles** per hour.

7 Pixels: pixel

The optimum display setting is 1024 x 768 **pixels**.

Skill Practice

A Listen to the following conversation and fill in the blanks with the correct words. Then, listen to the sentences and check your answers.

07-02

W Student: Let's review for the test. How big is Saturn? Mark, can you answer?

M Student: How big? Well, its diameter is about _____ kilometers, and it weighs _____ times more than Earth. Actually, it is the _____ largest planet in size.

W: Well done. And how far from the sun is it?

M: It is 1.4 _____ kilometers away from the sun, and it moves at a speed of _____ kilometers per _____.

B Choose the right units in the box and fill in the blanks. Then, listen to the units and . check your answers.

07-03

| meter | kilogram | ampere | Kelvin | Newton | Pascal | joule | lux | hertz | hectare |

1 energy: _____

2 force: _____

3 area: _____

4 temperature: _____

5 illuminance: _____

6 mass: _____

7 frequency: _____

8 distance: _____

9 pressure: _____

10 electric current: _____

C Listen to part of a lecture and fill in the blanks with suitable words or numbers.

W Professor: The Nile River is about _____, or _____, in length and is the longest river both in Africa and in the world. The river begins in the mountains of Africa and flows north to the Mediterranean Sea. The Nile originates in Burundi, south of the equator, and flows northward through northeastern Africa. It eventually flows through Egypt and finally drains into the Mediterranean Sea. The construction of the Aswan Dam in the _____ meant that from _____, the annual floods were controlled. Its average discharge is _____, or _____, per second.

07-04

Basic Drill

Listen to parts of conversations or lectures and answer the questions.

Drill 1

Q What can be inferred about the student's homework habits?

07-05

    Ⓐ She does her homework once class ends.

    Ⓑ She rarely does not do her homework.

    Ⓒ She forgets to do her homework all the time.

    Ⓓ She prefers doing homework at the library.

Check-Up Listen again and choose the correct words.

M Professor: I am a little (concerned / discerned) that you (did return / didn't turn) in your homework today.

W Student: I'm sorry. I promise I'll (make up / make it up).

M: Is everything okay? We've been in school for four months now, and this is the first time you (have done / haven't done) your homework.

W: I've been (a bit distressed / a little stressed) by my parents' divorce. I'll turn this (work in / work out) tomorrow. I promise.

Drill 2

Q Indicate whether each of the following statements describes sedimentary or metamorphic rocks.

Click on the correct box for each statement.

07-06

	Sedimentary Rocks	Metamorphic Rocks
☐1 Include limestone		
☐2 Are rocks that have changed from other types of rocks		
☐3 Include quartz, marble, and slate		
☐4 Form in layers		

Check-Up Listen again and choose the correct words.

M Student: I (was confused / get confused) between sedimentary rocks and metamorphic rocks at times.

W Professor: You shouldn't. Sedimentary rocks form (in layers / in layoffs). And metamorphic rocks are those that have undergone changes from other types of rocks.

M: Ah, (heated pressure / heat and pressure) can make them do that, right?

W: Correct. Quartz, marble, and slate (are examples / are samples) of metamorphic rocks. Do you know any sedimentary rocks?

M: I know limestone is one. I don't know (another / any others).

Q Indicate which statements about the Indus Valley Civilization are facts and which are not.

Click in the correct box for each sentence.

07-07

	Fact	Not a Fact
1 It was located between present-day Pakistan and India.		
2 It was located between the Ganges and Jamuna rivers.		
3 Scholars think it was the only ancient civilization in history.		
4 Its ruins were found by a British man.		

Check-Up Listen again and choose the correct words.

W Professor: Another ancient civilization is the (India Valley / Indus Valley) Civilization. It was (located in / looked in) the area that is now Pakistan and the northwest part of India. The majority of (its ruins / it's ruined) are found between two rivers. (These rivers / These reverse) are the Indus River and Ghaggar-Hakra River. Scholars believe that the Indus Valley Civilization (flowered from / flourished from) 3300 B.C. to 1700 B.C. Its ruins (were first found / were first founded) by a British man in the early 1920s.

Q What can be inferred about how hot springs water is heated?

Ⓐ The sun is the main reason it is warm.

Ⓑ It is heated in different ways.

Ⓒ It is always heated by volcanoes.

Ⓓ It is heated artificially.

07-08

Check-Up Listen again and choose the correct words.

M Professor: Hot springs are a natural, (wonderful / wonder of) the world. They are (found / drowned) worldwide. Hot springs (are places / are placed) where hot water comes out of the ground and forms a pool or pond. At some hot springs, the water is hot because it is heated by the Earth's (inner heat / internal faces). Other hot springs happen because the (water nears / water is near) a volcano. This water is heated because it comes in (contact / can't act) with molten rocks.

Exercises with Short Conversations & Lectures

Exercise 1 Listen to part of a conversation and answer the questions.

07-09

Service Encounter

1 What can be inferred about the conductor?
- Ⓐ He thinks the students need more practice.
- Ⓑ He wants the students to select their parts.
- Ⓒ He is going to cancel orchestra practice today.
- Ⓓ He is too busy to talk to the student now.

2 What is the likely outcome of the student attending orchestra practice?
- Ⓐ The student will choose a new musical instrument.
- Ⓑ The student will get to lead the orchestra.
- Ⓒ The student will prepare for a solo concert.
- Ⓓ The student will know what music to play.

Words & Phrases

orchestra Ⓝ a group of musicians, especially stringed-instrument players
valid adj well-grounded; justifiable

Dictation Exercise Listen to the conversation again and fill in the blanks.

W Student: Hi, Mr. Jones. May I ask you a _____ ?

M Campus Orchestra Conductor: Of course.

W: I just _____ _____ the music we're playing for _____, and I have some questions about it.

M: Okay.

W: Well, I play _____ in the orchestra, and I got the _____ _____ for the first violin part and the second violin part. So I'm a little _____ because I can't play _____ parts at the same time.

M: Of course, you can't. _____ got both parts. We'll be picking our parts _____ _____ today.

W: Oh, okay. That makes _____. I feel kind of _____ now that I've asked about it.

M: Don't worry about it. It was a _____ question. Just _____ _____ you look over both parts before _____.

Exercise 2 Listen to part of a conversation and answer the questions.

07-10

Office Hours

1 What does the professor imply about the student?
- Ⓐ He should have studied more foreign languages.
- Ⓑ He may not be able to afford to study in Europe.
- Ⓒ He can learn how to paint by going abroad.
- Ⓓ He needs to work harder to improve his grade.

2 What is the student concerned about?
- Ⓐ Not having enough money
- Ⓑ Not speaking a foreign language
- Ⓒ Not learning enough in Europe
- Ⓓ Not knowing anyone abroad

Words & Phrases

consider v to think about doing something
pricey adj costly; expensive
negatively adv in a bad manner
afford v to have enough money to pay for something

Dictation Exercise Listen to the conversation again and fill in the blanks.

M Student: Professor Folsom, I could use some _____, please.

W Professor: Of course. What do you _____ to talk about?

M: I'm _____ studying abroad for a year, but I don't know if I should.

W: Hmm . . . You'd get to experience a _____, but study abroad programs can be a bit _____.

M: That's true. Would it affect my major _____?

W: I don't think so. You're an _____ major. Go to Europe, and you'll be able to see many works of art _____.

M: Ah, that's a _____. But I don't speak any _____

_____.

W: You'll _____ if you go abroad. If you can _____ it, you should try it.

Exercise 3 Listen to part of a lecture and answer the questions.

07-11

Biology

1   What can be inferred about endangered species?
   Ⓐ They can recover their numbers quickly.
   Ⓑ They are common in many countries.
   Ⓒ They are close to completely dying out.
   Ⓓ They are usually mammals or birds.

2   What is the likely outcome of humans cutting down a forest?
   Ⓐ People will build homes and farms there.
   Ⓑ Animals in it will move to other areas.
   Ⓒ Fires will start more easily during dry seasons.
   Ⓓ Many animals there will have no place to live.

> **Words & Phrases**
>
> **endangered** adj in danger of extinction
> **extinct** adj no longer in existence
> **species** n a biological grouping of like creatures

Dictation Exercise   Listen to the lecture again and fill in the blanks.

W Professor: All right, guys, it's _____ the end of the year, and I know you're all a little _____. So I think we should talk about _____ _____ today. I'd like to discuss _____ animals. A species qualifies as endangered for _____ _____. The first is that there are so _____ of them that they may become _____. The second reason is that _____ factors may cause them to become extinct. Environmental factors _____ things that people do to the environment that _____ _____ killing these animals. For example, when people cut down entire _____, they cause a lot of different animals to lose _____ and to die.

07-12

History

1 What can be inferred about Christopher Columbus?
   Ⓐ He sailed to the New World several times.
   Ⓑ He brought diseases to the New World.
   Ⓒ He wanted to find Asia when he sailed from Europe.
   Ⓓ He introduced Europeans to the New World.

2 What does the professor imply about smallpox?
   Ⓐ It was very deadly to Native Americans.
   Ⓑ Christopher Columbus had it.
   Ⓒ It killed everyone who got it.
   Ⓓ It caused problems for people who survived it.

Words & Phrases

explore Ⓥ to travel around an area to learn about it
immunity Ⓝ a state of being able to resist a disease
trace Ⓥ to follow or study

Dictation Exercise Listen to the lecture again and fill in the blanks.

M Professor: I'm sure you have _____ why there are so _____ Native Americans in America. We can _____ one answer to that question all the way back to Christopher Columbus. _____ _____ was that the Native Americans had been living on this _____ for centuries. Then, the Europeans, starting with Columbus, began to _____ and _____ in the New World. When they came over, the Europeans brought all kinds of _____, such as smallpox. These diseases didn't _____ the Europeans because they had built up _____ to them. But the Native Americans weren't _____. So these diseases ended up killing _____ of Native Americans.

Exercises with Mid-Length Conversations & Lectures

Exercise 1 Listen to part of a conversation and answer the questions.

07-13

Office Hours

1 Indicate whether each of the following statements describes the anthropology course or the international relations course.
Click in the correct box for each statement.

	Anthropology Course	International Relations Course
1 Has an excellent lecturer		
2 Can be taken in the summer		
3 Has a professor the student has taken before		
4 Is necessary for the student's major		

2 What does the student say about the international relations class?
- Ⓐ The class meets three times a week.
- Ⓑ It has a long waiting list of students.
- Ⓒ It is only offered one time a year.
- Ⓓ The teacher is a very hard grader.

📖 **Words & Phrases**

sort of phr a bit; somewhat
style n a way of doing something

decision n a choice
campus n the area where a school and its facilities is located

📝 Summary Note

A Look at the summary note and recall what you heard.

Student	Professor
• Can't decide which class to take • Points out international relations class offered one time a year; needs it to graduate	• Suggests student should take international relations; he can take other class in summer • Expects student will like lecturer in anthropology class

B Complete the following summary with the words below.

the student's major	in summer	the international relations class
next semester	one time	the anthropology class

The student is trying to decide which class to take _____.
_____ is an elective, but the lecturer is excellent. The international relations
class is needed for _____. It's also offered just _____
a year. The student says he should probably take _____. The professor
agrees and recommends taking the other class _____.

Dictation Exercise Listen to the conversation again and fill in the blanks.

M Student: I can't _____ between taking an anthropology course and an international
relations course _____ _____.

W Professor: The anthropology course would be an _____, right?

M: Yes. I'm sort of _____ in it. The _____ will be Professor Kensley.

W: He's an _____ lecturer. You'd _____ enjoy his class.

M: I wasn't _____ of that.

W: _____ _____ the international relations class?

M: I _____ that class for my major. It's only _____ once a year, uh, during the fall
semester.

W: I see. Who is the _____?

M: It's Professor Chamberlain. I've taken two of her classes in the _____.

W: Then you _____ _____ her style. Which one do you think you should take?

M: I should _____ take Professor Chamberlain's class.

W: That's a _____ _____. You can take the other class in _____. I know
you like _____ around campus each summer vacation.

Exercise 2 Listen to part of a conversation and answer the questions.

07-14

Service Encounter

1 What can be inferred about Stacy Blair?
- Ⓐ She works in the same office as the student.
- Ⓑ She is currently in a class now.
- Ⓒ She lives in the student's dormitory.
- Ⓓ She is majoring in sociology.

2 Why did the student visit the woman?
- Ⓐ To show up for his next shift
- Ⓑ To ask about getting some time off
- Ⓒ To respond to her email
- Ⓓ To let her know his schedule for next week

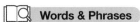 **Words & Phrases**

obviously adv for sure; clearly
position n a job

contact v to get in touch with
understanding adj sympathetic

Summary Note

A Look at the summary note and recall what you heard.

Student
- Can't work shift tomorrow
  ➜ has to do biology lab

Woman
- Agrees to let student skip work shift

Student
- Says Stacy Blair could work; offers to contact her

Woman
- Says she can call Stacy Blair herself

B Complete the following summary with the words below.

work his shift	not busy	will call
tomorrow morning	do a lab	not work

The student visits the office to tell the woman that he cannot _____
tomorrow. He has to _____, and the only time available is
_____. The woman agrees to let the student _____.
The student mentions that Stacy Blair is _____ tomorrow. He states that
he could call her, but the woman says that she _____ Stacy and ask her
to work.

Dictation Exercise Listen to the conversation again and fill in the blanks.

M Student: Hello, Ms. Sanderson. How are you _____ today?

W Sociology Department Office Employee: I'm _____, Keith. But what
are you doing here? You're not _____ to work any hours here today.

M: Actually, I need to talk to you about _____ tomorrow.

W: What's up?

M: My biology teacher just told me I need to do a _____ for the class. The _____
_____ I can do it is tomorrow morning. So . . .

W: I see. Well, you should _____ put your studies _____ of your part-time position.

M: Thanks for _____. I appreciate that.

W: No problem.

M: Um . . . You know, Stacy Blair doesn't have _____ to do tomorrow morning. If you want, I
could _____ her and ask if she can _____ my shift.

W: I didn't _____ that you knew her.

M: Oh, yeah. We've been _____ for a couple of years.

W: That's interesting. Well, don't worry about _____ her. I'll _____ her a call and
ask her if she's _____ in making a few extra dollars tomorrow.

M: Thanks so much, Ms. Sanderson. I'm glad that you're an _____.

Exercise 3 Listen to part of a lecture and answer the questions.

07-15

Geology

1   What does the professor imply about glaciers?
     Ⓐ They form by pressure and snow over thousands of years.
     Ⓑ Little pressure is needed for them to be created.
     Ⓒ They are many tiny granules all pressed together.
     Ⓓ They can be created in just a few weeks.

2   In the lecture, the professor describes a number of facts about a glacier. Indicate whether of the following is a fact about a glacier.
     Click in the correct box for each sentence.

	Fact	Not a Fact
1 The incline of a land determines how a glacier moves.		
2 A glacier moves because of gravity.		
3 A glacier does not make any imprints in the ground.		
4 It takes a relatively short time for a glacier to be formed.		

📖 **Words & Phrases**

accumulate Ⓥ to grow or increase
gravity Ⓝ a force that makes things fall to the ground
pressure Ⓝ the force produced by pressing against something
thaw Ⓥ to melt

📝 **Summary Note**

A   Look at the summary note and recall what you heard.

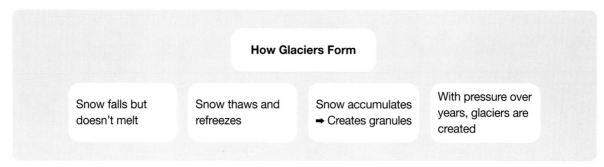

B Complete the following summary with the words below.

the world was like	leave imprints	the slope of
create pressure	rivers of ice	completely melts

Glaciers are _____ that move slowly with gravity. The way a glacier moves depends on _____ the land. They are created over many thousands of years. Snow falls and accumulates. But it never _____. Instead, it thaws a bit and then refreezes. Years and years of snowfall _____. This pressure forms sheets of ice. Over time, glaciers _____ in the ground like fossils. This way, scientists can tell what _____ during the last ice age.

Dictation Exercise Listen to the lecture again and fill in the blanks.

W Professor: Yesterday, we started talking about how geological _____ take a long time to be _____. One formation is called the glacier. Does anyone know what a glacier is?

M Student: It's a lot of _____!

W: Well, kind of. It's _____ a lot of ice, but it's _____ just that. A glacier is like a _____ of ice that moves slowly. The way a glacier moves _____ on the slope of the land. A glacier moves with _____. I need to talk about _____ these glaciers are formed. What happens is that _____ covers mountainous regions. This snow _____ completely melts. It might thaw a little and then _____ a bit though. So you have this thawing and _____, which changes the _____ to granules. Then, more snow _____. Can anyone _____ what happens to the snow that's at the _____ of this pile?

M: Wouldn't it get really firm from all the _____?

W: _____. So over thousands of years, from lots and lots of pressure, these _____ of slow-moving ice form. That's how a glacier is _____. The _____ about these glaciers is that they leave _____ in the ground kind of like fossils. So scientists can tell what the world _____ when it was _____ by glaciers back during the last ice age.

Exercise 4 Listen to part of a lecture and answer the questions.

07- 16

History of Science

1   What does the lecturer imply about Leonardo da Vinci?
    Ⓐ He was not very good at painting or sculptures.
    Ⓑ He built the first airplane that took flight.
    Ⓒ He had patents on all of his inventions.
    Ⓓ He was a man with many talents.

2   What can be inferred about Leonardo da Vinci's inventions?
    Ⓐ They used highly advanced technology.
    Ⓑ Most of them were too advanced for his time.
    Ⓒ They were loved by people during the Renaissance.
    Ⓓ They changed the lives of many people.

🔍 Words & Phrases

device Ⓝ a tool or gadget used to do something
famous adj well-known
invention Ⓝ a new creation

📝 Summary Note

A   Look at the summary note and recall what you heard.

Leonardo da Vinci

As an artist
• Painted *Mona Lisa* and *The Last Supper*

As an inventor
• Drew sketches of airplanes
• Created the anemoscope

B Complete the following summary with the words below.

going to change	he invented	many famous pieces
which direction	a famous inventor	way ahead

Leonardo da Vinci was _____. He lived during the Renaissance. Aside from inventing things, Leonardo also created _____ of art. The *Mona Lisa* is his most famous painting. Leonardo's inventions were _____ of his time. This is why he rarely made the things _____. Some of his inventions were created though. One of them is called the anemoscope. This is a device that tells _____ the wind is blowing. It also tells how the wind is _____ to before it ever does. People do not use anemoscopes anymore, but they did a long time ago.

Dictation Exercise Listen to the lecture again and fill in the blanks.

W1 Professor: All right, class, so we've been talking about _____ this week. One of the most famous inventors of the Renaissance was Leonardo da Vinci. Who knows _____ Leonardo was famous for?

W2 Student: Paintings! He did the *Mona Lisa*!

W1: That's absolutely right. Leonardo was the _____ who painted the famous *Mona Lisa*. He also painted *The Last Supper* and was famous for _____, sculptures, and so many different _____. In addition to all this, he was a very famous _____. He drew _____ of airplanes 400 years before the first plane took flight. _____ was, though, that most of these inventions were way ahead of his time. So they didn't _____ much during his time. Yes?

M Student: What do you mean by "way ahead of his time?"

W1: Well, he _____ these things _____, but the technology back then wasn't _____ enough to create most of these inventions. Anyway, some of his inventions were _____. For example, Leonardo created the anemoscope. An anemoscope is a _____ that tells you which direction the wind is _____. It also is supposed to tell you what direction the wind is going to _____ to before it even does.

W2: So does the anemoscope still _____?

W1: No one really uses it _____. But they did a long time ago.

Integrated Listening & Speaking

A Listen to a lecture on geology while looking at the summary note. Then, answer the questions in your own words.

07-17

Geology

📝 Summary Note

How Glaciers Form

| Snow falls but doesn't melt | Snow thaws and refreezes | Snow accumulates ➡ Creates granules | With pressure over years, glaciers are created |

1 How long does it take a glacier to form?

   a. It takes _____ to form.

   b. Glaciers take _____ to form.

2 What causes glaciers to move?

   a. Glaciers move _____.

   b. The thing that makes glaciers move is _____.

3 What can scientists learn from reading glacier imprints?

   a. Glacier imprints can tell scientists _____.

   b. Reading glacier imprints lets scientists know _____.

B Listen to a lecture on history of science while looking at the summary note. Then, answer the questions in your own words.

07-18

History of Science

📝 **Summary Note**

Leonardo da Vinci

As an artist
- Painted *Mona Lisa* and *The Last Supper*

As an inventor
- Drew sketches of airplanes
- Created the anemoscope

1 What were some of Leonardo da Vinci's talents?

a. He was good at _____ .

b. His talents included _____ .

2 What was Leonardo da Vinci's most famous painting?

a. His _____ was the *Mona Lisa*.

b. He _____ *Mona Lisa*.

3 What was one of Leonardo da Vinci's inventions that was actually created?

a. The anemoscope was _____ .

b. _____ was the anemoscope.

Mini TOEFL iBT Practice Test

Listen to part of a conversation between a student and a cafeteria assistant.

1 What is the purpose of the assistant's survey?

Ⓐ To educate students about the benefits of new menu items

Ⓑ To determine which new menu items are the most nutritious

Ⓒ To find out what students think about the new menu items

Ⓓ To discuss the purpose of changing the cafeteria's menu

2 How do many students feel about the taco bar?

Ⓐ They want more ingredients to choose from.

Ⓑ They think the food is not good.

Ⓒ They believe it is a bad idea.

Ⓓ They think the tacos are delicious.

3 What can be inferred about the man?

Ⓐ He is a manager at the cafeteria.

Ⓑ He is friends with the woman.

Ⓒ He sometimes eats the food in the cafeteria.

Ⓓ He created the survey questions himself.

Listen to part of a lecture in an ecology class.

07-20

Ecology

Lake

4 What is the lecture mainly about?

    Ⓐ Fish living in lakes

    Ⓑ The formation of lakes

    Ⓒ How lakes are divided

    Ⓓ Different types of lakes

5 Based on the information in the lecture, indicate which zone the following statements refer to.

Click in the correct box for each statement.

	The Center of the Lake	Along the Lakeshore	The Deepest Part of the Lake
1 Is close to the surface			
2 May have nothing living in it			
3 May not have any sunlight			
4 Is where the land slopes down			

6 Listen to part of the lecture again. Then answer the question.

What does the professor mean when she says this: 🎧

    Ⓐ She does not have time to give the student an answer.

    Ⓑ She thinks that the student's question is very insightful.

    Ⓒ She will answer the student's question later in the class.

    Ⓓ She wants the class to answer the student's question.

Vocabulary Check-Up

A Choose the correct words that match the definitions.

1 require •   • Ⓐ to travel around a new area to learn about it

2 decision •   • Ⓑ to grow well and to be healthy

3 sculpture •   • Ⓒ costly; expensive

4 pricey •   • Ⓓ to need

5 pressure •   • Ⓔ a way of doing something

6 flourish •   • Ⓕ to grow or increase

7 immunity •   • Ⓖ well-grounded; justifiable

8 contact •   • Ⓗ having a lot of mountains

9 endangered •   • Ⓘ a statue

10 style •   • Ⓙ in danger of extinction

11 accumulate •   • Ⓚ a resolution of choices

12 valid •   • Ⓛ the force produced by pressing against something

13 explore •   • Ⓜ to search for; to track

14 trace •   • Ⓝ the state of being able to resist disease

15 mountainous •   • Ⓞ to get in touch with

B Complete the sentences by choosing the correct words.

> Ⓐ ingredients   Ⓑ invention   Ⓒ position   Ⓓ obviously   Ⓔ direction

1 She applied for a _____ at a consulting firm.

2 The _____ in this dish are all very nutritious.

3 He does not know which _____ he should travel.

4 The computer is a(n) _____ that has changed the world.

5 They are _____ tired after running ten kilometers.

08 Making Inferences

Overview

Introduction

Making Inference questions requires you to reach a conclusion based on facts presented in the listening passage. In other words, you are to see read between the lines in the passage and predict the outcome. The questions may be about different things from a simple process to a cause and effect to a comparison and contrast.

Question Types

◆ What does the professor imply about X?

◆ What will the student probably do next?

◆ What can be inferred about X?

◆ What does the professor imply when he says this: (replay)

Useful Tips

▶ While taking notes, try to add up the details from the passage to reach a conclusion.

▶ Make efforts to generalize about what you hear in the listening passages.

▶ Try to find out the meanings of directly stated words.

▶ Focus on answer choices that use vocabulary not found in the listening passages.

Script

M Professor: In animals, the brain is the control center of the central nervous system. In most animals, the brain is located in the head, protected by the skull, and close to the primary sensory apparatuses of vision, hearing, taste, and smell. In humans, it is an organ of thought. While all vertebrates have a brain, invertebrates have either a centralized brain or collections of individual ganglia. Brains can be extremely complex. The human brain also has a massive number of synaptic connections. This allows for a great deal of parallel processing. For example, the human brain contains more than 100 billion neurons, each linked to as many as 10,000 others.

08-01

Q What can be inferred about the human brain?

Ⓐ It is an involuntary organ.

Ⓑ It is a secondary organ.

Ⓒ It is a primary organ.

Ⓓ It is a vulnerable organ.

✅ **Correct Answer**

The correct answer is Ⓒ. The professor first talks about the brains of all the animals and their importance. Then, he implies to the students that the human brain is a primary organ in the human body.

Skill & Tip | Sound Modification

Introduction to the Skill

Sound modification refers to the ways spoken sounds are altered compared to their original forms. These changes occurs due to the influence of surrounding sounds and how we naturally produce speech. There are two main types of sound modifications:

A Assimilation

Assimilation is defined as the process of replacing one sound by another sound under the influence of a third sound that is near it in the word or sentence.

Written Form	Spoken Form	Assimilation
that man	→ ðæp mæn	t → p
that cap	→ ðæk kæp	t → k
ten minutes	→ tem minits	n → m
can go	→ kəŋ gow	n → ŋ
goodbye	→ gub bai	d → b
good girl	→ gug gərl	d → g
tell me	→ tem mi	l → m
give me	→ gim mi	v → m

When the negative n't is attached to an auxiliary verb, the /t/ is often changed to a short sound at the same place of articulation as the following consonant, and the /n/ assimilates to this consonant.

Written Form	Spoken Form	Assimilation
I can't believe it.	→ ay kæmp bəliyv ət	nt → mp
I can't go.	→ ay kæŋk gow	nt → ŋk

B Deletion of Consonants

The final consonants of underlined words are usually unreleased and can even be deleted as shown below. However, clusters created by the addition of grammatical endings are not simplified.

Example	Pronunciation	Example	Pronunciation
band shell	bæn ʃel	canned peaches	kænd piytshəz
left field	lɛf fiyld	laughed hard	læft hard
next month	nɛks mʌnθ	missed chances	mist tʃænsəz

Skill Practice

A Listen and fill in the blanks with the correct words.

08-02

1 We _____ get the magazine to write something.

2 I _____ believe you're right, and I feel much better about the _____ progress.

3 Really _____ professors _____ bring the sense of wonder in a _____ way.

4 His parents plan to move to their new home _____ week.

B Listen to the following conversation and underline where sound modifications happen.

08-03

W Professor: Come in and have a seat. How are you?

M Student: I'm fine. Thanks. Have you had a chance to look at my proposal?

W: Yes, I have. That's what I mainly want to talk about.

M: I wasn't sure whether it was exactly the kind of thing you wanted.

W: Oh, have no worries. It's precisely what we need, and you did really good work.

M: Well, I must say that's a great relief.

C Listen to part of a lecture and underline where sound modifications happen.

08-04

W Professor: You'd think Mars would be easier to understand. Like Earth, Mars has polar ice caps and clouds in its atmosphere, seasonal weather patterns, volcanoes, canyons, and other recognizable features. However, conditions on Mars vary wildly from what we experience on our own planet. Over the past three decades, spacecraft have shown us that Mars is rocky, cold, and sterile beneath its hazy pink sky.

Basic Drill

Listen to parts of conversations or lectures and answer the questions.

Drill 1

Q What can be inferred about the student?
- Ⓐ She is worried that her books are too heavy.
- Ⓑ She is concerned that she will be late to her classes.
- Ⓒ She is sure that she will do well in all of her classes.
- Ⓓ She is afraid that she will get lost at her new school.

08-05

| Check-Up | Listen again and choose the correct words.

M Student Affairs Office Employee: We always tell (you students / new students) a bit about the school before they start class. (Something / One thing) you need to know is that you have ten minutes between classes to get to your next (class / craft).

W Student: But this school's so big! What if (ten minutes isn't / the time isn't) enough? I mean, how can it be if we have to go all the way across campus?

M: Most (students cart / students carry) books for a couple of classes at a time. That makes it a little easier.

W: I think I might have to make (a cup of / a couple of) practice runs. I don't want to be late for class.

Drill 2

Q What will the man probably do next?
- Ⓐ Check out a book
- Ⓑ Go to a higher floor
- Ⓒ Search for a book on the computer
- Ⓓ Turn a book in

08-06

| Check-Up | Listen again and choose the correct words.

M Student: (Can you / Can't you) help me find a book I need?

W Librarian: Sure. What are (you looking / you cooking) for?

M: I need a book about (snow / volcanoes) for a report that I'm writing for one of my classes.

W: Good luck with (the retort / your report). You will find our books on volcanoes in the science (series / section) on the second floor. Just go up the stairs and make a left.

M: (Thanks / Thank you) so much!

188 Part **III**

Drill 3

Q What can be inferred about the food pyramid?

    Ⓐ It tells people what to eat all the time.

    Ⓑ It is a useful tool for eating nutritious meals.

    Ⓒ All doctors believe in its usefulness.

    Ⓓ It is not helpful for keeping people healthy.

08- 07

❙Check-Up❙ Listen again and choose the correct words.

W Professor: Today, we're going to start talking about (nutrition / nutrients). It is really important to eat healthy foods so that we get the nutrients (are bodies / our bodies) need to function. An easy way to make sure we get the nutrients we need is (to fall on / to follow) the food pyramid. The (food pyramid / use pyramid) is a chart that tells us how much of which (kinds of foods / kinder foods) we should eat every day. The groups on the food pyramid (include grains / induce pains), fruits, vegetables, dairy products, meat, and fats.

Drill 4

Q What does the professor imply about depression?

    Ⓐ It happens to around half of all people.

    Ⓑ It can last for a person's entire life.

    Ⓒ There are other symptoms he did not name.

    Ⓓ It can be cured by taking various kinds of medicine.

08- 08

❙Check-Up❙ Listen again and choose the correct words.

M Professor: One of the most common psychiatric (disc odors / disorders) is depression. Depression (affects as / effect is) much as ten percent of the population at any given time. The most (common / come on) symptoms of depression are (half moons / sad moods) and lack of pleasure from previously enjoyable activities. Other symptoms include changes in appetite, changes in sleep, (feels guilty / feelings of guilt), and loss of energy. (People / Peep hole) who suffer from depression aren't able to function well on a day-to-day basis.

Exercises with Short Conversations & Lectures

Exercise 1 Listen to part of a conversation and answer the questions.

08-09

Service Encounter

1 What does the woman imply about the yearbooks?
- Ⓐ They are not currently available.
- Ⓑ They are being made for the first time.
- Ⓒ They are cheaper than last year.
- Ⓓ They include pictures of every student.

2 What will the student probably do next?
- Ⓐ Go to class
- Ⓑ Visit the library
- Ⓒ Pose for a picture
- Ⓓ Order a yearbook

Words & Phrases

in advance phr early
recommend v to suggest

Dictation Exercise Listen to the conversation again and fill in the blanks.

M Student: Hi, Ms. Olson. May I ask you a question?

W Registrar's Office Employee: _____ _____. What can I do for you?

M: I was _____ about our yearbooks. I know we have to _____ them in _____, but I don't know when the _____ is, how much they cost, _____ to pick them up, or anything.

W: I can give you all that _____. You can _____ your yearbook, or you can just buy one when they _____. The _____ _____ is in a week. You just have to drop off your _____ and check here. The yearbooks are fifty dollars. They'll be here in two months, and you can _____ yours _____ here.

M: So I still have some time to _____ whether or not I want to preorder?

W: Absolutely. But if you know you _____ want a yearbook, I would _____ preordering. That way, everything will be _____ you just to pick it up when it gets here.

M: You know, I think I'll _____ _____ and do that.

Exercise 2 Listen to part of a conversation and answer the questions.

08-10

Office Hours

1 What can be inferred about the student?
- Ⓐ She has decided to major in computer programming.
- Ⓑ She does not have perfect attendance in the class.
- Ⓒ She is getting an A in the professor's class.
- Ⓓ She has studied with the professor in the past.

2 What will the student probably do next?
- Ⓐ Visit the computer laboratory
- Ⓑ Talk more with her professor
- Ⓒ Ask a classmate for assistance
- Ⓓ Read chapter two in her book

Words & Phrases

formula Ⓝ a set recipe for a function
function Ⓝ a computer routine
tackle Ⓥ to approach aggressively

Dictation Exercise Listen to the conversation again and fill in the blanks.

W Student: Professor Andrews?

M Professor: Yes, Catherine?

W: I have a question about _____ today.

M: What can I _____ you with?

W: Well, we _____ the different Excel functions today, but some of the stuff didn't _____ to me. I think the _____ is that this is only my second class. I believe I _____ from an earlier class.

M: All right. We did cover some of the _____ for this lesson last week.

W: That makes sense. I didn't _____ how everyone already knew which formulas to _____ .

M: Of course. If you take a look at chapter two in your book, I think it will help you _____ . Then, if you're still having _____ , we can tackle that _____ .

W: Thanks, Mr. Andrews!

Exercise 3 Listen to part of a lecture and answer the questions.

08- 11

Public Health

1 What can be inferred about water?
  Ⓐ It can help prevent heart attacks.
  Ⓑ It is useful for giving people more energy.
  Ⓒ It is of great importance to good health.
  Ⓓ It makes up less than half of the human body.

2 Why does the professor mention dehydration?
  Ⓐ To point out that it is easy to avoid
  Ⓑ To call it a problem people suffer from
  Ⓒ To note how many people die from it
  Ⓓ To state that drinking water prevents it

Words & Phrases

benefit ⓝ an advantage; a good point
dehydration ⓝ the act of becoming dried out
improve ⓥ to make better
maintain ⓥ to keep

Dictation Exercise Listen to the lecture again and fill in the blanks.

M Professor: I'm sure many of you have heard about the _____ of drinking water. You know, you're supposed to drink several cups of water _____. Have you ever asked why? The _____ is not just that the body is around sixty percent water. There are _____ to drinking it. It _____ the dehydration of the body. It also helps _____ oxygen through the body. Water makes the skin _____ and improves how it looks. It _____ waste from the body and also helps you maintain regular _____. I'd say that drinking water is _____, wouldn't you?

Exercise 4 Listen to part of a lecture and answer the questions.

08-12

Drama

1 What can be inferred about love in Greek theater?
- Ⓐ It was the main topic of most plays.
- Ⓑ It was frequently used in tragedies.
- Ⓒ It appeared in the best Greek plays.
- Ⓓ It was uncommon in the early years.

2 What does the professor imply about the three periods of Greek theater?
- Ⓐ They lasted for hundreds of years.
- Ⓑ They were loved by most Greeks.
- Ⓒ They focused on tragedies.
- Ⓓ They had differing topics.

Words & Phrases

ancient adj very old; from a past era
comedy n a humorous drama with a happy ending
tragedy n a serious drama with a sad ending

Dictation Exercise   Listen to the lecture again and fill in the blanks.

W Professor: Today, we're going to talk about _____ Greek theater. The ancient Greeks mostly did comedies and _____. The first _____ we're going to talk about is comedy. Greek comedy is _____ into three divisions. They are old comedy, _____ comedy, and new comedy. One of the ways that those _____ of comedy are _____ is in the topics they covered. Old comedy poked _____ at real people from that time. Middle comedy mostly _____ _____ reviewing the way society was. It made fun of the _____ people lived. New comedy covered _____ as middle comedy. But it also started to add aspects of _____.

Exercise 1 Listen to part of a conversation and answer the questions.

08-13

Office Hours

1 What can be inferred about the professor?

Ⓐ He intends to meet all of his students.

Ⓑ He is an expert on bird migrations.

Ⓒ He disapproves of the student's topic.

Ⓓ He will check the student's paper for her.

2 What does the student imply about geese?

Ⓐ They mostly live in Hawaii.

Ⓑ They can fly for hours at a time.

Ⓒ They live in the same place all year long.

Ⓓ They do not migrate long distances.

Words & Phrases

compare Ⓥ to judge different things side by side
migration Ⓝ the mass movement of animals, especially birds, from one area to another
pattern Ⓝ a sequence
specific adj precise or definite

📝 Summary Note

A Look at the summary note and recall what you heard.

> Topic of Report: Short-Distance Bird Migrations
>
> Goose migration in general
>
> Comparison of different species' migrations

B Complete the following summary with the words below.

zoology report	different species	goose migration
focus the report	a lot of information	general migration pattern

The professor is speaking with a student about her _____. The student tells the professor that she will _____ on short-distance bird migrations. The main reason she chose this topic is that she found _____ about it. The student will begin her report by talking about _____ in general. She states that most geese have the same _____. She will then compare _____ of geese.

Dictation Exercise Listen to the conversation again and fill in the blanks.

W Student: Hello, Professor Adams. You _____ to see me?

M Professor: Hi, Sara. Yes, I want to talk about your zoology _____. I'm making _____ with everyone to talk about their papers.

W: Oh, okay.

M: What are you _____ your report on now?

W: I'm looking at _____ _____.

M: That's a great topic. Are you focusing on _____?

W: I think I've _____ it _____ to birds that do short-distance migrations. You know, geese and other _____.

M: Was there a reason you chose that _____ topic?

W: Actually, a _____ of the decision just came from the _____ that I found the most information on short-distance migration. I also found a lot of _____ on geese.

M: That's a pretty _____ to go with that. So _____ are you taking this report?

W: I thought I'd write about goose migration _____. I found out that all geese have the _____ general migration pattern. So I'm going to _____ that first. Then, I'm going to talk about the _____ of specific geese. I thought I'd _____ a few different species, like the Canadian goose and the Hawaiian goose.

M: That sounds good. I'm _____ to reading your paper.

Exercise 2 Listen to part of a conversation and answer the questions.

08-14

> ## Service Encounter
>
> 1   What can be inferred about the student?
>   - Ⓐ He is a poor swimmer.
>   - Ⓑ He is not interested in exercising.
>   - Ⓒ He is on the swim team.
>   - Ⓓ He enjoys playing all kinds of sports.
>
> 2   What will the student probably do next?
>   - Ⓐ Speak with his friend
>   - Ⓑ Find a gym teacher
>   - Ⓒ Go to a bank to get money
>   - Ⓓ Have lunch

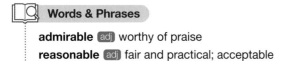

Words & Phrases

admirable adj worthy of praise
reasonable adj fair and practical; acceptable

📝 Summary Note

A   Look at the summary note and recall what you heard.

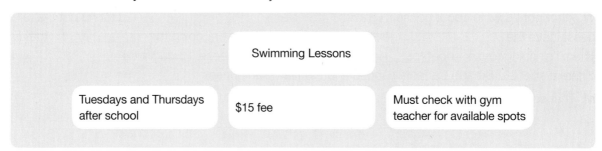

Swimming Lessons

| Tuesdays and Thursdays after school | $15 fee | Must check with gym teacher for available spots |

B Complete the following summary with the words below.

fifteen dollars	how to swim	take swimming lessons
available spots	after-school activities	see the gym teacher

The student is asking about certain _____. He would like to

_____ because he never learned _____ properly

as a kid. The employee tells him that swimming lessons are on Tuesdays and Thursdays after

school. They will cost _____. The employee tells the student to

_____ and to ask if there are any _____ open for

the lessons. He is grateful for the woman's help.

Dictation Exercise Listen to the conversation again and fill in the blanks.

W Student Activities Office Employee: Hi, Steve. What can I help you with?

M Student: I'm looking into some _____ activities, and I was _____ if I could get
some information about them.

W: Definitely. Is there anything in _____ you're interested in?

M: I really want to do the after-school _____ lessons. I mean, I _____
_____ how to swim properly when I was younger.

W: That's an admirable _____. Let me grab the information about the swimming, and we'll
_____ what you need to know.

M: Great!

W: Okay, swimming lessons _____ twice a week on Tuesdays and Thursdays. Can you
_____ those days?

M: Yeah, I've got those days _____.

W: There's a _____ involved. You get lessons for the _____
_____ for fifteen dollars.

M: That's really _____.

W: Okay, great. Well, I don't know if there are still any _____ available for the lessons. So what
you should do right away is see one of the _____ _____. Let him know you want
to _____. It would help if you could take the fifteen dollars with you so that
your spot will be _____.

M: Do you think there will still be _____ left?

W: There should be. It's still _____ in the semester. Just make sure you get
to the gym _____ _____.

M: All right, I'll do that. Thanks for your help!

Exercise 3 Listen to part of a lecture and answer the questions.

08- 15

Psychology

1 What can be inferred about developmental psychology?

Ⓐ It covers the development of a human's entire life.

Ⓑ It is the most popular field in psychology nowadays.

Ⓒ It is a relatively new field of study.

Ⓓ It primarily focuses on the development of infants.

2 What does the professor imply about babies?

Ⓐ Their bodies develop slower than their brains.

Ⓑ Some of them can walk before they are a year old.

Ⓒ They all develop at roughly the same rate.

Ⓓ Those six months old can see as well as adults.

Words & Phrases

blind adj unable to see

develop v to grow and change over time

infant n a baby from birth until the child starts talking

vision n the ability to see

Summary Note

A Look at the summary note and recall what you heard.

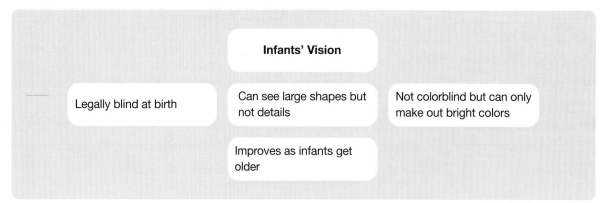

Infants' Vision

Legally blind at birth

Can see large shapes but not details

Not colorblind but can only make out bright colors

Improves as infants get older

B Complete the following summary with the words below.

a baby is born	make out detail	make out differences
field of psychology	their growth	as an adult's

Developmental psychology is a _____ that looks at how people grow.
One thing this field looks at is infants and _____. For example, when
_____, the child has very poor vision. The baby cannot
_____, only large shapes. Infants can also only
_____ in bright colors. Vision improves as infants get older. At six months,
an infant's vision is almost the same _____.

Dictation Exercise   Listen to the lecture again and fill in the blanks.

W Professor: Yesterday, I told you that we were going to _____ about a
field of psychology called developmental psychology. This _____ of psychology looks at the
many ways people's _____ and _____ develop from before they're even born until
they die. So we should just start at the _____. Let's start with infants. When a baby is born up
until he or she starts _____, the baby is _____ to as an infant. Infants can't do a lot
of things that _____ can do.
Let's look at the _____ side of things. Babies are born with really _____
_____. Actually, they're legally _____ when born. Infants can mostly make out
_____ shapes and stuff, but they can't tell _____. Their sense of _____
also isn't very good. For a long time, psychologists thought infants were _____ right after birth.
As it turns out, research has shown that most babies can, in fact, _____ _____
bright colors. For example, an infant can tell the _____ between a bright red ball and a bright
blue ball. But it would be _____ for an infant to tell the difference between
a light blue ball and a dark blue ball. As infants get older, their _____ of _____
improves. Some psychologists think that by the age of six months, an infant's vision is almost
_____ as an adult's.

08-16

Writing

1 What can be inferred about the middle of an essay?

Ⓐ It the information stated in the introduction.

Ⓑ It is supposed to support the essay's topic.

Ⓒ It is the least important piece of the essay.

Ⓓ It is made up of introductory material.

2 Listen again to part of the lecture. Then answer the question.
What does the professor imply when he says this: 🎧

Ⓐ The writer can impress readers with his knowledge in the middle part.

Ⓑ This beginning part is where the writer gets to know the reader.

Ⓒ This is the part where the writer shows the reader his words.

Ⓓ The middle part is where the reader gets to know the writer.

Words & Phrases

argument Ⓝ a point of view or case

convince Ⓥ to prove something to someone

topic Ⓝ a subject

📝 Summary Note

A Look at the summary note and recall what you heard.

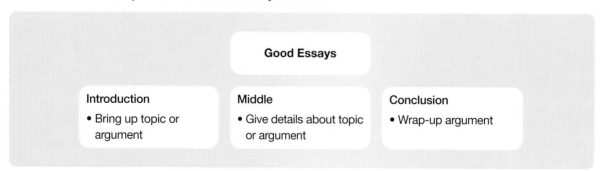

Good Essays

Introduction	Middle	Conclusion
• Bring up topic or argument	• Give details about topic or argument	• Wrap-up argument

B Complete the following summary with the words below.

at the end	the most important	a good essay
brings up	the writer convinces	his arguments

A professor is teaching his class how to write _____. The three main parts of an essay are the introduction, the middle, and the conclusion. The introduction is the beginning of the essay. In this part, the writer first _____ his topic and arguments. He might begin to talk briefly about _____. The conclusion is the part of the essay that comes _____. The writer wraps up his argument in the conclusion. The middle of the essay is _____ part. This is where _____ the readers that his point of view is correct.

Dictation Exercise   Listen to the lecture again and fill in the blanks.

M Professor: We're going to spend the _____ of the month writing different kinds of _____. First though, we need to talk about what _____ an essay _____. There are certain things that every essay, _____ what you'll be writing about, needs to have. Who can tell me one thing that an essay _____?

W Student: Um, doesn't every essay need an _____?

M: Of course. _____ must have an introduction. In the intro, you'll talk about the _____ of your essay. You might also talk about some of your _____ or subtopics. But if you do, you have to make sure that you're _____ about them. Your introduction shouldn't be _____ a paragraph. What else does an essay need to have?

W: A _____?

M: Absolutely! If you're introducing your topic at the beginning, you must _____ your argument at the end. The conclusion talks about _____ _____ as the introduction, but it's not _____ the same. Here, you have to _____ your topic. You have to make sure that the reader is _____ that your _____ of view is right. Yes, do you have a question?

W: So what happens in the middle?

M: The middle's the _____ part. That's where you tell _____ _____ all the reasons that they should agree with you. That's where you really get to _____ what you know.

Integrated Listening & Speaking

A Listen to a lecture on psychology while looking at the summary note. Then, answer the questions in your own words.

Psychology

08-17

📝 **Summary Note**

Infants' Vision

Legally blind at birth

Can see large shapes but not details

Not colorblind but can only make out bright colors

Improves as infants get older

1 What is the focus of developmental psychology?

    a. The focus of developmental psychology

    ....

    b. Developmental psychology ....

2 What does this lecture teach about an infant's vision at birth?

    a. At birth, ... is very poor.

    b. An infant .... at birth.

3 When does an infant's vision get to be as good as an adult's?

    a. An infant's vision is almost .... by six months.

    b. By six months, an infant can see ....

B Listen to a lecture on writing while looking at the summary note. Then, answer the questions in your own words.

08-18

Writing

📝 **Summary Note**

Good Essays

Introduction
- Bring up topic or argument

Middle
- Give details about topic or argument

Conclusion
- Wrap-up argument

1 What are the three main parts of an essay?

  a. The three main parts of an essay are _____.

  b. _____ are the three main parts of an essay.

2 What happens in the introduction?

  a. In the introduction, the writer first _____.

  b. The writer first _____ in the introduction.

3 What is the purpose of the conclusion?

  a. The purpose of the conclusion is _____.

  b. The writer _____ in the conclusion.

Mini TOEFL iBT Practice Test

Listen to part of a conversation between a student and a student housing office employee.

08-19

1 What is the student's problem?
- Ⓐ He cannot afford to move to another dorm.
- Ⓑ He does not have enough time to study.
- Ⓒ He does not get along with his roommate.
- Ⓓ He is doing poorly in some of his classes.

2 What does the student say about his roommate?
Click on 2 answers.
- Ⓐ He is not very friendly.
- Ⓑ He goes to bed late.
- Ⓒ He does not study hard.
- Ⓓ He plays loud music.

3 What will the student probably do next?
- Ⓐ Call his roommate
- Ⓑ Sign the form the woman gave him
- Ⓒ Return to his dormitory
- Ⓓ Learn more about changing rooms

Listen to part of a lecture in a psychology class.

08-20

4 What is the lecture mainly about?

   Ⓐ The most common personality disorders

   Ⓑ Developmental problems

   Ⓒ Narcissistic personality disorders

   Ⓓ Ways to treat psychological problems

5 How does a person with narcissistic personality disorder act?

   Ⓐ In a confident way

   Ⓑ In a way that is easy to make friends

   Ⓒ In an egotistical manner

   Ⓓ In a harmless way

6 What is the professor's attitude toward the student?

   Ⓐ She believes the student needs to study more.

   Ⓑ She likes the way the student answers questions.

   Ⓒ She wants the student to try her best every class.

   Ⓓ She thinks the student talks too much.

Vocabulary Check-Up

A Choose the correct words that match the definitions.

1 recommend •   • Ⓐ to approach aggressively

2 disruptive •   • Ⓑ a desire to eat

3 vision •   • Ⓒ an advantage; a good point

4 migration •   • Ⓓ disturbing or upsetting

5 disorder •   • Ⓔ a baby from the time he is born until he starts speaking

6 tackle •   • Ⓕ the mass movement of animals, especially birds, from one area to another

7 admirable •   • Ⓖ to suggest

8 appetite •   • Ⓗ a state of being untidy; badly prepared

9 ancient •   • Ⓘ to prove something to someone

10 luck •   • Ⓙ worthy of praise

11 benefit •   • Ⓚ unwilling to change one's mind

12 tragedy •   • Ⓛ the ability to see

13 infant •   • Ⓜ fortune

14 convince •   • Ⓝ old or from a past era

15 stubborn •   • Ⓞ a serious drama that has a sad ending

B Complete the sentences by choosing the correct words.

Ⓐ absolutely	Ⓑ reasonable	Ⓒ narcissistic	Ⓓ blind	Ⓔ develop

1 She is so _____ that she only thinks of herself.

2 We are _____ interested in attending the concert.

3 A dog is leading the _____ man across the street.

4 She paid a(n) _____ price for her new clothes.

5 It can take time to _____ new skills.

Actual Test

Actual Test

09-01

Listening Section Directions

This section measures your ability to understand conversations and lectures in English.

The listening section is divided into separately timed parts. In each part, you will listen to 1 conversation and 1 or 2 lectures. You will hear each conversation or lecture only **one** time.

After each conversation and lecture, you will answer some questions about it. The questions typically ask about the main idea and supporting details. Some questions ask about a speaker's purpose or attitude. Answer the questions based on what is stated or implied by the speakers.

You may take notes while you listen. You may use your notes to help you answer the questions. Your notes will not be scored.

If you need to change the volume while you listen, click on the **Volume** icon at the top of the screen.

In some questions, you will see this icon: 🎧 This means that you will hear, but not see, part of the question.

Some of the questions have special directions. These directions appear in a gray box on the screen.

Most questions are worth 1 point. If a question is worth more than 1 point, it will have special directions that indicate how many points you can receive.

A clock at the top of the screen will show you how much time is remaining. The clock will not count down while you are listening. The clock will count down only while you are answering the questions.

09-02

Listening Directions

In this part, you will listen to 1 conversation and 1 lecture.

You must answer each question. After you answer, click on **Next**. Then click on **OK** to confirm your answer and go on to the next question. After you click on OK, you cannot return to previous questions.

You may now begin this part of the Listening Section. You will have **7 minutes** to answer the questions.

Click on **Continue** to go on.

09-03

1 What is the student's problem?

    Ⓐ Her grade in a class is very low.

    Ⓑ A class she signed up for was canceled.

    Ⓒ She does not get along with her professor.

    Ⓓ One of her classes changed times.

2 Why does the student have to take English 2?

    Ⓐ Her parents want her to write better.

    Ⓑ She did not get an A in English 1.

    Ⓒ She is planning to major in English.

    Ⓓ Her advisor insisted that she take it.

3 Why does the man discuss Professor Watson?

    Ⓐ To state that many students enjoy her classes

    Ⓑ To explain why she is not teaching this semester

    Ⓒ To say that her class has an opening in it

    Ⓓ To agree with the student's opinion of her

4 What will the student probably do next?

    Ⓐ Pay a fee

    Ⓑ Talk to her professor

    Ⓒ Make a new ID card

    Ⓓ Register for a class

5 Listen again to part of the conversation. Then answer the question.

What does the student mean when she says this: 🎧

    Ⓐ She wants to take English 2 this semester.

    Ⓑ The proposed class does not fit her schedule.

    Ⓒ She is willing to take a class another semester.

    Ⓓ She wishes she did not have to take English 2.

09-04

Biology

6 What is the main topic of the lecture?

Ⓐ Fish species

Ⓑ Fish fins

Ⓒ Fish speed

Ⓓ Fish size

7 Why does the professor explain finlets?

Ⓐ So that the students understand how some fish lose fins during evolution

Ⓑ So that the students understand that fast fish have them

Ⓒ So that the students understand they are not important

Ⓓ So that the students understand that small fish need them

8 What are caudal fins?

Ⓐ Part of the pectoral fins

Ⓑ Finlets

Ⓒ Part of the dorsal fins

Ⓓ Tails

9 What does the professor imply about the dorsal fins on whales?

   Ⓐ They are important for identifying individual whales.

   Ⓑ They are important for speed.

   Ⓒ They are not very important, especially for bowhead whales.

   Ⓓ They should be bigger for extra speed.

10 What can be inferred about the mako shark?

   Ⓐ It usually swims very slowly.

   Ⓑ It should be feared due to its speed.

   Ⓒ It resembles the great white shark.

   Ⓓ It is larger than a male orca.

11 In the lecture, the professor describes a number of facts about the fins on a fish. Indicate whether each of the following sentences is a fact about the fins on a fish. Click in the correct box for each sentence.

	Fact	Not a Fact
1 Fins are unnecessary for most fish.		
2 Fish use fins for stability.		
3 Fins are necessary to escape predators.		
4 Fish need fins for identification.		

Listening Directions

09- 05

In this part, you will listen to 1 conversation and 2 lectures.

You must answer each question. After you answer, click on **Next**. Then click on **OK** to confirm your answer and go on to the next question. After you click on OK, you cannot return to previous questions.

You may now begin this part of the Listening Section. You will have **10 minutes** to answer the questions.

Click on **Continue** to go on.

09-06

1   Why did the professor ask to see the student?
   Ⓐ To discuss her recent class performance
   Ⓑ To find out her plans for the next semester
   Ⓒ To ask her to give him some assistance
   Ⓓ To offer her a job during summer vacation

2   What does the student say about her class schedule?
   Ⓐ She has classes every day of the week.
   Ⓑ She has too many classes this semester.
   Ⓒ She is taking one evening class.
   Ⓓ She finishes her classes in the afternoon.

3   What can be inferred about the student?
   Ⓐ She is looking for a second job.
   Ⓑ She is very good at astronomy.
   Ⓒ She does not remember the professor.
   Ⓓ She is doing poorly this semester.

4   What does the professor ask the student to do?
   Ⓐ Help tutor students in his class
   Ⓑ Sign up for an astronomy class
   Ⓒ Apply to some graduate schools
   Ⓓ Quit her part-time job at the library

5   What is the professor's attitude toward the student?
   Ⓐ He is very respectful of her.
   Ⓑ He is slightly impolite to her.
   Ⓒ He praises her choice of major.
   Ⓓ He hopes she will study with him again.

09-07

Zoology

6 What is the main topic of the lecture?

   Ⓐ Bird banding

   Ⓑ Hummingbird nesting habits

   Ⓒ Hummingbird migration

   Ⓓ Birds of the tropics

7 Why does the professor explain banding?

   Ⓐ To describe how flocks of birds gather

   Ⓑ To make clear the nesting habits of birds

   Ⓒ To show the need for better study tools

   Ⓓ To discuss how individual birds are studied

8 According to the professor, what is one way that weather could affect hummingbird migration?

   Ⓐ Cold weather forces hummingbirds to migrate northward.

   Ⓑ Most hummingbirds leave the tropics when the weather gets too warm.

   Ⓒ Severe weather has the potential to destroy an entire species.

   Ⓓ Hummingbirds do not migrate in the rainy season.

9 What does the professor imply about banding?

    Ⓐ A more up-to-date method of recording hummingbird migrations is needed.

    Ⓑ Banding provides many details about individual and group migrations.

    Ⓒ Banding is the most suitable tracking device for hummingbirds.

    Ⓓ More researchers should band hummingbirds for more reliable information.

10 In the lecture, the professor describes a number of facts about the ruby-throated hummingbird. Indicate whether each of the following sentences is a fact about the ruby-throated hummingbird.

Click in the correct box for each sentence.

	Fact	Not a Fact
1 Its popularity is less now than in past years.		
2 It loves to eat insects.		
3 It can fly 500 miles without stopping.		
4 It is studied so much because of its range.		

11 What can be inferred about the professor?

    Ⓐ She enjoys studying hummingbirds in the field.

    Ⓑ She is planning to do research on bird migration this winter.

    Ⓒ She thinks hummingbirds are more interesting than other birds.

    Ⓓ She believes there is more to be learned about hummingbirds.

VOLUME

09-08

Psychology

Bonding

12 What is the lecture mainly about?
- Ⓐ Paternal bonding
- Ⓑ Maternal bonding
- Ⓒ Mother-father-baby bonding
- Ⓓ Sibling rivalries

13 What is a pacifier?
- Ⓐ Something a baby sleeps on
- Ⓑ Something a baby plays on
- Ⓒ Something a baby sucks on
- Ⓓ Something a baby learns with

14 Why does the professor discuss colic?
- Ⓐ To show the more positive aspects of the topic
- Ⓑ To show the class that babies suffer from stress
- Ⓒ To show the class a negative aspect of it
- Ⓓ To show the class that babies enjoy crying

15 What does the professor imply about breastfeeding?

    Ⓐ It should be done by all mothers.

    Ⓑ It is the most important form of bonding.

    Ⓒ It is not as important as touching.

    Ⓓ Mothers who do not do it do not bond with their babies.

16 Why does the professor bring up the Velcro bonding theory?

    Ⓐ To introduce more positive bonding examples

    Ⓑ To cover the negative aspects of bonding

    Ⓒ To review the topic for an upcoming exam

    Ⓓ To compare it with the baby blues

17 Listen again to part of the lecture. Then answer the question.

What does the professor imply when he says this: 🎧

    Ⓐ Most mothers want good relationships with their children.

    Ⓑ The mother and the child will have a poor relationship.

    Ⓒ Mothers need to spend more time with their children.

    Ⓓ Some children reject the care that their mothers provide.

Appendix

Mastering Word List

This part provides lists of important vocabulary words in each unit. They are essential words for understanding any academic scripts. Many of the words are listed with their derivative forms so that students can expand their vocabulary in an effective way. These lists can be used as homework assignments.

Step A

- ☐ aerial
- ☐ aerosol
- ☐ atmosphere
- ☐ bombardment
- ☐ civilian
- ☐ climatology
- ☐ display
- ☐ geography
- ☐ masterpiece
- ☐ mixture
- ☐ participation
- ☐ portion
- ☐ rediscover
- ☐ symbolism
- ☐ tapestry
- ☐ wrench

Step B

- ☐ *n.* act
- ☐ *v.* activate
- ☐ *adj.* active
- ☐ *adv.* actively

- ☐ *n.* advice
- ☐ *v.* advise
- ☐ *adj.* advisable
- ☐ *adv.* advisably

- ☐ *n.* brutality
- ☐ *v.* brutalize
- ☐ *adj.* brutal
- ☐ *adv.* brutally

- ☐ *n.* comfort
- ☐ *v.* comfort
- ☐ *adj.* comfortable
- ☐ *adv.* comfortably

- ☐ *n.* curiosity
- ☐ *adj.* curious
- ☐ *adv.* curiously

- ☐ *n.* division
- ☐ *v.* divide
- ☐ *adj.* divisive
- ☐ *adv.* divisively

- ☐ *n.* expense
- ☐ *adj.* expensive
- ☐ *adv.* expensively

- ☐ *n.* explanation
- ☐ *v.* explain
- ☐ *adj.* explanatory
- ☐ *adv.* explanatorily

- ☐ *n.* history
- ☐ *adj.* historical
- ☐ *adv.* historically

- ☐ *n.* inhumanity
- ☐ *adj.* inhumane
- ☐ *adv.* inhumanely

- ☐ *n.* interest
- ☐ *v.* interest
- ☐ *adj.* interesting
- ☐ *adv.* interestingly

- ☐ *n.* monument
- ☐ *v.* monumentalize
- ☐ *adj.* monumental
- ☐ *adv.* monumentally

- ☐ *n.* nerve
- ☐ *adj.* nervous
- ☐ *adv.* nervously

- ☐ *n.* prediction
- ☐ *v.* predict
- ☐ *adj.* predictive
- ☐ *adv.* predictively

- ☐ *n.* radiation
- ☐ *v.* radiate
- ☐ *adj.* radiate
- ☐ *adv.* radiately

- ☐ *n.* religion
- ☐ *adj.* religious
- ☐ *adv.* religiously

- ☐ *n.* reality
- ☐ *v.* realize
- ☐ *adj.* real
- ☐ *adv.* really

- ☐ *n.* symbol
- ☐ *v.* symbolize
- ☐ *adj.* symbolic
- ☐ *adv.* symbolically

Step A

- ☐ access
- ☐ assassinate
- ☐ audience
- ☐ autologous
- ☐ carbon
- ☐ clot
- ☐ dignify
- ☐ donation
- ☐ emphasis
- ☐ facial
- ☐ fluid
- ☐ gland
- ☐ hormone
- ☐ injustice
- ☐ instinctive
- ☐ kidney
- ☐ mineral
- ☐ negotiation
- ☐ organism
- ☐ oxygen
- ☐ plasma
- ☐ platelet
- ☐ regulate
- ☐ resolve
- ☐ resource
- ☐ status
- ☐ tissue
- ☐ transport

Step B

- ☐ *n.* access
- ☐ *v.* access
- ☐ *adj.* accessible
- ☐ *adv.* accessibly

- ☐ *n.* affection
- ☐ *v.* affect
- ☐ *adj.* affective
- ☐ *adv.* affectively

- ☐ *n.* argument
- ☐ *v.* argue
- ☐ *adj.* argumentative
- ☐ *adv.* argumentatively

- □ *n.* benefit
- □ *v.* benefit
- □ *adj.* beneficial
- □ *adv.* beneficially

- □ *n.* blood
- □ *v.* bleed
- □ *adj.* bloody
- □ *adv.* bloodily

- □ *n.* capability
- □ *adj.* capable
- □ *adv.* capably

- □ *n.* difference
- □ *v.* differ
- □ *adj.* different
- □ *adv.* differently

- □ *n.* digestion
- □ *v.* digest
- □ *adj.* digestive
- □ *adv.* digestively

- □ *n.* familiarity
- □ *v.* familiarize
- □ *adj.* familiar
- □ *adv.* familiarly

- □ *n.* instinct
- □ *adj.* instinctive
- □ *adv.* instinctively

- □ *n.* intention
- □ *v.* intend
- □ *adj.* intentional
- □ *adv.* intentionally

- □ *n.* nourishment
- □ *v.* nourish
- □ *adj.* nourishing

- □ *n.* peace
- □ *adj.* peaceful
- □ *adv.* peacefully

- □ *n.* prime
- □ *adj.* primary
- □ *adv.* primarily

- □ *n.* transportation
- □ *v.* transport
- □ *adj.* transportable
- □ *adv.* transportably

UNIT 03 Listening for Major Details

Step A

- □ anaphase
- □ anthropologist
- □ charcoal
- □ chromatin
- □ chromosome
- □ dissolve
- □ equatorial
- □ hinder
- □ identical
- □ inward
- □ mediator
- □ membrane
- □ metaphase
- □ microtubule
- □ mitosis
- □ nutrient
- □ Paleolithic
- □ patriarchal
- □ photosynthesis
- □ pinch
- □ prophase
- □ racism
- □ respiration
- □ revolution
- □ tremendously
- □ tribal
- □ schematic
- □ shaman

Step B

- □ *n.* completion
- □ *v.* complete
- □ *adj.* complete
- □ *adv.* completely

- □ *n.* demonstration
- □ *v.* demonstrate
- □ *adj.* demonstrative
- □ *adv.* demonstratively

- □ *n.* duplicate
- □ *v.* duplicate
- □ *adj.* duplicable

- □ *n.* expansion
- □ *v.* expand
- □ *adj.* expansive
- □ *adv.* expansively

- □ *n.* insight
- □ *adj.* insightful
- □ *adj.* insightfully

- □ *n.* interpretation
- □ *v.* interpret
- □ *adj.* interpretable
- □ *adv.* interpretably

- □ *n.* nature
- □ *v.* naturalize
- □ *adj.* naturalistic
- □ *adv.* naturalistically

- □ *n.* origin
- □ *v.* originate
- □ *adj.* original
- □ *adv.* originally

- □ *n.* politics
- □ *adj.* political
- □ *adv.* politically

- □ *n.* research
- □ *v.* research
- □ *adj.* researchable

- □ *n.* respect
- □ *v.* respect
- □ *adj.* respectful
- □ *adv.* respectfully

- □ *n.* respiration
- □ *v.* respire
- □ *adj.* respiratory

- □ *n.* rotation
- □ *v.* rotate
- □ *adj.* rotative
- □ *adv.* rotatively

- □ *n.* segregation
- □ *v.* segregate
- □ *adj.* segregated

UNIT 04 Understanding the Function of What Is Said

Step A

- andante
- architecture
- authority
- awareness
- bullying
- conceit
- consistent
- damage
- enroll
- fluctuation
- human
- hygiene
- generation
- geometry
- minuet
- narrative
- negatively
- participation
- passion
- pollution
- precisely
- preserve
- rectangular
- reverse
- sonata
- tuition
- variation

Step B

- *n.* accuracy
- *adj.* accurate
- *adv.* accurately

- *n.* authority
- *v.* authorize
- *adj.* authoritative
- *adv.* authoritatively

- *n.* competition
- *v.* compete
- *adj.* competitive
- *adv.* competitively

- *n.* consideration
- *v.* consider
- *adj.* considerate
- *adv.* considerately

- *n.* contamination
- *v.* contaminate
- *adj.* contaminative

- *n.* horror
- *v.* horrify
- *adj.* horrifying
- *adv.* horrifyingly

- *n.* information
- *v.* inform
- *adj.* informative
- *adv.* informatively

- *n.* intensity
- *v.* intensify
- *adj.* intense
- *adv.* intensely

- *n.* mass
- *adj.* massive
- *adv.* massively

- *n.* mentality
- *adj.* mental
- *adv.* mentally

- *n.* norm
- *v.* normalize
- *adj.* normal
- *adv.* normally

- *n.* prevention
- *v.* prevent
- *adj.* preventive
- *adv.* preventively

- *n.* randomness
- *v.* randomize
- *adj.* random
- *adv.* randomly

- *n.* society
- *v.* socialize
- *adj.* social
- *adv.* socially

- *n.* visualization
- *v.* visualize
- *adj.* visual
- *adv.* visually

UNIT 05 Understanding the Speaker's Attitude

Step A

- adjust
- attendance
- biography
- candidate
- charter
- cholesterol
- consume
- criteria
- cultural
- elect
- emotion
- enhance
- establish
- fable
- fiber
- fiction
- gender
- homicide
- institution
- moist
- poetry
- president
- request
- revise
- subsidy
- suicide
- vital
- vitamin

Step B

- *n.* abuse
- *v.* abuse
- *adj.* abusive
- *adv.* abusively

- *n.* colony
- *v.* colonize
- *adj.* colonial

- *n.* creation
- *v.* create
- *adj.* creative
- *adv.* creatively

□ *n.* definition
□ *v.* define
□ *adj.* definitive
□ *adv.* definitively

□ *n.* digestion
□ *v.* digest
□ *adj.* digestive
□ *adv.* digestively

□ *n.* essence
□ *adj.* essential
□ *adv.* essentially

□ *n.* imagination
□ *v.* imagine
□ *adj.* imaginary
□ *adv.* imaginarily

□ *n.* intensity
□ *v.* intensify
□ *adj.* intense
□ *adv.* intensely

□ *n.* motivation
□ *v.* motivate
□ *adj.* motivational
□ *adv.* motivationally

□ *n.* negligence
□ *v.* neglect
□ *adj.* neglectful
□ *adv.* neglectfully

□ *n.* property
□ *adj.* proper
□ *adv.* properly

□ *n.* qualification
□ *v.* qualify
□ *adj.* qualifying

□ *n.* seriousness
□ *adj.* serious
□ *adv.* seriously

□ *n.* suicide
□ *v.* suicide
□ *adj.* suicidal

UNIT 06 Understanding Organization

Step A

□ adjacent
□ appreciate
□ bacteria
□ blob
□ chromosome
□ conserve
□ contain
□ controversial
□ courtesan
□ dehydration
□ endure
□ enormous
□ epicenter
□ evaporation
□ helix
□ hump
□ hypocenter
□ insulation
□ interview
□ lava
□ molecule
□ nucleotide
□ pillow
□ protein
□ rescue
□ scandalous
□ submarine
□ strand
□ tortoise

Step B

□ *n.* amazement
□ *v.* amaze
□ *adj.* amazing
□ *adv.* amazingly

□ *n.* completeness
□ *v.* complete
□ *adj.* complete
□ *adv.* completely

□ *n.* controversy
□ *v.* controvert
□ *adj.* controversial
□ *adv.* controversially

□ *n.* experiment
□ *v.* experiment
□ *adj.* experimental
□ *adv.* experimentally

□ *n.* explosion
□ *v.* explode
□ *adj.* explosive
□ *adv.* explosively

□ *n.* location
□ *v.* locate
□ *adj.* local
□ *adv.* locally

□ *n.* multiple
□ *v.* multiply
□ *adj.* multiple

□ *n.* organism
□ *v.* organize
□ *adj.* organic
□ *adv.* organically

□ *n.* popularity
□ *v.* popularize
□ *adj.* popular
□ *adv.* popularly

□ *n.* remark
□ *v.* remark
□ *adj.* remarkable
□ *adv.* remarkably

□ *n.* symbiosis
□ *v.* symbiose
□ *adj.* symbiotic
□ *adv.* symbiotically

□ *n.* tolerance
□ *v.* tolerate
□ *adj.* tolerant
□ *adv.* tolerantly

□ *n.* variety
□ *v.* vary
□ *adj.* various
□ *adv.* variously

Step A

- [ ] anemoscope
- [ ] civilization
- [ ] device
- [ ] endangered
- [ ] extinct
- [ ] flourish
- [ ] fossil
- [ ] glacier
- [ ] gravity
- [ ] imprint
- [ ] international
- [ ] microscopic
- [ ] mountainous
- [ ] orchestra
- [ ] oxygen
- [ ] practical
- [ ] pressure
- [ ] promise
- [ ] qualify
- [ ] realize
- [ ] sculpture
- [ ] slope
- [ ] species
- [ ] stuff
- [ ] thaw
- [ ] trace
- [ ] zone

Step B

- [ ] *n.* absoluteness
- [ ] *adj.* absolute
- [ ] *adv.* absolutely

- [ ] *n.* accumulation
- [ ] *v.* accumulate
- [ ] *adj.* accumulative
- [ ] *adv.* accumulatively

- [ ] *n.* creation
- [ ] *v.* create
- [ ] *adj.* creative
- [ ] *adv.* creatively

- [ ] *n.* division
- [ ] *v.* divide
- [ ] *adj.* divisive
- [ ] *adv.* divisively

- [ ] *n.* existence
- [ ] *v.* exist
- [ ] *adj.* existent

- [ ] *n.* exploration
- [ ] *v.* explore
- [ ] *adj.* exploratory

- [ ] *n.* fame
- [ ] *v.* fame
- [ ] *adj.* famous
- [ ] *adv.* famously

- [ ] *n.* immunity
- [ ] *v.* immunize
- [ ] *adj.* immune

- [ ] *n.* invention
- [ ] *v.* invent
- [ ] *adj.* inventive
- [ ] *adv.* inventively

- [ ] *n.* prevention
- [ ] *v.* prevent
- [ ] *adj.* preventive
- [ ] *adv.* preventively

- [ ] *n.* reason
- [ ] *v.* reason
- [ ] *adj.* reasonable
- [ ] *adv.* reasonably

- [ ] *n.* ruin
- [ ] *v.* ruin
- [ ] *adj.* ruinous
- [ ] *adv.* ruinously

- [ ] *n.* suggestion
- [ ] *v.* suggest
- [ ] *adj.* suggestive
- [ ] *adv.* suggestively

- [ ] *n.* validity
- [ ] *v.* validate
- [ ] *adj.* valid
- [ ] *adv.* validly

Step A

- [ ] ancient
- [ ] appetite
- [ ] aspect
- [ ] bother
- [ ] colorblind
- [ ] convince
- [ ] dairy
- [ ] depression
- [ ] disorder
- [ ] disruptive
- [ ] goose
- [ ] grain
- [ ] formula
- [ ] inconsiderate
- [ ] infant
- [ ] narcissistic
- [ ] nutrition
- [ ] poke
- [ ] psychiatric
- [ ] psychology
- [ ] pyramid
- [ ] recommend
- [ ] symptom
- [ ] stubborn
- [ ] tackle
- [ ] tragedy

Step B

- [ ] *n.* comedy
- [ ] *adj.* comic
- [ ] *adv.* comically

- [ ] *n.* comparison
- [ ] *v.* compare
- [ ] *adj.* comparative
- [ ] *adv.* comparatively

- [ ] *n.* conclusion
- [ ] *v.* conclude
- [ ] *adj.* conclusive
- [ ] *adv.* conclusively

- ☐ *n.* conviction
- ☐ *v.* convince
- ☐ *adj.* convincing
- ☐ *adv.* convincingly

- ☐ *n.* development
- ☐ *v.* develop
- ☐ *adj.* developmental
- ☐ *adv.* developmentally

- ☐ *n.* formula
- ☐ *v.* formularize
- ☐ *adj.* formulaic
- ☐ *adv.* formulaically

- ☐ *n.* function
- ☐ *v.* function
- ☐ *adj.* functional
- ☐ *adv.* functionally

- ☐ *n.* interaction
- ☐ *v.* interact
- ☐ *adj.* interactive
- ☐ *adv.* interactively

- ☐ *n.* legality
- ☐ *v.* legalize
- ☐ *adj.* legal
- ☐ *adv.* legally

- ☐ *n.* migration
- ☐ *v.* migrate
- ☐ *adj.* migrant

- ☐ *n.* narrowness
- ☐ *v.* narrow
- ☐ *adj.* narrow
- ☐ *adv.* narrowly

- ☐ *n.* psychology
- ☐ *adj.* psychological
- ☐ *adv.* psychologically

- ☐ *n.* recommendation
- ☐ *v.* recommend
- ☐ *adj.* recommendatory

- ☐ *n.* tragedy
- ☐ *adj.* tragic
- ☐ *adv.* tragically

MEMO

MEMO

How to Master Skills for the

TOEFL® iBT

LISTENING

▌ Answers, Scripts, and Translations

Second Edition

Basic

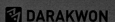 DARAKWON

How to
Master Skills for the

Second Edition

TOEFL® iBT

LISTENING

Basic

Answers, Scripts,
and Translations

 DARAKWON

UNIT **01** Listening for Main Ideas

Skill & Tip ··· p.14

Skill Practice

A

1 We went over the course requirements the last time.
2 Each place on the Earth has different patterns of weather events.
3 She wants to help children by doing a fundraising campaign.
4 They can tutor other students who need help for the preparation of the course and the test.

B

W Student: Would you tell me why it is so important to understand Greek mythology in your class? I don't know why I should write a paper about the birth of Aphrodite.

M Professor: Hey, Cindy. Greek myths are not simple and funny old stories. They have tons of characters and events, which have fertilized our lives, culture, and environment for two thousand years. So you can get the essential feeling from that topic for your work just like former great writers did.

C

W Professor: As you know, the center of opera was Italy, especially Florence in the northern part of Italy. It gradually spread to many places throughout Europe by the 1600s. However, for many years, or even centuries, Italian opera was thought to be ideal, and many non-Italian composers kept using Italian words in their works.

Basic Drill ··· p.16

Drill 1 Ⓐ

Script 🎧 01-05

W Student: Hello. I heard there's a shuttle bus on campus. How can I use it?

M Student Activities Office Employee: It's very easy. Just go to one of the bus stops. When the bus arrives, scan your student ID card, and you can ride on it.

W: Great. Do you know how often the shuttle bus arrives?

M: We have several shuttles on campus. So they usually arrive at each bus stop within five minutes.

해석

W Student: 안녕하세요. 캠퍼스에 셔틀 버스가 다닌다고 들었어요. 어떻게 이용할 수 있나요?

M Student Activities Office Employee: 매우 간단해요. 버스 정류장 한 곳으로 가세요. 버스가 도착하면 학생의 학생증을 대고 탑승하면 되죠.

W: 그렇군요. 셔틀 버스가 얼마나 자주 오는지 아시나요?

M: 여러 대의 셔틀 버스가 캠퍼스를 돌아다녀요. 그래서 각 정류소에 보통 5분 이내의 간격으로 도착을 해요.

Drill 2 Ⓑ

Script 🎧 01-06

W Student: Mr. Jenkins, I've finished the first draft of my term paper. I was hoping you could check it over for me.

M Professor: You're already done? That may be the fastest anyone's ever completed a first draft.

W: Well, I like to get started early on my projects. So is it possible for you to look it over and tell me what needs to be rewritten?

M: Sure, but I don't have time now. How about if I return it to you next week?

해석

W Student: Jenkins 교수님, 학기 보고서의 초안을 완성했어요. 교수님께서 한번 봐 주셨으면 좋겠어요.

M Professor: 벌써 끝냈다고요? 아마도 초안을 가장 빨리 작성한 학생이 되겠군요.

W: 음, 프로젝트를 일찍 시작하고 싶어서요. 그래서 한번 보시고 다시 작성해야 할 부분이 어디인지 말씀해 주시겠어요?

M: 그래요, 하지만 지금은 시간이 없어요. 다음 주에 돌려 줘도 될까요?

Drill 3 Ⓒ

Script 🎧 01-07

W Professor: There is a small town in Belgium called Waterloo. This small town became very famous because of Napoleon's last battle. A lot of his soldiers were killed and injured at Waterloo. As a result, he was removed from his emperor's throne and sent to Saint Helena. He died there in 1821.

해석

W Professor: 벨기에에는 워털루라고 불리는 작은 마을이 있습니다. 이 작은 마을은 나폴레옹의 마지막 전투 덕분에 매우 유명해졌어요. 그의 많은 병사들이 워털

루에서 사망하고 부상을 당했습니다. 그 결과 그는 황제의 자리에서 물러나게 되었고 세인트 헬레나로 유배되었죠. 그는 1821년에 그곳에서 숨을 거두었습니다.

Drill 4 Ⓑ

Script 🎧 01-08

> **M Professor**: The atmosphere is a mixture of different gases and aerosols. We usually call it air. The atmosphere is very important to our lives, and we cannot live without it. Almost every living creature on the Earth breathes it. It surrounds the Earth and protects us from deadly rays and radiation from space.

해석

M Professor: 대기에는 다양한 기체들과 연무질이 섞여 있습니다. 보통은 이를 공기라고 부르죠. 대기는 우리 삶에 매우 중요하며, 우리는 대기 없이 살 수가 없습니다. 지구상의 거의 모든 생명체들이 호흡을 합니다. 대기는 지구를 둘러싸고 있으며 우주에서 오는 치명적인 광선과 방사선으로부터 우리를 보호해 줍니다.

Exercises with Short Conversations & Lectures

Exercise 1 1 Ⓓ 2 Ⓑ   p.18

Script 🎧 01-09

> **M Student**: Hello, Professor Nightengale. May I speak with you for a moment, please?
>
> **W Professor**: Of course, James. What can I do for you?
>
> **M**: The first two classes of the semester have been a bit hard for me. I wonder if I am in a level that's too high.
>
> **W**: Hmm . . . Didn't you take Spanish in high school? I seem to recall you said that. So taking Spanish II shouldn't be too hard.
>
> **M**: Yes, I did take it. I guess you're right. I'll just have to study harder to make sure I can do well.
>
> **W**: That's a good attitude. Just try your best. Come to me if you have any problems.

해석

M Student: 안녕하세요, Nightengale 교수님. 잠시 이야기를 나눌 수 있을까요?

W Professor: 물론이죠, James. 어떻게 도와 드리면 될까요?

M: 이번 학기의 첫 번째 수업 두 개가 제게 약간 어려워요. 제가 너무 높은 레벨의 수업을 듣는 것이 아닌지 궁금해서요.

W: 흠… 고등학교 때 스페인어 수업을 듣지 않았나요? 학생이 그렇게 이야기한 것으로 기억해요. 그렇다면 스페인어 II 수업이 그렇게 어렵지는 않을 텐데요.

M: 네, 수업을 들었어요. 교수님 말씀이 맞는 것 같아요. 공부를 더 열심히 해서 꼭 좋은 결과를 내도록 할게요.

W: 자세가 좋군요. 최선을 다하세요. 문제가 생기면 저한테 오세요.

Exercise 2 1 Ⓑ 2 Ⓐ   p.19

Script 🎧 01-10

> **M Student**: I am going to take Mathematical Ideas this semester. I am a bit nervous of that subject because I am not really good at math.
>
> **W Residential Assistant**: Mathematical Ideas? Don't worry. I had that class my sophomore year. The lectures were very interesting, and the teacher made the students feel comfortable in the course. You will love the class.
>
> **M**: Well, I don't know. Weren't the tests difficult?
>
> **W**: Not at all. If you listen carefully to the lectures and do the homework, the tests will be easy. The teacher would hand out a summary of his lecture every class. If you study them thoroughly, you will not even need to read the textbook. I was bad at math, but I got a good grade.
>
> **M**: I see. Thank you so much for your advice. It has really helped me.

해석

M Student: 저는 이번 학기에 수학적 사고를 들을 거예요. 사실 수학을 잘하는 편이 아니라서 이 수업에 대해 약간 걱정이 들지만요.

W Residential Assistant: 수학적 사고요? 걱정하지 마세요. 저도 2학년 때 그 수업을 들었어요. 강의도 매우 흥미로웠고, 선생님도 수업에서 학생들을 편안하게 대해 주셨어요. 수업이 정말 마음에 들 거예요.

M: 음, 잘 모르겠어요. 시험은 어렵지 않았나요?

W: 전혀 어렵지 않았어요. 강의를 주의 깊게 듣고 과제를 잘 수행한다면 시험은 쉬울 거예요. 선생님께서 수업 시간마다 강의 요약문을 나누어 주실 거예요. 이것만 제대로 공부하면 교재는 보지 않아도 될 정도이죠. 저도 수학을 잘 못했지만 좋은 성적을 받았어요.

M: 알겠어요. 충고해 줘서 정말 고마워요. 정말로 큰 도움이 되었어요.

Exercise 3 1 Ⓑ 2 Ⓑ   p.20

Script 🎧 01-11

> **W Professor**: Hello. My name is Jenny Smith. I will be your physical geography teacher this semester. Um . . . Since this is your first class, I want to talk about what physical geography is. What is physical geography? Does anybody have any ideas . . . ? Well, uh, basically, it's a science about the Earth. But it is unique because it uses ideas from other sciences profoundly. For example, you will find information from chemistry, biology, climatology, astronomy, and many other sciences in physical geography. Does that sound scary? Actually, you don't really need to worry about it. Fundamentally, this is a geography class. So we just will use what we already know in those areas. We will not go into too many details about those subjects. Okay . . . now let me show you

some examples . . . Please turn to page eleven. Chapter one. Energy.

해석

W Professor: 안녕하세요. 제 이름은 Jenny Smith입니다. 제가 이번 학기에 여러분의 자연 지리학 수업을 맡을 거예요. 음… 첫 수업이기 때문에 자연 지리학이 무엇인지에 대해 이야기하고 싶군요. 자연 지리학이 무엇일까요? 아시는 분이 있나요…? 어, 음, 기본적으로 자연 지리학은 지구에 관한 학문입니다. 하지만 다른 과학에서 비롯된 아이디어들을 많이 사용한다는 점이 특징이죠. 예를 들어 여러분은 화학, 생물학, 기후학, 천문학, 그리고 기타 과학에서 알려진 내용들을 자연 지리학에서 접하게 될 것입니다. 무시무시하게 들리나요? 사실 그에 대해 걱정할 필요는 없어요. 기본적으로 이번 수업은 지리학 수업이에요. 그렇기 때문에 그러한 분야에서 우리가 이미 알고 있는 내용만을 이용할 거예요. 그러한 주제에 대해서는 그다지 상세히 다루지 않을 것이고요. 좋아요… 그럼 몇 가지 예를 보여 드리면… 11페이지를 봐 주세요. 1장입니다. 에너지.

Exercise 4 1 ⓓ 2 ⓐ   p.21

Script 🎧 01-12

M Professor: Okay . . . Now let's talk about tests and grades. There will be two written tests and one oral test this semester. Each written test will have forty multiple-choice questions. The oral test will have five questions. Uh . . . Some of you may think the tests are too difficult with too many questions. But that is not so. As a matter of fact, there will be a summary handout every class this semester. And if you study them well, then the tests will be very easy. And speaking about grades, the written and oral tests will be just a small portion of your final grade. Active class participation is the most important thing to get a good grade. So please listen to my lectures carefully, ask many questions, and discuss the topics with your classmates and me during the class. It will be very good for you to prepare for each unit before class, too.

해석

M Professor: 좋아요… 이제 시험과 점수에 대해 얘기해 보죠. 이번 학기에는 두 번의 필기 시험과 한 번의 구두 시험이 있을 예정입니다. 필기 시험은 각각 객관식 40문항으로 구성될 거예요. 구두 시험에는 5문항이 출제됩니다. 어… 여러분 중 일부는 문제가 너무 많아서 시험이 어렵다고 생각할 수도 있을 거예요. 하지만 그렇지 않습니다. 사실 이번 학기에는 수업 시간마다 수업 요약 자료를 나누어 줄 예정입니다. 그것만 잘 공부한다면 시험은 아주 쉬울 거예요. 그리고 점수에 대해 이야기하면, 필기 시험과 구두 시험은 최종 결과의 극히 일부에 지나지 않을 것입니다. 좋은 성적을 얻기 위해서는 무엇보다 적극적으로 수업에 참여해야 합니다. 그러니 강의를 잘 듣고, 질문도 많이 하고, 수업 시간에 급우들 및 저와 주제에 대한 토론을 해 주시기 바랍니다. 수업 시간 전에 각 단원을 미리 예습해 두면 큰 도움이 될 거예요.

Exercise 1 1 ⓒ 2 ⓒ   p.22

Script 🎧 01-13

W Student: Professor Gibbs, I didn't do well on the midterm exam. What should I do?

M Professor: Did you study the material, Tiffany? I notice that you take notes in class, so I know you are paying attention.

W: Yes, I did study. I studied for three days before the test. But when I took the test, I just couldn't remember any of the answers.

M: Hmm . . . Maybe you should get a tutor. A tutor might be able to help you remember the information in the class.

W: A tutor? How would I do that?

M: You can go to the academic affairs office. It's located in Briar Hall. Tell the receptionist what class you are taking. She should be able to recommend a tutor for you.

W: Okay. That sounds like a good idea. But . . . um . . . tutors are pretty expensive, aren't they? I don't know if I can actually afford to pay for one.

M: There's nothing to worry about. This is a free service that the university provides. So you won't have to pay a thing.

W: What a relief. Thanks so much for letting me know.

해석

W Student: Gibbs 교수님, 제 중간 고사 성적이 좋지 못했어요. 어떻게 해야 할까요?

M Professor: 수업 내용을 공부했나요, Tiffany? 수업 시간에 학생이 필기하는 모습을 봐서 학생이 주의를 기울이고 있다는 점은 알고 있어요.

W: 네, 했어요. 시험 보기 전 3일 동안 공부를 했죠. 하지만 시험을 볼 때 어떤 답도 기억해 낼 수가 없었어요.

M: 흠… 아마도 개인 지도가 필요할 것 같아요. 개인 지도 교사가 수업에서 배운 내용을 기억할 수 있도록 도움을 줄 수 있을 거예요.

W: 개인 지도요? 어떻게 개인 지도를 받을 수 있죠?

M: 교무처로 가면 되어요. Briar 홀에 위치해 있죠. 그곳 직원에게 학생이 어떤 수업을 듣고 있는지 알려 주세요. 그녀가 학생에게 개인 지도 교사를 추천해 줄 거예요.

W: 알겠어요. 좋은 아이디어인 것 같군요. 하지만… 음… 개인 지도는 상당히 비싸죠, 그렇지 않나요? 제가 실제로 그에 대한 비용을 감당할 수 있을지 잘 모르겠어요.

M: 전혀 걱정할 필요가 없어요. 대학에서 제공하는 무료 서비스니까요. 그러니 학생이 낼 비용은 없을 거예요.

W: 다행이군요. 알려 주셔서 정말 고맙습니다.

The student did poorly on the midterm exam even though she studied for three days. The professor recommends that the student get a tutor. She can find one at the academic affairs office. The student is pleased with the idea. But she says she cannot afford a tutor. The professor says that the tutors are a free service provided by the school.

Exercise 2 1 Ⓐ 2 Ⓓ   p.24

Script 🎧 01-14

> **M1 Professor**: Jamie, you seem tired these days. Is everything all right?
>
> **M2 Student**: You know I do some volunteer work in my free time, don't you? Well, I've been preparing a lot for a special event coming up next week. Right now, I'm making a banner for it.
>
> **M1**: Really? What event are you talking about?
>
> **M2**: I do a lot of work with underprivileged children. The kids don't have enough money to buy clothes or school supplies. So my organization is going to hold a fundraiser to try to raise some money for them.
>
> **M1**: It's so good of you to try to help other people who don't have the same opportunities that others do.
>
> **M2**: Yes, I just hope it can help them a bit.
>
> **M1**: Are there many students at our school that are members of the organization?
>
> **M2**: Not really. I wish there were more of them.
>
> **M1**: Well, if you want, you can make a short presentation at the end of class tomorrow. Maybe some other students in the class will volunteer to help.
>
> **M2**: That would be great. Thanks so much, Professor Worthy.

해석

M1 Professor: Jamie, 요즘 피곤해 보이는군요. 괜찮은 거죠?

M2 Student: 제가 시간이 날 때 자원봉사를 하고 있다는 점은 알고 계시죠? 음, 저는 다음 주에 있을 특별 행사를 위해 많은 것들을 준비하고 있어요. 지금은 행사용 배너를 제작하고 있고요.

M1: 그런가요? 어떤 행사를 말하는 거죠?

M2: 저는 소외 계층의 아이들과 함께 많은 일을 하고 있어요. 이 아이들은 옷이나 학교 준비물을 구입하기에 충분한 돈을 가지고 있지 않죠. 그래서 제 단체에서 그들을 위한 기금을 마련하기 위해 모금 행사를 개최할 거예요.

M1: 다른 사람들과 동일한 기회를 갖지 못하는 사람들을 도우려고 한다니 멋지군요.

M2: 네, 그들에게 약간의 도움이라도 되기를 바라고 있어요.

M1: 그 단체에 우리 학교의 학생들이 많이 있나요?

M2: 그렇지는 않아요. 더 많으면 좋겠지만요.

M1: 음, 학생이 원한다면 오늘 수업이 끝날 무렵에 프레젠테이션을 짧게 해도 좋아요. 수업을 듣는 다른 학생들이 자원해서 도움을 줄 수도 있을 거예요.

M2: 그러면 좋을 것 같아요. 정말 고맙습니다, Worthy 교수님.

Summary Note B

The student is preparing for an upcoming fundraiser to help underprivileged children who need help. He is making a banner that will advertise the event. At the fundraiser, he is planning to raise some money to buy children various things that they need. The professor offers to let the student talk about the organization at the end of the next class.

Exercise 3 1 Ⓓ 2 Ⓐ   p.26

Script 🎧 01-15

> **M Professor**: The Renaissance began in Italy in the late 1300s and lasted until the 1500s. By then, it had spread around Europe. It was a time when there was a rebirth of learning from ancient Greece and Rome. Many fields were affected during the Renaissance. Art then was influenced greatly by the ancient Greeks and Romans. As a result, art in the Renaissance was much different from art in the Middle Ages. For instance, the subject matter changed. Renaissance artists still painted religious scenes like people did in the Middle Ages. However, they also started making more secular paintings. They painted scenes from mythology. They also painted portraits, uh, you know, pictures of people. Renaissance artists used a more realistic style as well. The main reason was that they rediscovered certain painting techniques from the past. This enabled them to paint realistic-looking people in paintings. Here, uh, take a look at this painting by Leonardo da Vinci. It's called *The Last Supper*. Do you see what I'm talking about?

해석

M Professor: 르네상스는 1300년대 후반 이탈리아에서 시작되어 1500년대까지 지속되었습니다. 이 시기에는 르네상스가 유럽 전역에 퍼져 있었죠. 이때는 고대 그리스 및 로마의 지식이 부활한 때였습니다. 르네상스 기간 동안 여러 분야가 영향을 받았습니다. 당시 미술은 고대 그리스 및 로마인들로부터 막대한 영향을 받았죠. 그 결과 르네상스 시대의 미술은 중세 시대 미술과 크게 달랐어요. 예를 들어 주제가 바뀌었습니다. 르네상스 시대의 화가들도 중세 시대 사람들이 그렸던 것처럼 여전히 종교적인 장면을 그렸습니다. 하지만 보다 세속적인 그림들도 그리기 시작했어요. 신화 속 장면들을 그렸습니다. 또한 초상화, 어, 아시다시피 사람들의 그림도 그렸습니다. 르네상스 화가들은 또한 보다 사실주의적인 기법을 사용했어요. 주로 과거의 특정 회화 기법들을 재발견했기 때문이었죠. 이로써 그들은 그림에서 보다 사실적으로 보이는 사람들을 그릴 수 있었습니다. 여기, 어, 레오나르도 다빈치가 그린 이 그림을 봐 주세요. *최후의 만찬*이라는 그림입니다. 제가 말하는 바를 아시겠어요?

Summary Note B

The Renaissance lasted from the late 1300s to the 1500s.

It involved a rebirth of learning from ancient Greece and Rome. Artists were greatly affected by it. They made paintings different from those in the Middle Ages. They painted more secular works such as scenes from mythology and portraits. They painted people who looked realistic, like the people in *The Last Supper* by Leonardo da Vinci.

Exercise 4 1 ⒟ 2 Ⓑ   p.28

Script 🎧 01-16

> **W Professor**: Okay, class. Now, before we start going into the details of climatology, we need to know about climate. What is climate? What is the definition of climate? Do you have any ideas?
>
> **M Student**: I think it is a collection of weather.
>
> **W**: Yes, that is a correct answer. Actually, climate is the overall collected weather in a certain place on the Earth. Let's take some examples and make it clearer. Hmm . . . Do you know the aurora that happen in the Arctic Circle? Do you think it is a climate? No, it is not a climate. It is not even weather. What about global climate? Is there such a thing as a global climate? Yes, there is. It's the sum of all of the climates on the planet added up. For example, when the Earth is getting hotter, we can say, "The global climate is increasing in temperature." So there is a global climate. Hmm . . . Actually, there are many types of climates on the Earth. And we live in one of them or one that is a combination of two. As the seasons gradually change, the climate also changes each year. It can get warmer or colder. Or there can be more or less rain. There can even be more or less sunlight.

해석

W Professor: 좋아요. 여러분. 자, 기후학을 자세히 살펴보기 전에, 기후에 관해 알아야 합니다. 기후란 무엇일까요? 기후의 정의가 무엇일까요? 아시는 분이 있나요?

M Student: 날씨로 이루어지는 것이라고 생각합니다.

W: 네, 정답입니다. 실제로 기후는 지구상의 특정 지역에서 나타나는 전체적인 날씨로 이루어집니다. 몇 가지 예를 들어서 보다 구체적으로 말씀을 드리죠. 흠… 북극권에서 나타나는 오로라를 아시나요? 이것이 기후라고 생각하시나요? 아니죠, 기후가 아닙니다. 날씨도 아니에요. 지구 기후는 어떨까요? 지구 기후와 같은 것이 존재할까요? 네, 존재합니다. 지구에서 나타나는 모든 기후를 합산한 것이에요. 예를 들어 지구가 점점 더워지는 시기에는 "지구 기후의 온도가 상승하고 있다."고 말할 수 있습니다. 따라서 지구 기후는 존재합니다. 흠… 사실 지구에는 다양한 유형의 기후가 존재해요. 그리고 우리는 그중 하나, 혹은 두 개가 조합된 환경에서 살고 있습니다. 서서히 계절이 바뀌기 때문에 기후 또한 매년 바뀌죠. 점점 따뜻해지거나 점점 추워질 수 있어요. 혹은 비가 더 많이 내릴 수도, 더 적게 내릴 수도 있죠. 햇빛이 더 많을 때도, 더 적을 때도 있을 수 있고요.

📝 Summary Note Ⓑ

The lecturer says that climate is the general pattern of collected weather in a certain place on the Earth. There are a wide variety of climates on the planet, and people live in one type of climate or another. The climate gradually changes every year in accordance with seasonal changes.

Integrated Listening & Speaking   p.30

A

Script 🎧 01-17

> **M Professor**: The Renaissance began in Italy in the late 1300s and didn't conclude until the 1500s. By then, it had spread to countries all around Europe. It was a time when there was a rebirth of learning of knowledge from ancient Greece and Rome. Many fields were affected during the Renaissance. As an example, art was influenced greatly by the ancient Greeks and Romans. As a result, art in the Renaissance was much different from art made during the Middle Ages. For instance, the subject matter changed. Renaissance artists still painted religious scenes similar to what people did in the Middle Ages. However, they also started to make more secular paintings. They painted scenes from mythology and also painted portraits, uh, you know, pictures of people. Renaissance artists used a more realistic style in their work as well. The main reason was that they rediscovered certain painting techniques from the past. This enabled them to paint realistic-looking people in paintings.

1 a. There was a rebirth of learning from ancient Greece and Rome.
   b. Art was influenced greatly by the ancient Greeks and Romans.

2 a. They painted religious scenes like people did in the Middle Ages.
   b. They made secular paintings such as scenes from mythology and portraits.

3 a. Renaissance artists used a more realistic style.
   b. Renaissance artists painted realistic-looking people in paintings.

B

Script 🎧 01-18

> **W Professor**: Okay, class, the last time, I told you about the climate. Some of you may still be confused about climate and weather. So I want to explain the difference again. From the viewpoint of time, weather is an event that occurs for a short period of time. For example, if we

want to take a trip, we are curious about the weather because we go on a trip for just a short period of time. So this is weather. Now for climate . . . Climate is a collection of weather, so it affects people's lives longer compared to weather. For example, sometimes we see people moving to other countries. When they move, they want to know what the local climate is like because they will live there for a certain period of time. So this is climate. There are many types of climates on the Earth. These climates change over a long period of time. It could be years, decades, or even centuries. Now I hope you aren't confused about the climate anymore.

1   **a.** They often get confused about climate and weather.
     b. The confusion is mostly about climate and weather.

2   **a.** It is a collected weather condition.
     b. Climate is a collection of weather.

3   **a.** The climate changes over a long period of time.
     b. It changes gradually over years, decades, or even centuries.

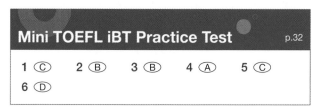

Mini TOEFL iBT Practice Test   p.32

1 ⓒ   2 Ⓑ   3 Ⓑ   4 Ⓐ   5 ⓒ
6 Ⓓ

[1-3]

Script 🎧 01-19

M Student: Pardon me, but I'm a first-year student. Do you mind if I ask some questions?

W Librarian: Not at all. But you should have taken the library orientation tour a few days ago. Didn't you do that?

M: I didn't arrive at school until yesterday.

W: Ah, that explains it. Well, what questions do you have for me?

M: Is this the desk I need to come to when I want to borrow books? And how many books can students check out at one time?

W: Yes, this is the circulation desk. When you want to check out a book, just bring the book here. Make sure you have your student ID card. That's all you need.

M: That's pretty easy.

W: It sure is. In addition, you can check out up to 100 books at a time.

M: 100? I don't think I'll need that many.

W: You might not, but there are students and professors who check out dozens of books. They need lots of books for the research they are doing.

M: Ah, that makes sense. One more question . . . How do I search for a book on the computer system?

W: Just find an available terminal. You can see some over there. Type the title of the book or the author. If you don't know either, type the subject. You'll get various recommendations.

M: If I have a problem, should I come back here?

W: Actually, you want to speak with the reference librarian. He's right over at that desk. If you can't find something, he can give you a hand.

해석

M Student: 죄송하지만 제가 신입생이라서요. 몇 가지 질문을 드려도 될까요?

W Librarian: 그럼요. 하지만 며칠 전에 도서관 오리엔테이션을 들었어야 했을 텐데요. 듣지 않았나요?

M: 저는 어제 학교에 도착했어요.

W: 아, 그럼 설명이 되는군요. 음, 질문이 무엇인가요?

M: 책을 대출하려고 할 때 이곳 데스크로 와야 하나요? 그리고 학생들은 한 번에 몇 권까지 도서를 대출할 수 있나요?

W: 네, 이곳이 대출 데스크예요. 대출을 하고 싶으면 책을 이곳으로 가지고만 오세요. 학생증 잊지 마시고요. 해야 할 일은 그게 다예요.

M: 정말 간단하군요.

W: 맞아요. 또한 한 번에 최대 100권까지의 도서를 대출할 수 있어요.

M: 100권이요? 그렇게 많이 필요할지는 잘 모르겠군요.

W: 그렇지는 않겠지만 책을 수십 권씩 대출하는 학생과 교수님들도 계세요. 진행 중인 연구에 많은 책들이 필요한 경우이죠.

M: 아, 이해가 가네요. 한 가지 질문이 더 있는데… 컴퓨터로 책을 어떻게 검색하나요?

W: 비어 있는 단말기를 찾기만 하세요. 보시다시피 저쪽에 몇 대가 있어요. 책 제목이나 저자 이름을 치세요. 둘 다 모르는 경우에는 주제를 치시고요. 다양한 추천 도서를 보게 될 거예요.

M: 문제가 생기는 경우 여기로 오면 되나요?

W: 사실 참고 사서와 이야기하고 싶을 거예요. 그분은 저쪽 데스크에 계세요. 무언가를 찾지 못하는 경우에는 그분께서 도움을 주실 거예요.

[4-6]

Script 🎧 01-20

W Professor: Okay, class. Today, I am going to tell you about one of Pablo Picasso's greatest masterpieces . . . *Guernica*. As you know, Guernica is also the name of a Basque town.

In order to understand this picture, we need to go over some of the historical background of this town. The Basque town is a city located in northern Spain. During the Spanish Civil War, the German air force bombed the city. It was a massive aerial bombardment of a civilian population. It happened since the Nazis were helping Spain's dictator Francisco Franco.

Hundreds of civilians were killed in the raid. It shocked the world. It also prompted Picasso to begin painting. He completed it in fewer than two months and hung it in the Spanish Pavilion at the Paris International Exposition of 1937. The painting became a timely and predictive vision of the Second World War.

There is a complexity of symbolism in the painting as it does not portray the event directly. Instead, Picasso used imagery such as suffering people, animals, and buildings wrenched by violence. It certainly shows the chaos of carpet-bombing. We can feel the inhumanity, brutality, and hopelessness of war from it. Picasso really expressed his outrage very well with this monumental painting.

People say *Guernica* is the last great historical painting. It is now recognized as an international icon for peace. You can also see a tapestry copy of it displayed on the wall of the United Nations building in New York City. It is often described as the most important work of art in the twentieth century, but its meaning is still beyond the understanding even of some well-known scholars.

해석

W Professor: 자, 여러분. 오늘은 피카소의 가장 위대한 걸작 중 하나인… *게르니카*에 대해 이야기를 하고자 해요. 아시다시피 게르니카는 바스크에 있는 도시의 이름이기도 합니다.

이 그림을 이해하기 위해서는 이 도시에 관한 몇 가지 역사적 사실을 살펴봐야 해요. 바스크는 스페인 북부에 위치한 도시입니다. 스페인 내전 당시 독일 공군이 이 도시를 폭격했어요. 시민들을 대상으로 한 대규모 공중 폭격이었습니다. 나치가 스페인의 독재자인 프란시스코 프랑코를 돕고 있었기 때문에 그런 일이 벌어진 것이었죠.

공습으로 수백 명의 민간인들이 사망했습니다. 이는 전 세계를 경악하게 만들었어요. 또한 피카소로 하여금 그림을 그리도록 만들었습니다. 그는 채 두 달도 안되어서 그림을 완성시키고 이를 1937년 파리 국제 박람회의 스페인 전시관에 전시했습니다. 이 그림은 2차 세계 대전의 모습을 적절한 시기에 예측한 그림이 되었습니다.

이 그림은 사건을 직접적으로 묘사하지는 않는데, 그림 속에 복잡한 상징들이 존재합니다. 피카소는 고통스러워하는 사람들, 동물들, 그리고 폭력으로 부서진 건물들과 같은 이미지를 사용했어요. 이는 융단 폭격으로 인한 참사를 확실하게 보여 줍니다. 우리는 그림으로부터 비인간성, 잔인함, 그리고 전쟁의 절망적인 상황을 느낄 수 있습니다. 피카소는 이 기념비적인 회화 작품으로 자신의 분노를 매우 잘 표현해 냈어요.

사람들은 *게르니카*가 마지막 위대한 역사화라고 말합니다. 오늘날에는 국제적인 평화의 아이콘으로 통합니다. 또한 뉴욕의 UN 건물 벽에서 이 그림을 보여주는 태피스트리 작품을 볼 수도 있죠. 이 그림은 종종 20세기의 가장 중요한 예술 작품이라고 평가되지만, 그 의미는 아직 가장 저명한 학자들조차도 완전히 이해하지 못하고 있습니다.

Vocabulary Check-Up ———— p.35

A

1	①	2	⑩	3	⑪	4	⑭	5	⑧
6	④	7	⑮	8	⑫	9	⑬	10	③
11	②	12	⑤	13	⑥	14	⑩	15	⑦

B

| 1 | ② | 2 | ④ | 3 | ① | 4 | ③ | 5 | ⑤ |

UNIT 02 Listening for Main Purpose

Skill & Tip p.38

Skill Practice

A

1 I can run in that race.
2 Sorry, but I can't figure out what the right answer is.
3 You should also record the call number of the book.
4 You shouldn't talk so loudly in the hospital.

B

M Student: Professor Kimball, I didn't know you were going to hang around school in summer.

W Professor: Actually, I'm preparing to teach a class. What are you doing here?

M: I'm attending summer school. I want to get some credits out of the way. So I signed up for Economics 23.

W: I have some great news for you. I'm going to be your instructor in that class.

C

W Professor: Okay, students. We'll look at Beethoven's deafness today. It is not known for sure when he began to go deaf. But he kept the fact a secret until 1801, when he wrote a friend about his "miserable life." Can you imagine how deeply he suffered from that? He was totally deaf by 1818. That means his greatest work, the *Ninth Symphony*, was done without him being able to hear. That symphony was written in 1822. The fact that one of the greatest symphonies in the world was made up by an old deaf person should be kept in our minds.

Basic Drill p.40

Drill 1 Ⓑ

Script 🎧 02-05

M Student: Professor Starling, I'm having trouble finding a book for my final paper. The library doesn't have it, and the book is out of print.

W Professor: What's the title of the book? As you can see, I have a large collection here in my office.

M: It's *Classical Economic Theory* by Theordore Randolph. It was printed in the early 1900s.

W: Ah, yes, I do have a copy of that book. You can borrow it, but please make sure nothing happens to it.

해석

M Student: Starling 교수님, 기말 보고서 작성을 위한 책을 찾고 있는데 문제가 생겼어요. 도서관에는 없고, 책은 절판되었어요.

W Professor: 책 제목이 뭐죠? 알겠지만 이곳 제 사무실에 책이 많이 있거든요.

M: 시어도어 랜돌프가 쓴 *고전 경제학 이론*이에요. 1900년대 초에 출판되었고요.

W: 아, 그래요, 그 책이 한 권 있어요. 빌려가도 좋지만, 책에 아무런 문제도 생기지 않아야 해요.

Drill 2 Ⓒ

Script 🎧 02-06

W Student: Hello. I want to get some copies of my transcript, please. I need to send them to companies I'm applying to.

M Registrar's Office Employee: We can send them directly to the firms if you want. Just provide us with the addresses.

W: Oh, that's wonderful. I had no idea. Is there a form that I should fill out?

M: Here you are . . . In addition, each copy of your transcript will cost five dollars.

해석

W Student: 안녕하세요. 제 성적표 사본을 몇 부 받고 싶어서요. 제가 지원한 기업에 보내야 하거든요.

M Registrar's Office Employee: 원하시는 경우 직접 회사로 보내 드릴 수 있어요. 주소만 알려 주세요.

W: 오, 잘 되었군요. 몰랐어요. 제가 작성해야 하는 서류가 있을까요?

M: 여기 있어요… 그리고 발급 비용은 성적표 사본 한 장당 5달러예요.

Drill 3 Ⓒ

Script 🎧 02-07

W Professor: People of all cultures share food to create and maintain friendships with one another. When we invite others into our homes, we often expect to have fun eating together. We also go out to have dinner or to meet for lunch for many social reasons. Sharing food indicates affection, familiarity, and good will.

해석

W Professor: 모든 문화의 사람들은 서로 친분을 맺고 이를 유지하기 위해 함께 음식을 먹습니다. 다른 사람들을 집으로 초대하는 경우, 우리는 종종 다같이 재미있는 시간을 보낼 것으로 예상합니다. 또한 여러 가지 사회적인 이유들로 저녁을 먹으러 밖으로 나가거나 점심에 모임을 갖기도 하죠. 함께 음식을 먹는다는 것은 애정, 친밀감, 그리고 선의를 나타냅니다.

Drill 4 Ⓑ

Script 🎧 02-08

M Professor: It would be boring if there were no sound when you watched a movie. But most films were silent before the late 1920s. Films required a greater emphasis on body language and facial expressions so that the audience could understand better what actors were feeling and portraying on screen.

해석

M Professor: 영화를 볼 때 소리가 없으면 지루할 것입니다. 하지만 1920년대 후반까지 대부분의 영화는 무성 영화였어요. 영화 화면에서 배우가 느끼는 것과 표현하려는 것을 관객들이 더 잘 이해할 수 있도록 몸짓과 얼굴 표정이 더 크게 강조되어야 했습니다.

Exercises with Short Conversations & Lectures

Exercise 1 1 Ⓓ 2 Ⓐ p.42

Script 🎧 02-09

W Student: Hello, Professor Ozuna. I heard you want to speak with me. What can I do for you?

M Professor: Good morning, Alanis. I remember you said you were looking for a job during summer. Have you found one yet?

W: Not yet. It appears that most of the jobs on campus have already been filled.

M: Well, how would you like to be my research assistant this summer? I need someone to translate a bunch of documents from Greek. I know you speak it very well.

W: That sounds like a lot of fun. It's a paid position, right?

M: Yes, it is. You'll receive fifteen dollars an hour and will work for around twenty-five hours a week. How does that sound?

해석

W Student: 안녕하세요, Ozuna 교수님. 저와 이야기를 나누고 싶어하신다고 들었어요. 제가 어떻게 하면 되나요?

M Professor: 좋은 아침이에요, Alanis. 학생이 여름에 할 일을 찾고 있다고 말했던 것이 기억나서요. 일자리를 찾았나요?

W: 아직 못 찾았어요. 교내의 대부분의 일자리는 이미 채워진 것 같더군요.

M: 음, 이번 여름에 제 연구 조교가 되어 보는 것은 어떨까요? 그리스어로 작성된 많은 서류들을 번역할 사람이 필요하거든요. 학생이 그리스어를 매우 잘 한다고 알고 있어요.

W: 정말 재미있을 것 같아요. 급여가 지급되는 일이죠, 그렇죠?

M: 네, 그래요. 시간당 15달러를 받게 될 것이고, 일주일에 25시간 정도 일하게 될 거예요. 어떻게 들리나요?

Exercise 2   1 Ⓒ   2 Ⓑ   p.43

Script 🎧 02-10

W Professor: Have you chosen your topic for your sociology presentation yet, Karl?

M Student: Yes, I have. I intend to discuss cloning ethics.

W: That sounds good. But remember that you need to discuss both sides of the subject. By that, I mean talk about how people are both for and against it. How are you going to develop the topic?

M: Well, I plan to focus on the bad side and the good side. For example, some people say it is good because it will enable scientists to grow vital body parts for sick people. But others say it is unethical to experiment with human body parts. Moreover, people say it should be stopped because there could be unexpected consequences.

W: Hmm . . . That sounds interesting. I'm looking forward to hearing your presentation.

해석

W Professor: 사회학 발표를 위한 주제를 정했나요, Karl?

M Student: 네, 정했습니다. 복제 윤리에 대해 이야기할 생각이에요.

W: 괜찮게 들리는군요. 하지만 주제의 양면을 모두 논의해야 한다는 점을 기억하세요. 제 말은 찬성하는 사람들과 반대하는 사람들 모두에 대해 이야기해야 한다는 뜻이에요. 주제를 어떻게 전개할 생각인가요?

M: 음, 나쁜 면과 좋은 면에 초점을 맞출 계획이에요. 예를 들어 어떤 사람들은 그로 인해 아픈 사람에게 꼭 필요한 신체 부위를 과학자들이 만들 수 있게 될 것이라는 점에서 그것이 좋다고 주장을 하죠. 하지만 다른 사람들은 인간의 신체 부위로 실험을 하는 일은 비윤리적이라고 주장을 해요. 게다가 사람들은 예상치 못한 결과가 일어날 수 있으니 이를 중단해야 한다고 주장하죠.

W: 음… 흥미롭게 들리는군요. 학생의 발표를 기대하고 있을게요.

Exercise 3   1 Ⓐ   2 Ⓑ   p.44

Script 🎧 02-11

M Professor: Okay, class. Today, I want to talk about Roman doctors at the beginning of the first century. As I noted in our previous class, there was a fifteen-year-long war after Julius Caesar was assassinated. The war was severe. Many people were injured. There were so many injured that it became one of the top priorities of the new emperor to give medical care to those in need. It was around this time that the new emperor, Augustus, started thinking about upgrading the status of doctors. He realized that medical care was key to the empire and especially the army. In order to improve the medical system, he needed better doctors. So he started making the profession look more enticing. All army doctors were entitled to attend the new army medical school. They were given dignified titles, land grants, and special retirement benefits. Before that, doctors had a fairly low status.

해석

M Professor: 자, 여러분. 오늘은 1세기 초의 로마 의사들에 대한 이야기를 하고자 합니다. 이전 시간에 살펴본 것처럼 줄리어스 시저가 암살되고 난 뒤 15년 동안 전쟁이 지속되었습니다. 전쟁은 끔찍했어요. 많은 사람들이 부상을 입었죠. 너무 많은 사람들이 부상을 입어서 도움이 필요한 사람들을 치료하는 일이 신임 황제의 최우선 과제가 되었습니다. 이 무렵 신임 황제인 아우구스투스가 의사의 지위 향상에 대해 생각하기 시작했습니다. 그는 의료 서비스가 제국과 특히 군대에게 매우 중요하다 점을 깨달았어요. 의료 시스템을 개선시키기 위해서는 보다 뛰어난 의사들이 필요했습니다. 그래서 그는 이 직업이 보다 매력적으로 보이도록 만들었어요. 모든 군의관에게는 새로 생긴 군 의과 대학에 입학할 자격이 주어졌습니다. 위엄 있는 호칭, 토지, 그리고 특별 퇴직금도 주어졌고요. 그 전까지만 해도 의사의 지위는 상당히 낮은 편이었습니다.

Exercise 4   1 Ⓒ   2 Ⓐ   p.45

Script 🎧 02-12

W Professor: Okay, now let's talk about handball violations. I bet you all know that you aren't supposed to use your hands when you play soccer. It is called a handball violation. You cannot touch any part of the ball with your hands unless you are the goalkeeper. Only the goalkeeper can touch the ball with his hands. A handball violation includes using any part of the body from the fingers to the shoulders. Now, I want to ask you some questions. First, picture this situation. In the middle of the game, a player kicks the ball, and the ball touches the hand of a player on the opposing team. But he didn't touch it intentionally. Now, is that a handball violation? I want you to think about it. Here is another question. What if the kicker did that intentionally? Is that a handball violation?

W Professor: 좋아요, 이제 핸드볼 파울에 대해 얘기해 보죠. 축구를 할 때 손을 사용해서는 안 된다는 점은 분명 여러분 모두가 건 알고 계실 거예요. 이것이 핸드볼 파울이라는 것입니다. 골키퍼가 아닌 이상 공의 어떤 부분에도 손을 대서는 안 됩니다. 골키퍼만이 공에 손을 댈 수가 있죠. 손가락부터 어깨까지의 신체 어느 부분을 사용해도 핸드볼 파울에 해당됩니다. 자, 제가 몇 가지 질문을 드리죠. 먼저, 다음과 같은 상황을 상상해 보세요. 경기 도중 한 선수가 공을 차서 그 공이 상대 팀 선수의 손에 닿습니다. 그가 고의로 공을 건드린 것은 아니죠. 자, 이것도 핸드볼 파울일까요? 생각해 보세요. 또 한 가지 질문을 드릴게요. 만약 공을 찬 사람이 의도적으로 그렇게 한 경우라면 어떨까요? 이것도 핸드볼 파울일까요?

Exercises with Mid-Length Conversations & Lectures

Exercise 1 1 Ⓑ 2 Ⓑ, Ⓓ p.46

Script 🎧 02-13

M Student: Hello. I'm here to look for a job. What do I need to do?

W Student Employment Office Worker: Good afternoon. We have a couple of binders over there on that table. They list a lot of the jobs that are available.

M: Ah, okay. So . . . what exactly do I need to do?

W: The best thing is to look through the binders. Find a couple of jobs you are interested in. Then, talk to the contact person listed on the form.

M: Do the forms include how many hours a week are needed and the pay?

W: Yes, they do. Is there anything else?

M: One more question . . . What are some of the better jobs on campus?

W: Hmm . . . If you're an outdoor person, you could work for Buildings and Grounds. You might cut grass or do something similar. You'd be outside most of your shift.

M: That's not something I'm particularly interested in.

W: Ah, you're an indoor person then. In that case, try to get a job at the library. Or look for a job in one of the departmental offices. Good luck.

해석

M Student: 안녕하세요. 일자리를 구하고 싶어서 왔어요. 제가 어떻게 하면 되나요?

W Student Employment Office Worker: 안녕하세요. 저쪽에 있는 테이블 위에 두 개의 바인더가 있어요. 거기에 지원이 가능한 여러 일자리들이 나와 있어요.

M: 아, 그렇군요. 그러면… 제가 정확히 어떻게 하면 될까요?

W: 제일 좋은 방법은 바인더를 면밀히 살펴보는 것이에요. 관심이 가는 일자리를 두 개 정도 찾으세요. 그런 다음에 양식에 적혀 있는 연락 가능한 사람과 이야기를 나누어 보세요.

M: 일주일에 몇 시간을 일해야 하는지, 그리고 급여도 양식에 포함되어 있나요?

W: 네, 그래요. 질문이 또 있나요?

M: 한 가지 더 있어요… 교내 일자리 중에서 어떤 것들이 더 좋은가요?

W: 흠… 밖에서 일하는 것을 좋아하는 경우에는 건물 및 운동장 관리부에서 일할 수 있을 거예요. 잔디를 깎는 등의 일을 하게 되죠. 근무 시간 대부분을 야외에서 보내게 될 거예요.

M: 특별히 관심이 가는 일은 아니네요.

W: 아, 그러면 안에서 일하는 것을 좋아하겠군요. 그런 경우라면 도서관에서 일자리를 찾아보세요. 아니면 교내 부서의 사무실 중 한 곳에서 일자리를 찾아보세요. 행운을 빌어요.

📝 Summary Note Ⓑ

The student visits the office to ask about a job. The woman say he can look in the binders. He can find jobs he likes and speak with the contact person. The woman says that information such as the number of hours per work and the pay are on the forms. The student asks about popular jobs. The woman recommends working outdoors for Buildings and Grounds or indoors at the library or a departmental office.

Exercise 2 1 Ⓐ 2 Ⓒ p.48

Script 🎧 02-14

W Professor: Are you ready to go on tomorrow's expedition to the riverside, Jason?

M Student: I sure am. I've never gone searching for fossils before. It should be an exciting experience.

W: I take my students to the fossil beds there every year. They always come away with some nice fossils.

M: What are we probably going to find?

W: Hmm . . . Most of the time, we find trilobites and other shells. We also find small bones from various creatures.

M: I hope I find something interesting. Oh, what do we do with the fossils that we find?

W: That's the fun part. Next week, we'll be working in the lab to try to identify them. Some, such as trilobites and ammonites, are easy to identify. But the pieces of bone are much harder.

M: That sounds fascinating. I can't wait to go.

W: Just make sure you are in front of Matterhorn Hall by six thirty in the morning. That's when the bus is leaving. And we won't wait for latecomers.

M: I'll be there. Don't worry.

해석

W Professor: 내일 강가로 현장 학습을 떠날 준비가 되었나요, Jason?

M Student: 물론이죠. 저는 이전에 화석 발굴 조사를 해 본 적이 없어요. 흥미진진한 경험이 될 거예요.

W: 저는 매년 그곳 화석층으로 학생들을 데리고 가죠. 학생들은 항상 멋진 화석들을 가지고 그곳을 떠나고요.

M: 혹시 무엇을 발견하게 될까요?

W: 흠… 대부분의 경우 삼엽충과 기타 조개류들을 발견해요. 또한 다양한 생물들의 작은 뼈들도 발견하고요.

M: 제가 흥미로운 것을 찾아내면 좋겠어요. 오, 우리가 찾은 화석으로는 무엇이 하나요?

W: 그게 바로 재미있는 부분이죠. 다음 주 실험실에서 그것이 무엇인지 확인할 거예요. 삼엽충과 암모나이트와 같은 몇몇 화석들은 식별하기가 쉬운 편이죠. 하지만 뼈 조각들은 식별이 훨씬 더 까다로워요.

M: 흥미롭게 들리는군요. 당장이라도 가고 싶어요.

W: 잊지 말고 오전 6시 30분까지 Matterhorn 홀 앞으로 오세요. 그때 버스가 떠날 거예요. 그리고 우리는 지각생들을 기다리지 않을 거예요.

M: 꼭 갈게요. 걱정하지 마세요.

📝 Summary Note **B**

The student is looking forward to going to the riverside to search for fossils. The professor says they usually find trilobites, other shells, and small bones. She adds that they will attempt to identify the fossils in the lab next week. The student thinks that is fascinating. The professor reminds him to be on time tomorrow because the bus will not wait for latecomers.

Exercise 3   1 ⓓ   2 ⓒ   p.50

Script 🎧 02-15

> **W Professor**: Why do countries go to war? That is a complicated question. There have been thousands of wars throughout human history. Each one has its own causes. In general, wars between nations and societies start a lot like fights between two people. There is a disagreement over something. When people disagree, they usually try to resolve their differences peacefully through negotiations; Sometimes they clear the air; other times they don't. With countries, you cannot just put a wall between you and your neighbors when things go wrong. Wars happen when nations have disagreements that can't be resolved peacefully. There are many things that nations argue over: borders, rights to natural resources, injustices in the past, and human rights, among others. The list goes on and on. War is as old as organized society. Hunter-gatherer tribes from thousands of years ago fought with one another over access to food and water. Some psychologists believe war is the human version of instinctive animal behavior.

해석

W Professor: 국가들은 왜 전쟁을 할까요? 까다로운 질문입니다. 인류 역사상 수많은 전쟁이 있었습니다. 전쟁 마다 나름의 이유가 있어요. 일반적으로 국가 및 사회 간의 전쟁은 두 사람 사이의 다툼과 매우 비슷하게 시작됩니다. 무언가에 관해 의견이 달라지죠. 의견이 다르면 사람들은 대부분 협상을 통해 평화로

운 방법으로 의견 차이를 해소하려고 합니다. 때로는 오해를 풀기도 하고, 때로는 그렇지 못하기도 하죠. 국가의 경우 상황이 악화되면 이웃 간에 벽을 세울 수가 없습니다. 국가들의 의견 차이가 평화롭게 해결될 수 없는 경우에 전쟁이 일어나는 것이에요. 국가들의 논쟁 대상이 되는 것으로는 국경, 천연 자원에 대한 권리, 과거에 행해졌던 불의, 그리고 인권 등이 있습니다. 나열하자면 끝이 없죠. 전쟁은 조직된 사회만큼이나 오랫동안 존재했습니다. 수천 년 전 사냥과 채집 생활을 했던 사람들도 식량과 물을 확보하기 위해 서로 싸움을 했어요. 일부 심리학자들은 전쟁이 동물적인 본능을 따르는 인간의 행동이라고 생각합니다.

📝 Summary Note **B**

A war is a fight between nations when there is a disagreement. It is like a fight between two people. Nations argue over borders, natural resources, injustices in the past, and human rights. There are so many issues that it is hard to list everything. Animals have instinctive behavior, and war is the human version of animal behavior. Since humans organized society, wars have happened.

Exercise 4   1 ⓒ   2 ⓑ   p.52

Script 🎧 02-16

> **M Professor**: Birds and mammals, despite being different, have a few similarities with each other. For instance, both of them are warm-blooded animals. This is unlike reptiles and amphibians, which are cold blooded. Birds and mammals can therefore regulate their own body temperature, primarily through consuming food. They are both vertebrates. This means that they have backbones. Like all creatures, they breathe oxygen. And one more important characteristic is this one: They take care of their young by feeding them. Of course, there are many other differences. For instance, birds have feathers on their bodies. Mammals, on the other hand, have hair or fur instead. Birds have wings and are capable of flying. Sure, not all birds can fly. Penguins and ostriches are two flightless birds. But in general, birds can fly. Other than bats, mammals are not able to achieve flight. Birds lay eggs, too, which is different from mammals. Mammals give birth to live young.

해석

M Professor: 조류와 포유류는 비록 다르지만 몇 가지 유사성을 지니고 있어요. 예를 들어 둘 다 온혈 동물입니다. 이는 냉혈 동물인 파충류 및 양서류와 다른 점이죠. 따라서 조류와 포유류는 주로 먹이를 섭취함으로써 자신의 체온을 조절합니다. 이들은 둘 다 척추 동물입니다. 그들이 등뼈를 가지고 있다는 점을 의미하죠. 모든 생물들과 마찬가지로 이들도 산소를 들이마십니다. 그리고 또 한가지 중요한 특성은 이들이 새끼에게 먹이를 주면서 새끼들을 돌본다는 점이에요. 물론 그 밖의 차이점들도 많이 있습니다. 예를 들면 조류의 신체에는 깃털이 있죠. 반면에 포유류들은 그 대신 머리털이나 털을 가지고 있고요. 조류는 날개를 가지고 있으며 날 수가 있습니다. 물론 모든 조류들이 다 날 수 있는 것은 아니에요. 펭귄과 타조는 날지 못하는 조류입니다. 하지만 일반적으로 조류는 날 수가 있습니다. 박쥐를 제외한 포유류들은 비행을 하지 못합니다. 또한 새들은 알을 낳는데, 이 역시 포유류와 다른 점입니다. 포유류는 살아 있는 상태의 새끼를 낳습니다.

Summary Note B

The professor says birds and mammals have some similarities. They are both warm-blooded vertebrates that breathe oxygen. They also both take care of their young. However, birds have wings and feathers and aside from a few animals, can fly. Mammals have hair or fur and except for bats, cannot fly. Birds also lay eggs, but mammals give birth to live young.

Integrated Listening & Speaking   p.54

A

Script 🎧 02-17

> **W Professor**: In our last class, we talked about war. Have you ever had a disagreement with your friends or neighbors? I am sure you have at least once. That happens a lot with some people. When it happens, we usually try to talk and resolve the problem peacefully. But what do we do if that does not work? Well, that is a tough question, right? That probably happens to us in our daily lives. When nations have disagreements over something and cannot solve them peacefully . . . war happens. War has existed since humans started living together in societies. War happens when nations defend their territories, have problems over access to natural resources and human rights, and have various other issues. There are an unlimited number of reasons for war, and there have been thousands of wars in human history. I feel bad about people killing each other in wars. I wonder why it can't be avoided . . . It is human nature, similar to instinctive animal behavior. When you get down to it, it is usually related to survival.

1 a. They go to war when they can't resolve problems peacefully.
   b. They go to war when disagreements between countries cannot be resolved peacefully.

2 a. They argue over borders, natural resources, and human rights.
   b. There are many reasons for war.

3 a. War happens because humans have a version of instinctive animal behavior.
   b. Animals sometimes kill each other to survive, and so do humans.

B

Script 🎧 02-18

> **M Professor**: Birds and mammals are different yet also share a few similarities with each other. For instance, both of them are warm-blooded animals. This is unlike reptiles and amphibians, which are cold blooded. Birds and mammals can therefore regulate their own body temperature, primarily by eating food. They are both vertebrates. This means that they have backbones. Like all creatures, they must breathe oxygen to survive. And one more important characteristic is this one: They take care of their young by feeding them. Of course, there are quite a few other differences. For instance, birds have feathers on their bodies. Mammals, on the other hand, have hair or fur instead. Birds have wings and are capable of flying. Sure, not all birds can fly. Penguins and ostriches, for example, are two flightless birds. But, in general, birds can fly. Other than bats, mammals are not able to achieve flight. Birds lay eggs, too, which is different from mammals. Mammals, on the other hand, give birth to live young.

1 a. Birds and mammals are warm-blooded animals, unlike reptiles and amphibians.
   b. Reptiles and amphibians are cold blooded, but birds and animals are not.

2 a. Both of them are vertebrates.
   b. Both of them have backbones.

3 a. Birds are capable of flying, but except for bats, mammals cannot.
   b. Birds lay eggs while mammals give birth to live young.

Mini TOEFL iBT Practice Test   p.56

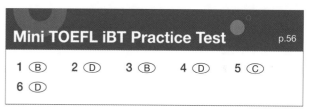

1 Ⓑ   2 Ⓓ   3 Ⓑ   4 Ⓓ   5 Ⓒ
6 Ⓓ

[1-3]

Script 🎧 02-19

> **M Student**: Professor Berry, I would like to speak with you for a moment.
>
> **W Professor**: Sure, Richard. What's on your mind today?
>
> **M**: I decided that I'd like to write a senior honors thesis next year. I wonder if you could be my advisor for it.
>
> **W**: I'd love to, but are you aware that it's a lot of work? It requires the entire school year.
>
> **M**: One of my friends is currently writing one. He said it's not easy, but he is learning a lot from the process. I think it will be a good experience.
>
> **W**: As long as you know how much work you will be doing, that's fine with me.
>
> **M**: Thank you so much for accepting. I'm really looking

forward to this.

W: Okay. So . . . what's your topic? What are you interested in researching?

M: Um . . . I was hoping you would assist me with that.

W: Don't you have a general area of interest? You know, something that you like to learn about?

M: Ah, yes, of course. I am really interested in ancient Roman fortifications. When I lived in Europe, my family traveled around a lot, and I saw many of them.

W: That's a good start. Why don't you narrow the topic down a bit? Maybe you can explore just a couple of fortifications or some located in a specific part of Europe.

M: Okay. I can do that.

W: Come back with a thesis proposal in a few days, and then we can start working together.

해석

M Student: Berry 교수님, 교수님과 잠시 이야기를 나누었으면 해요.

W Professor: 그래요, Richard. 오늘은 무슨 일인가요?

M: 저는 내년에 졸업 논문을 쓰기로 결심했어요. 교수님께서 그에 대한 지도 교수가 되어 주실 수 있는지 궁금합니다.

W: 그러면 좋겠는데, 해야 할 일이 많다는 점도 알고 있나요? 한 학년 전체가 필요할 거예요.

M: 제 친구 중 한 명이 현재 쓰고 있는 중이에요. 그가 쉽지 않다고 말했지만, 그러한 과정을 통해 그는 많은 것을 배우고 있어요. 제 생각에 좋은 경험이 될 것 같아요.

W: 학생이 하게 될 일이 얼마나 많은지 알고 있다면야 저로서는 괜찮아요.

M: 승낙해 주셔서 정말 감사합니다. 정말로 기대가 되는군요.

W: 좋아요. 그러면… 주제가 무엇인가요? 무엇을 연구해 보고 싶으세요?

M: 음… 그 점에 대해서는 교수님께서 도움을 주시기를 바라고 있었어요.

W: 관심이 가는 분야가 없나요? 알겠지만, 학생이 공부하고 보고 싶은 것이 있나요?

M: 아, 네, 물론 있어요. 저는 고대 로마의 방어 시설에 큰 관심을 가지고 있어요. 유럽에서 살 때 저희 가족이 여행을 많이 해서 여러 군데를 볼 수 있었죠.

W: 시작이 좋군요. 주제를 약간 좁혀 보면 어떨까요? 두어 곳의 방어 시설을 조사해 볼 수도 있고, 아니면 유럽의 특정 지역에 위치한 몇몇 방어 시설을 조사해 볼 수도 있을 거예요.

M: 좋아요. 그럴 수 있을 것 같아요.

W: 며칠 후에 연구 계획서를 가지고 다시 오면 같이 시작할 수 있을 거예요.

[4-6]

Script 🎧 02-20

W Professor: The average adult has about five liters of blood flowing inside his body. **Blood is the fluid of life, growth, and health.** It transports oxygen from the lungs to body tissue and carbon dioxide from body tissue to the lungs. It transports nourishment from digestion and

hormones from glands throughout the body. It transports disease-fighting substances to tissues and waste to the kidneys.

Blood is alive because it contains living cells. Red blood cells and white blood cells are responsible for nourishing and cleansing the body. Since the cells are alive, they need nourishment. Vitamins and minerals keep the blood healthy. Blood cells have a definite life cycle just as all living organisms do. Approximately fifty-five percent of blood is plasma, a straw-colored, clear liquid. Liquid plasma carries solid cells and platelets. When the human body loses a bit of blood through a minor wound, platelets help the blood clot so that the bleeding stops. You would bleed to death without the platelets. Your body is always making new blood inside your bones.

When the human body loses a lot of blood through a major wound, that blood has to be replaced through a blood transfusion from another person. But everybody's blood is not the same. There are four different blood types. Plus, your blood has Rh factors which make it even more unique. Blood received through a transfusion must match your own. Sometimes patients donate their own blood when they are scheduled to have major surgery so that they will have a perfect match. It is called an autologous blood donation.

해석

W Professor: 평균적인 성인의 경우 체내에 5리터 정도의 혈액이 들어 있어요. 혈액은 생명, 성장, 그리고 건강에 필요한 액체입니다. 폐에 있는 산소를 신체 조직에 가져다 주고, 신체 조직에 있는 이산화탄소는 폐로 가지고 오죠. 소화로 얻은 영양분과 선에서 나오는 호르몬들을 신체 곳곳에 가져다 줍니다. 질병과 싸우는 물질을 조직으로 보내고 노폐물은 신장에 가져다 주기도 하죠.

혈액은 살아 있는 세포를 가지고 있기 때문에 살아 있습니다. 적혈구와 백혈구는 신체에 영양분을 공급하며 신체를 깨끗하게 만들어요. 이 세포들은 살아 있기 때문에 영양분을 필요로 합니다. 비타민과 무기질이 혈액의 건강을 유지시킵니다. 모든 생명체와 마찬가지로 혈액 세포 역시 일정한 수명을 지닙니다. 혈액의 약 55%는 담황색을 띠는 맑은 액체인 혈장이에요. 액체인 혈장은 고형 세포와 혈소판을 가지고 다니죠. 작은 상처 때문에 인체에서 약간의 혈액이 빠져나가면 혈소판은 출혈이 멈추도록 혈액의 응고를 돕습니다. 혈소판이 없다면 출혈 때문에 사망하게 될 거예요. 신체 내의 뼈 안에서는 항상 새로운 피가 만들어집니다.

큰 부상 때문에 인체에서 다량의 혈액이 빠져나가면 다른 사람으로부터 수혈을 받음으로써 빠져 나간 혈액을 보충해야 합니다. 하지만 모든 사람의 혈액이 같은 것은 아니에요. 네 개의 혈액형이 존재합니다. 게다가 혈액에는 혈액을 보다 독특하게 만드는 Rh 인자가 들어 있어요. 수혈을 통해 받는 혈액은 여러분의 혈액과 반드시 일치해야 합니다. 때때로 중요한 수술을 앞둔 환자들의 경우 혈액이 완벽하게 일치할 수 있도록 자신의 혈액을 미리 뽑아 놓기도 하죠. 이를 자가 수혈이라고 부릅니다.

Vocabulary Check-Up

p.59

A
1 ⓛ	2 ⒣	3 ⒜	4 ⒤	5 ⒝
6 ⓜ	7 ⒞	8 ⓞ	9 ⒟	10 ⒥
11 ⒠	12 ⓝ	13 ⓚ	14 ⒡	15 ⒢

B
1 ⒟	2 ⒠	3 ⒜	4 ⒞	5 ⒝

UNIT 03 Listening for Major Details

Skill & Tip p.62

Skill Practice

A

1 A man cannot be said to have succeeded in this life if he does not satisfy one friend.

2 He has been a potter, and he's not bad as a sculptor.

3 Money is merely a convenient medium of exchange.

4 Better be wise by the misfortunes of others than by your own.

5 Due to the kindness of friends, we have an apartment to stay in here and can easily reach the hospital.

B

W Student: Professor Boyle, can I ask a favor of you?

M Professor: Of course. What can I do for you?

W: Actually, I was so sick that I couldn't attend your class yesterday. Can I have yesterday's material?

M: Why not? Here you are.

C

W Professor: Okay, so if you have no further questions on this, let's look at the makeup of the atom. An atom consists of an extremely small positively charged nucleus surrounded by a cloud of negatively charged electrons. Although the nucleus is typically less than one ten-thousandth the size of the atom, the nucleus contains more than 99.9 percent of the atom's mass. The nuclei consist of positively charged protons and electrically neutral neutrons held together by the so-called strong, or nuclear, force.

Basic Drill

p.64

Drill 1 ⒟

Script 🎧 03-05

> **W1 Student**: Hi. I need to check out some books today, but I lost my library card. Did anyone return it by any chance?
>
> **W2 Librarian**: Let me check the lost and found. What's your name?
>
> **W1**: Kelly Hamm.
>
> **W2**: Give me a second . . . Sorry. Nobody turned it in. I think we have to cancel your previous card and issue you a new one.
>
> **W1**: Oh, thanks. Please do whatever it takes. Oh . . . By the way, can you check if anyone has checked out a book with my card?
>
> **W2**: Certainly. I'll do that. Meanwhile, just fill out this application.

해석

W1 Student: 안녕하세요. 오늘 책을 몇 권 대출해야 하는데 도서관 카드를 잃어버렸어요. 혹시 누군가 가지고 오지 않았나요?

W2 Librarian: 분실물 보관소를 확인해 볼게요. 이름이 어떻게 되죠?

W1: Kelly Hamm입니다.

W2: 잠시만요… 유감이네요. 가지고 온 사람이 없었어요. 학생의 예전 카드를 취소하고 새로 발급을 해야 할 것 같아요.

W1: 오, 고맙습니다. 그렇게 해 주세요. 오… 그건 그렇고 누군가 제 카드로 책을 대출했는지 확인해 주실 수 있나요?

W2: 그럼요. 확인해 드릴게요. 그 동안 이 신청서를 작성해 주세요.

Drill 2 ⒝

Script 🎧 03-06

> **W Professor**: Speaking about your writing, you had a strong introduction and conclusion, but the body did not strongly support the theme.
>
> **M Student**: Can you explain in more detail?
>
> **W**: Sure. You need to explain and support your theme in the body. Some of the information didn't support the theme, and some parts were confusing.
>
> **M**: I see. Could you underline the parts that were confusing and misleading?
>
> **W**: I already did. I wrote down some comments in the margin.
>
> **M**: Thank you, Mrs. Larson. I'll redo it correctly this time.

해석

W Professor: 학생이 쓴 글에 대해 이야기하면, 도입부와 결론은 잘 썼는데 본론이 주제를 잘 받쳐 주지 못했어요.

M Student: 좀 더 자세히 설명해 주시겠어요?

W: 그럼요. 본론에서는 주제를 설명하고 뒷받침해 주어야 해요. 일부 내용들이 주제를 받쳐 주지 못했고, 어떤 부분들은 명확하지가 않았어요.

M: 알겠습니다. 명확하지 않고 오해의 소지가 있는 부분에 밑줄을 쳐 주실 수 있나요?

W: 벌써 그렇게 했죠. 여백에 몇 가지 의견들도 적어 놓았고요.

M: 감사합니다, Larson 교수님. 이번에는 제대로 수정하겠습니다.

Drill 3 Ⓐ

Script 🎧 03-07

> M Professor: In 1963, Martin Luther King, Jr. led a massive demonstration in Birmingham, Alabama. The protest was against racism in the United States. People, including children and teenagers, took to the streets to fight for their rights. However, tragically, police officers and firefighters tried to stop them with dogs and high-pressure water hoses. The protesters were brutally attacked by dogs and torrents of water from fire hoses. These scenes were shown in newspapers and on televisions around the world. Of course, these scenes touched people's hearts. So the demonstrators gained support against segregation.

해석

M Professor: 1963년 마틴 루터 킹 주니어가 앨라배마 버밍햄에서 대규모 시위를 이끌었습니다. 이 시위는 미국에서의 인종 차별을 반대하기 위한 것이었죠. 어린이와 십대들을 포함한 사람들이 자신의 권리를 찾기 위해 거리로 나왔습니다. 하지만 안타깝게도 경찰관과 소방수들은 개와 고압 호스를 이용해서 이들을 막으려고 했어요. 시위대는 개와 호스에서 쏟아져 나오는 물줄기에 의한 맹렬한 공격을 받았습니다. 이러한 장면은 전 세계의 신문과 TV에서 소개되었어요. 당연하게도 이러한 장면은 사람들의 마음을 움직였습니다. 그래서 시위 참가자들은 인종 차별 반대에 대한 지지를 얻게 되었습니다.

Drill 4 Ⓒ

Script 🎧 03-08

> W Professor: Both the rotation of the moon and its revolution around Earth take twenty-seven days, seven hours, and forty-three minutes to be exact. That's a bit less than a month. Because of its motion, the moon appears to move about thirteen degrees against the stars each day. That's around half a degree per hour. If you watch the moon over the course of several hours one night, you will notice that its position among the stars changes by a few degrees. The changing position of the moon with respect to the sun leads to lunar phases.

해석

W Professor: 달의 자전 주기와 지구 주위를 도는 공전 주기는 모두 정확히

27일 7시간 43분입니다. 한 달이 약간 되지 않는 시간이죠. 이러한 운동 때문에 달은 별을 기준으로 하루에 약 13도씩 이동합니다. 시간당 0.5도 정도 이동하는 것이죠. 하룻밤 동안 여러 시간에 걸쳐 달의 움직임을 관찰해 보면 별들 사이에서 달의 위치가 몇 도씩 바뀌는 것을 알게 될 것입니다. 태양을 상대로 한 달의 위치가 변하기 때문에 달의 위상이 나타납니다.

Exercises with Short Conversations & Lectures

Exercise 1 1 Ⓑ 2 Ⓐ   p.66

Script 🎧 03-09

> W Student: I have a problem with my political science class. I don't understand what you're talking about and regret taking it. I should have dropped the class.
>
> M Professor: Calm down, Jane. Students take classes to learn.
>
> W: I know. But I am so clueless. I am just not into politics, the Constitution, and laws. And again, the words are so confusing to me.
>
> M: Jane, let me tell you something. Based on my experience, you just need to try. You know, the words may sound difficult, but they are not really that hard. Once you become familiar with the vocabulary, the basic laws, and the events, political science is a very interesting and easy subject. On top of that, you have me to help you.
>
> W: Do you really think so?
>
> M: Yes, I'm sure. Everything's up to you. If you think positively and put effort into it, everything will become easy.

해석

W Student: 저는 정치학 수업에서 문제를 겪고 있어요. 교수님께서 하시는 말씀이 이해가 되지 않고 수업을 신청한 것을 후회하고 있어요. 수업을 취소해야 했어요.

M Professor: 진정해요, Jane. 학생들은 배우기 위해 수업을 듣는 거예요.

W: 저도 알아요. 하지만 제가 너무 멍청한 걸요. 정치학, 헌법, 그리고 법률에는 관심이 가지가 않아요. 게다가 용어들도 너무 헷갈리고요.

M: Jane, 제가 이야기를 할게요. 제 경험에 의하면 학생은 노력을 해야 해요. 알겠지만 용어들이 어렵게 들릴 수는 있어도 실제로 그처럼 어렵지는 않아요. 용어, 기본적인 법, 그리고 사건들에 친숙하면 정치학은 매우 흥미롭고 쉬운 과목이에요. 게다가 제가 도울 수도 있고요.

W: 정말로 그렇게 생각하시나요?

M: 네, 물론이죠. 모든 것은 학생에게 달렸어요. 긍정적으로 생각하고 노력하면 모든 것이 쉬워질 거예요.

Exercise 2 1 2   p.67

W Student: I've finally <u>decided</u> on my classes for next semester. Would you care to take a look?

M Professor: Sure, Caroline. What are you taking?

W: I'm <u>enrolling</u> in your archaeology class. I'll also <u>take</u> Roman Archaeology with Professor Hern.

M: You'll really <u>enjoy</u> his class. <u>What</u> <u>else</u> are you taking?

W: I'm enrolling in a class on Byzantine history <u>as well as</u> Math 202. I need to <u>complete</u> my math requirement.

M: Those look <u>fine</u>. Will you take <u>any</u> <u>more</u> classes?

W: One more. It's an <u>art</u> <u>history</u> class on Renaissance art. It looks <u>fascinating</u>.

M: I believe that Professor McCloud teaches it. You're really going to <u>enjoy</u> it. I <u>like</u> your schedule a lot.

해석

W Student: 드디어 다음 학기에 들을 수업을 정했어요. 한번 보시겠어요?

M Professor: 그럼요, Caroline. 무엇을 들을 건가요?

W: 교수님의 고고학 수업에 등록할 거예요. 또한 Hern 교수님의 로마 고고학 수업도 들을 거예요.

M: 그분 수업은 정말로 마음에 들 거예요. 그 외에 또 무엇을 들을 건가요?

W: 비잔틴 역사에 관한 수업과 수학 202 수업에도 등록할 거예요. 필수 수학 과목을 끝내야 하거든요.

M: 좋아 보이는군요. 수업을 더 들을 건가요?

W: 하나 더요. 르네상스 시대의 미술에 관한 미술사 수업이에요. 무척 재미있을 것 같아요.

M: McCloud 교수님께서 담당하실 것 같군요. 정말로 좋아하게 될 거예요. 학생 시간표가 마음에 들어요.

Exercise 3   1 Ⓑ   2 Ⓓ   p.68

Script 🎧 03-11

M Professor: It's <u>possible</u> to break down trees into two types: coniferous trees and deciduous trees. The main <u>difference</u> between them concerns their leaves. You see, uh, coniferous trees have leaves during <u>every</u> <u>season</u>. They <u>gradually</u> lose some, but then new ones grow to <u>replace</u> them. Deciduous trees are <u>different</u>. They are broad-leafed trees that <u>lose</u> their leaves during <u>part</u> of the year. For the most part, that season is <u>winter</u>. Then, deciduous trees go <u>dormant</u>. Their leaves don't grow again until <u>spring</u> comes. As a <u>general</u> rule, the leaves of coniferous trees are <u>pointed</u> like needles or have a waxlike coating. Deciduous trees, on the other hand, have <u>broad</u> leaves that change colors in <u>fall</u>. Coniferous trees have <u>seeds</u> produced in cones whereas deciduous trees produce <u>flowers</u>. These flowers then produce <u>various</u> fruits that <u>contain</u> seeds.

해석

M Professor: 나무는 두 가지 유형으로, 즉 침엽수와 낙엽수로 구분할 수 있습니다. 이들의 주요 차이점은 잎과 관련이 있어요. 아시다시피, 어, 침엽수에는 모든 계절에 잎이 달려 있습니다. 잎들은 서서히 떨어지기도 하지만, 새로운 잎들이 자라서 이들을 대체하게 되죠. 낙엽수는 다릅니다. 이들의 잎은 널찍하고 연중 특정 시기에 떨어집니다. 대체로 그러한 시기는 겨울이에요. 이때 낙엽수는 휴면기에 들어갑니다. 이들의 잎은 봄이 오기 전까지 다시 자라지 않아요. 일반적으로 침엽수의 잎은 바늘처럼 끝이 뾰족한 형태일 수도 있고, 왁스와 같은 물질로 코팅이 되어 있기도 합니다. 반면에 낙엽수는 널찍한 잎을 가지고 있으며, 가을이 되면 이들의 색이 변합니다. 침엽수의 씨앗은 방울에서 만들어지는 반면에 낙엽수에서는 꽃이 핍니다. 이 꽃들이 다양한 열매를 만들어 내는데, 그 안에 씨앗이 포함되어 있죠.

Exercise 4   1 Ⓐ   2 Ⓓ   p.69

Script 🎧 03-12

M Professor: In my opinion, Pocahontas was a <u>spy</u> for the colonists. Yes, she <u>served</u> as a mediator between the British colonists and the Native Americans, but she was <u>more</u> of a spy. As you know, she even provided <u>vital</u> food supplies to the colonists. However, she didn't think of <u>herself</u> as a spy. In addition, the colonists didn't <u>trust</u> her much despite her help. In a way, we could say she was a <u>sad</u> spy. <u>Unfortunately</u>, a war broke out <u>between</u> the Powhatans and the colonists. The colonists <u>captured</u> her and brought her to Jamestown. While she was in Jamestown as a <u>hostage</u>, she freely converted to Christianity and <u>married</u> John Rolfe. As we all know, this <u>marriage</u> brought the war to its <u>end</u>. What do you think? Was she a mediator or a spy? I believe she was a spy, a spy who <u>played</u> a role as a mediator.

해석

M Professor: 제 생각에 포카혼타스는 식민지 개척자들의 스파이였어요. 네, 그녀는 영국 식민지 주민들과 미 원주민 사이에서 중재자 역할을 맡았지만, 보다 스파이에 가까웠습니다. 여러분도 아시다시피 그녀는 식민지 주민들에게 필요한 식량을 제공하기도 했어요. 하지만 그녀는 자신을 스파이라고 생각하지 않았습니다. 또한 그녀의 도움에도 불구하고 식민지 주민들은 그녀를 그다지 신뢰하지 않았죠. 어떤 측면에서는 그녀가 슬픈 스파이였다고 말할 수도 있겠군요. 안타깝게도 포와탄족과 식민지 주민 사이에 전쟁이 일어났어요. 식민지 주민들은 그녀를 포로로 잡아 제임스타운으로 데리고 갔습니다. 인질로서 제임스타운에 머무르는 동안 그녀는 스스로 기독교로 개종했고 존 롤프와 결혼을 했어요. 우리 모두가 알고 있는 것처럼 이 결혼으로 인해 전쟁은 끝이 났습니다. 어떻게 생각하나요? 그녀가 중재자였을까요, 아니면 스파이였을까요? 저는 그녀가 스파이였다고, 중재자 역할을 맡았던 스파이였다고 생각합니다.

Exercises with Mid-Length Conversations & Lectures

Exercise 1   1 Ⓑ   2 Ⓐ   p.70

W Student: Hello. Is this the office I should go to for student clubs?

M Student Activities Office Employee: That's right. However, we already had our club day last week. All the school clubs were at the student center in order to introduce themselves to interested students.

W: Actually, I attended it, but there weren't any clubs I was interested in joining.

M: Ah, so you would like to start your own club?

W: Yes, I would. But I don't know what to do.

M: First, what kind of club would you like to start?

W: I'd like to have a hiking club. There are so many good trails in the mountains near here. I think it might be popular.

M: Hmm . . . You could be right. Okay, you can definitely start that club.

W: Great. What do I need to do?

M: Every club is required to have ten members. You need to have ten students sign this sheet here . . . Have them put down their names and student ID numbers. Do that by next week, and you can have your club.

W: Thanks so much for your help. See you next week.

M: Bye.

해석

W Student: 안녕하세요. 여기가 학생 동아리를 담당하는 사무실인가요?

M Student Activities Office Employee: 맞아요. 하지만 동아리 홍보 기간은 지난 주였어요. 교내의 모든 동아리들이 관심 있는 학생들에게 자신을 소개하기 위해 학생 회관에 모여 있었죠.

W: 실은 저도 참석을 했는데요, 하지만 가입을 하고 싶은 동아리가 없더군요.

M: 아, 그러면 학생이 동아리를 만들고 싶은 건가요?

W: 네, 그래요. 하지만 어떻게 해야할지 모르겠어요.

M: 먼저 만들고 싶은 동아리가 어떤 종류인가요?

W: 하이킹 동아리가 있으면 좋겠어요. 이곳 주변에 있는 산에는 멋진 산길들이 정말 많거든요. 인기가 있을 것 같아요.

M: 흠… 학생 말이 맞을 수도 있겠군요. 좋아요, 그런 동아리는 분명 만들 수 있을 거예요.

W: 잘 되었군요. 제가 어떻게 하면 될까요?

M: 모든 동아리에는 10명의 회원이 있어야 해요. 여기 이 종이에 10명 학생의 서명을 받아야 하는데… 자신의 이름과 학생증 번호를 적도록 하세요. 다음 주까지 그렇게 하면 동아리를 만들 수 있어요.

W: 도와 주셔서 정말 고맙습니다. 다음 주에 뵐 게요.

M: 잘 가요.

📝 **Summary Note** Ⓑ

The student visits the office to ask about clubs. She says that she wants to start her own club. She is interested in a hiking club because there are many good trails in the mountains nearby. The man tells her that she needs to have ten members. He gives her a form to have students sign up by next week.

Exercise 2 1 Ⓓ 2 Ⓐ   p.72

Script 🎧 03-14

W Student: Finally, the semester is over.

M Professor: Are you happy that you don't have to come to my class anymore?

W: Yes . . . I'm just kidding.

M: I'm sure that you are.

W: I actually want to say thank you. As you know, I was completely lost when this class started. I thought I wouldn't be able to pass this class, and look what I got.

M: Congratulations.

W: Thank you. Without your help, I probably would have failed this class. You made economics so easy and fun for me.

M: Well, you are the one who tried hard and put in the time and effort. If you weren't showing any effort, I probably wouldn't have helped you.

W: You encouraged me to put in the effort and try my best.

M: It's my job to help students learn and succeed in the future.

W: You are an amazing teacher. I wish you could teach all my classes.

M: I'm sure you are going to meet tremendously talented and helpful teachers throughout your school life. Come by whenever you need help.

W: I will. Thank you so much.

M: Enjoy your winter break.

해석

W Student: 드디어 이번 학기가 끝났네요.

M Professor: 더 이상 제 수업에 올 필요가 없어서 기분이 좋은가요?

W: 네… 농담입니다.

M: 그럴 줄 알았어요.

W: 사실 교수님께 감사하다는 말씀을 드리고 싶어요. 아시겠지만 이번 수업이 시작했을 때 저는 어떻게 해야 할지 전혀 몰랐거든요. 이번 수업을 통과하지 못할 것으로 생각했는데, 결과를 보세요.

M: 축하해요.

W: 감사합니다. 교수님 도움이 없었더라면 아마도 이번 수업에서 낙제했을 거예요. 교수님 덕분에 경제학이 너무 쉽고 재미있었어요.

M: 음, 학생은 열심히 공부하고 시간과 노력을 아끼지 않았던 사람 중 한 명이에요. 학생이 노력하는 모습을 보여 주지 않았다면 아마 저도 도와 주지 않았을 거

예요.

W: 교수님께서 제가 노력하고 최선을 다 할 수 있도록 격려해 주셨죠.

M: 학생들이 배우고 미래에 성공할 수 있도록 돕는 것이 제 일이에요.

W: 교수님께서는 정말 훌륭하신 분이세요. 제가 듣는 수업이 모두 교수님 수업이면 좋겠어요.

M: 학생은 분명 학교 다니는 동안 매우 뛰어나고 도움을 주실 수 있는 선생님을 만나게 될 거예요. 도움이 필요하면 언제든 오세요.

W: 그렇게 할게요. 정말 감사합니다.

M: 겨울 방학 잘 보내요.

📝 Summary Note Ⓑ

The fall semester is over, and the student is grateful to her economics professor for his help and encouragement throughout the semester. The student believes that without his help, she could not have completed the class. On the other hand, the professor insists that he doesn't help students who don't make an effort.

Exercise 3   1 Ⓐ   2 Ⓐ, Ⓓ   p.74

Script 🎧 03-15

W Professor: Today's topic is on plants and water. As you all know, water is very important for all the living things on the Earth. We can't live without water. Neither can plants. Water plays a very important part in the lives of plants. Too much water may cause root damage, and too little may dry them out. Depending on the species, some plants have the ability to store water for short periods of time while others can store water for longer periods of time. In addition, air movement and humidity play important roles in the respiration process of plants. Now, I want to talk about a process called photosynthesis.

M1 Student: I remember learning about it in junior high. Isn't it a process which involves water and sunlight?

W: Yes, exactly. Let's see how much you remember what you were taught in junior high. Who can tell me about photosynthesis in detail?

M2 Student: Water moves upward from the roots to the leaves. In doing that, it carries dissolved nutrients and minerals.

W: Anyone else?

M1: These nutrients, together with carbon dioxide, water, and sunlight, allow photosynthesis to take place. It produces both oxygen and a kind of sugar called glucose.

W: Very good!

해석

W Professor: 오늘의 주제는 식물과 물입니다. 여러분도 다 알고 있는 것처럼

물은 지구상의 모든 생명체에게 대단히 중요해요. 우리도 물 없이는 살 수가 없죠. 식물도 마찬가지입니다. 물은 식물의 삶에 있어서 매우 중요한 역할을 해요. 너무 물이 많으면 뿌리가 썩을 수 있고, 너무 적으면 뿌리가 마를 수도 있습니다. 종에 따라서 일부 식물은 짧은 기간 동안 물을 저장할 수 있는 반면 어떤 종은 보다 오랜 기간 동안 물을 저장할 수 있어요. 또한 식물의 호흡 과정에서는 공기의 이동과 습도가 중요한 역할을 합니다. 이제 광합성으로 불리는 과정에 대해 이야기해 볼게요.

M1 Student: 중학교 때 배웠던 기억이 나네요. 물과 햇빛이 관련된 과정 아닌가요?

W: 네, 맞아요. 중학교 때 배운 걸 얼마나 기억하고 있는지 확인해 보죠. 광합성에 대해 자세히 말해 볼 사람이 있나요?

M2 Student: 물이 뿌리에서 잎으로 올라갑니다. 그러한 과정으로 용해된 영양소와 무기질이 운반되고요.

W: 또 다른 사람이 있나요?

M1: 그 영양소들이 이산화탄소, 물, 그리고 햇빛과 함께 광합성을 일으킵니다. 이로써 산소와 포도당이라는 당이 만들어지고요.

W: 훌륭하군요!

📝 Summary Note Ⓑ

Plants cannot survive without water. One of the major respiration processes that requires water is called photosynthesis. During photosynthesis, water moves from the roots to leaves while carrying dissolved nutrient and minerals. Then, with these nutrients, carbon dioxide, water, and sunlight complete photosynthesis. They form oxygen and glucose.

Exercise 4   1 Ⓒ   2 Ⓒ   p.76

Script 🎧 03-16

M1 Professor: We are going to start chapter three today. It's on cave paintings. Who can tell me about cave paintings?

M2 Student: The drawings are mostly of animals.

M1: Correct. The animals are mostly bison, horses, and deer. The most common themes in cave paintings are large wild animals such as bison, horses, aurochs, and deer. Anthropologist Abbé Breuil interpreted the paintings as being hunting magic. That is to say, they were meant to increase the number of animals. Drawings of humans are rare and are usually schematic rather than the more naturalistic animal subjects. Who can guess when cave painting started?

W1 Student: Prehistoric times . . .

M1: Yes . . . the first paintings were made during the upper Paleolithic Period about 40,000 years ago. Let me ask you another question. Who drew the paintings?

W1: Artists . . .

M1: Good answer, but who were the artists? What were

their positions?

W2 Student: Tribal leaders?

M1: Close but incorrect. The artists were believed to be respected elders or shamans. The main colors of the paintings were yellow, brown, charcoal, and red.

해석

M1 Professor: 오늘은 3장을 들어갈 거예요. 동굴 벽화에 관한 내용이죠. 동굴 벽화에 대해 말해 볼 사람이 있나요?

M2 Student: 그 그림들은 주로 동물을 그린 그림들입니다.

M1: 맞아요. 주로 들소, 말, 그리고 사슴이죠. 동굴 벽화에 나오는 가장 흔한 소재는 들소, 말, 오록스, 그리고 사슴과 같이 몸집이 큰 야생 동물입니다. 인류학자 아베 브뢰이는 벽화를 사냥 주술로 해석했어요. 다시 말해서 동물의 수를 증가시키기 위해 그림이 그려진 것이었죠. 인간을 그린 그림은 드물고, 보다 자연주의적으로 그려진 동물들보다 도식적입니다. 동굴 벽화가 언제 그려지기 시작했는지 추측해 볼 사람이 있나요?

W1 Student: 선사 시대요…

M1: 네… 최초의 벽화는 약 40,000년 전 후기 구석기 시대에 그려졌어요. 또 다른 질문을 해 보죠. 누가 그림을 그렸을까요?

W1: 화가들이요…

M1: 좋은 답변이긴 한데, 화가들은 누구였을까요? 어떤 지위의 사람들이었을까요?

W2: 부족장들 아니었을까요?

M1: 비슷했지만 정답은 아닙니다. 화가들은 존경 받는 연장자나 주술사들이었어요. 벽화에 쓰인 색깔은 주로 노란색, 갈색, 암회색, 그리고 빨간색이었습니다.

📝 **Summary Note** Ⓑ

Cave paintings started approximately 40,000 years ago during the upper Paleolithic Period. The pictures are mainly of animals such as bison, horses, aurochs, and deer. The colors were mostly limited to yellow, brown, charcoal, and red. In contrast to naturalistic animal paintings, drawings of humans are schematic and rare. The artists were believed to be respected elders and shamans.

Integrated Listening & Speaking   p.78

A

Script 🎧 03-17

W Professor: As everyone knows, water is very important for living things on the Earth. We can't live without water. Neither can plants. Water plays a very important part in the lives of plants. For instance, too much water may cause root damage while too little may dry them out. Some species of plants have the ability to store water for short periods of time while others are able to store water for longer periods of time. In addition, air movement and humidity play important roles in the

respiration process of plants. Now, I would like to discuss photosynthesis with you. It's a process which involves water and sunlight. Water moves up the plant from the roots to the leaves. In doing that, the water carries dissolved nutrient and minerals. Then, these nutrients, carbon dioxide, water, and sunlight allow photosynthesis to take place. It produces both oxygen and a kind of sugar called glucose.

1 a. Too much water can damage plants.
   b. Air movement and humidity play important roles in the plant respiration process.

2 a. Water moves from the roots to the leaves.
   b. Water carries dissolved nutrients and minerals as it goes up.

3 a. Nutrients, carbon dioxide, water, and sunlight let photosynthesis happen.
   b. The photosynthesis process produces oxygen and a sugar called glucose.

B

Script 🎧 03-18

M Professor: Most cave paintings show animals. The animals are mainly bison, horses, and deer. The most common themes in cave paintings are large wild animals such as bison, horses, aurochs, and deer. Anthropologist Abbé Breuil interpreted the paintings as being hunting magic. In other words, they were meant to increase the number of animals. Drawings of humans are rare. They are also usually schematic rather than the more naturalistic animal subjects. The first paintings are believed to have been made during the upper Paleolithic Period. That was sometime around 40,000 years ago. The artists are thought to have been respected elders or shamans. The main colors of the paintings were yellow, brown, charcoal, and red.

1 a. She interpreted the paintings as being hunting magic.
   b. She interpreted the paintings as being drawn to increase the number of animals.

2 a. The paintings are mostly of large, wild animals.
   b. The paintings are mostly of bison, horses, aurochs, and deer.

3 a. The animal paintings are more naturalistic than the drawings of humans.
   b. The drawings of humans are rare and schematic compared to the animal paintings.

p.80

| 1 ⓑ | 2 ⓑ | 3 ⓓ | 4 ⓑ | 5 ⓑ |
| 6 ⓐ | | | | |

[1-3]

Script 🎧 03-19

M Student: Professor Verlander, I received your email. You need to talk to me?

W Professor: Hello, Allen. Please come in and have a seat.

M: Um . . . I'm not in trouble, am I? Oh, by the way, I didn't get my paper today. You handed one out to everyone but me.

W: That's why I want to talk to you, Allen.

M: Oh . . . That doesn't sound good.

W: On the contrary, it actually is good. You see, Allen, I was extremely impressed with your paper, so I wanted to give it to you in person. Here you are . . .

M: An A+? Wow. I've never gotten a grade like that before.

W: You deserved it. This was an extremely well-written paper. I loved the topic.

M: Thank you for saying that.

W: I'm curious . . . Where did you get the idea for your paper? Did you come up with it by yourself?

M: Uh . . . Yes, I did. It's something I have thought about a lot whenever I read Edmund Spenser's poetry. So I thought I would just write about it.

W: Well, it was rather insightful. Tell me, Allen . . . Are you an English literature major?

M: I haven't declared a major yet, but I'm strongly leaning toward getting a double major in English literature and chemistry.

W: That's a unique combination. Well, I have a proposal for you. Spenser is one of my favorite poets. How would you like to do a directed research course on Spenser next semester? You'd be the only student in the course, and you'd be studying directly with me.

M: Oh, wow. That sounds interesting. Can you tell me a bit more, please? I've never heard of this kind of course.

W: Sure. I can do that.

해석

M Student: Verlander 교수님, 교수님의 이메일을 받았어요. 제게 하실 말씀이 있으신가요?

W Professor: 안녕하세요, Allen. 들어와서 앉으세요.

M: 음… 저에게 문제가 있는 건 아니죠, 그렇죠? 오, 그건 그렇고, 저는 오늘 보고서를 받지 못했어요. 모두에게 나누어 주셨지만 저는 못 받았어요.

W: 바로 그 점 때문에 학생과 이야기를 하고 싶어요, Allen.

M: 오… 좋게 들리지는 않는군요.

W: 그와 반대로 사실은 좋은 일이에요. 알겠지만, Allen, 저는 학생의 보고서에 정말로 깊은 인상을 받았고, 그래서 직접 전해 주고 싶었어요. 여기 있어요…

M: A+인가요? 와. 이런 점수는 한 번도 받아본 적이 없어요.

W: 그럴 자격이 있어요. 정말로 잘 쓰여진 보고서였으니까요. 주제가 정말로 마음에 들었어요.

M: 그렇게 말씀해 주시다니 감사합니다.

W: 궁금해서 그런데… 보고서에 대한 아이디어는 어디에서 얻었나요? 혼자서 생각해 냈나요?

M: 어… 네, 그랬어요. 제가 에드먼드 스펜서의 시를 읽을 때마다 많이 생각했던 것이에요. 그래서 그에 대해 쓰면 되겠다고 생각을 했죠.

W: 음, 통찰력이 상당했군요. 말해 보세요, Allen… 영문학 전공인가요?

M: 아직 전공을 정하지는 못했지만, 영문학과 화학을 복수 전공하는 쪽으로 마음이 크게 기울어져 있어요.

W: 특이한 조합이군요. 음, 학생에게 제안할 것이 있어요. 스펜서는 제가 가장 좋아하는 시인 중 한 명이에요. 다음 학기에 스펜서에 관한 논문 연구 과정에 참여하는 것이 어떨까요? 그 과정에서는 학생이 유일한 학생이 될 텐데, 저와 함께 연구를 하게 될 거예요.

M: 오, 와. 흥미롭게 들리는군요. 좀 더 말씀해 주실 수 있으신가요? 그러한 과정에 대해서는 들어본 적이 없거든요.

W: 물론이에요. 그럴 수 있죠.

[4-6]

Script 🎧 03-20

W1 Professor: Now we will talk about Virginia Woolf. I'm sure you are all familiar with her and have read at least one of her books.

M Student: I read *The Lighthouse*. It was a fantastic book.

W1: Yes, of course. With *The Lighthouse* and *The Waves*, she established herself as one of the leading writers of modernism. She developed innovative literary techniques to reveal women's experiences and to find an alternative to male-dominated views of reality. Does anyone know about her philosophy?

W2 Student: She was a feminist.

W1: Yes, more in detail?

W2: She wrote *A Room of One's Own*, which deals with obstacles and prejudices that have hindered women writers.

W1: Exactly. To add to Jenny's comment, Woolf stated that there have been few great women in history because material circumstances limited women's lives and achievements. Because women were not educated and were not allowed to control wealth, they necessarily led lives that were less publicly significant than those of men. Until women can overcome these material limitations, women will continue to achieve less than men.

M: Women were unprivileged.

W2: But we are equal now.

W1: Are we? Actually, we still need to work on that more, and we have overcome so much. Anyway, what other books do you know?

M: *Three Guineas* examined the necessity for women to make a claim for their own history and literature.

W1: Yes, in this work, Woolf expresses an important idea which is the existence of a women's culture separate from men's. It is irrelevant not only from the patriarchal power but also from wars and from the culture of violence.

해석

W1 Professor: 이제 버지니아 울프에 대해 이야기해 보죠. 분명 여러분 모두는 그녀를 알고 있으며 최소한 그녀의 책중 한 권은 읽어 보았을 것으로 생각해요.

M2 Student: 저는 *등대로*를 읽었습니다. 정말 훌륭한 책이었어요.

W1: 네, 그럼요. *등대로*와 *파도*로 그녀는 선구적인 모더니즘 작가 중 한 명이 될 수 있습니다. 그녀는 혁신적인 문학적 기법을 개발해서 여성의 경험을 드러내고 남성 우위의 가치관에 대한 대안을 찾으려고 했어요. 그녀의 철학에 대해 아는 사람이 있나요?

W2 Student: 페미니스트였어요.

W1: 네, 더 자세히 이야기하면요?

W2: *자기만의 방*이라는 작품을 썼는데, 이는 여성 작가에게 방해가 되는 장애물과 편견을 다루고 있어요.

W1: 정확해요. Jenny의 말에 덧붙이자면, 울프는 물리적인 환경이 여성의 삶과 업적을 제한했기 때문에 역사상 위대한 여성이 극소수에 불과했다고 주장했어요. 여성들은 교육을 받지 못했고 재산을 관리할 수도 없었기 때문에 어쩔 수 없이 남성 보다 공공연하게 덜 중요한 삶을 살았던 것이죠. 여성들이 이러한 물리적인 제한을 극복하기 전까지는 여성들의 성과가 남성들보다 계속해서 적을 거예요.

M: 여성은 차별을 받았어요.

W2: 하지만 지금은 평등하잖아요.

W1: 그런가요? 사실 그에 대해 아직도 노력해야 하지만, 매우 많은 것을 극복해 냈죠. 그건 그렇고 다른 책을 아는 사람이 있나요?

M: *3기니*에서는 여성들이 자신의 역사와 문학에 대한 권리를 주장해야 할 필요성이 검토되었어요.

W1: 그래요, 그 책에서 울프는 남성의 문화와 별개인 여성의 문화가 존재한다는 중요한 아이디어를 제시하고 있죠. 이는 가부장적인 권력뿐만 아니라 폭력적인 문화 및 전쟁과도 무관한 것입니다.

Vocabulary Check-Up ——— p.83

A
1 ⓘ   2 ⓗ   3 ⓖ   4 ⓐ   5 ⓓ
6 ⓜ   7 ⓝ   8 ⓙ   9 ⓚ   10 ⓑ
11 ⓞ   12 ⓒ   13 ⓕ   14 ⓔ   15 ⓛ

B
1 ⓐ   2 ⓓ   3 ⓔ   4 ⓒ   5 ⓑ

PART II Pragmatic Understanding

UNIT 04 Understanding the Function of What Is Said

Skill & Tip p.88

Skill Practice

A

1 I never managed / to discuss this / with my father / while he lived.

2 I don't remember / when I got home / last night.

3 Which color do you like more, / black / or yellow?

4 When you're young, / there's almost no place / you can go / at night.

5 There's nothing / I can do / for them / except / what I can do / in the future.

6 Next month, / we are both / supposed to go / to Chicago / to visit my uncle.

B

W Resident Assistant: Hi, Jamie! / How was your presentation / in psychology class?

M Student: Oh, it was not so bad. I got the right answers / on every single question, / even from Professor Graham.

W: That sounds great. Actually, / Professor Graham is very strict / about students' presentations. I knew / you were so worried about it. Good job!

C

W Professor: Using common household materials, / you can make / a pinhole camera / like this. It can produce / real pictures, and it will provide / an inexpensive / and interesting way / to take pictures. To make a pinhole camera, / you only need a can / or box. If you take a picture / with the camera you build, / you'll be very proud of it.

Basic Drill ································ p.90

Drill 1 ⓓ

Script 🎧 04-05

M Student: Hello. I wonder if you can give me a hand.

W Math Department Office Employee: I'll do my best.

What do you need?

M: I was up at Professor Oaktown's office a moment ago. But the light was off, and the door was locked.

W: He just finished his office hours about half an hour ago.

M: Oh, I see. Will he be at school tomorrow?

W: Yes, he will. He has an early class, so why don't you come here around nine in the morning?

해석

M Student: 안녕하세요. 제게 도움을 주실 수 있는지 궁금해서요.

W Math Department Office Employee: 최선을 다하죠. 무엇이 필요한가요?

M: 조금 전에 Oaktown 교수님의 사무실에 갔다 왔어요. 하지만 불이 꺼지고 문이 잠겨 있더군요.

W: 그분의 사무실 근무 시간은 약 30분 전에 끝났어요.

M: 오, 그랬군요. 내일 학교에 오시나요?

W: 네, 오실 거예요. 수업이 이른 시간에 있어서 내일 오전 9시쯤 여기로 오는 것이 어떨까요?

Drill 2 Ⓓ

Script 04-06

M Student: Professor Dean, did you want to see me?

W Professor: Yes, Joseph. I just want to talk to you about your class participation.

M: I know. It has been pretty rough for me because of football practice.

W: I see. I hope you get plenty of rest every day. **It is great that you are playing sports, but don't let it get in the way of your studying.**

M: Yes, ma'am. I know that education is more important. I will pace myself.

해석

M Student: 학장님, 저를 보자고 하셨나요?

W Professor: 그래요, Joseph. 학생의 수업 참여에 대해 이야기하고 싶어요.

M: 저도 알아요. 축구 연습 때문에 제가 많이 힘들었거든요.

W: 그래요. 매일 충분히 쉬기를 바라요. 스포츠 경기에 참여하는 것은 멋진 일이지만, 운동이 학업에 방해가 되도록 놔두어서는 안돼요.

M: 네, 학장님. 학업이 더 중요하다는 건 저도 알고 있어요. 페이스를 조절할게요.

Drill 3 Ⓒ

Script 04-07

M Professor: Are we doing enough to protect the environment from pollution? The environment is suffering

---

from various kinds of pollution. These negatively affect the nature and well-being of all living organisms. Major pollutants include water, air, and noise pollution and soil containment. Unfortunately, all this pollution is manmade, and there is no sign of slowing down. **We, as humans, must work together to reverse the damage we have done to the environment.**

해석

M Professor: 환경 오염을 막기 위해 우리가 충분히 노력하고 있나요? 환경은 다양한 종류의 오염을 겪고 있습니다. 이는 자연 및 모든 생명체의 건강에 부정적인 영향을 미치죠. 주요한 오염으로는 수질 오염, 대기 오염, 그리고 소음 공해 및 토양 오염을 들 수 있습니다. 안타깝게도 이러한 모든 오염은 인간이 만든 것이며, 오염의 속도가 느려지고 있다는 징후는 존재하지 않습니다. 인간인 우리들이 환경에 가해진 피해를 복구하기 위해 함께 노력해야 합니다.

Drill 4 Ⓑ

Script 04-08

W Professor: In the past, bullying was considered a part of growing up. However, there is an increasing awareness of the harmful effects of bullying. It causes not only long-term social behavior problems but also leads to other types of violence. **Therefore, schools need to run active programs to prevent or stop bullying.**

해석

W Professor: 과거에는 따돌림이 성장 과정의 한 부분으로 생각되었어요. 하지만 따돌림의 해로운 결과에 대해 경각심이 높아지고 있습니다. 이는 장기적으로 사회적 행동의 문제를 일으킬 뿐만 아니라 또 다른 형태의 폭력으로 이어지죠. 따라서 학교들은 따돌림을 예방하거나 중지시키기 위한 적극적인 프로그램을 운영해야 합니다.

Exercises with Short Conversations & Lectures

Exercise 1 1 Ⓓ 2 Ⓓ p.92

Script 04-09

W Registrar's Office Employee: Hi. Can I help you?

M Student: I would like to find out how to register for summer school.

W: Are you currently enrolled in this school?

M: Yes, I am.

W: Okay, if not, I would have to ask you to register. Since you are already enrolled, look through this schedule of classes and decide which ones you would like to take. Then, either go to the school website or call the number on the schedule to enroll.

M: Great. How do I pay my tuition?

W: It's the same as in normal semesters. You can pay directly online while enrolling, mail your payment, or pay in person right in this office.

M: Thank you very much.

해석

W Registrar's Office Employee: 안녕하세요. 도와 드릴까요?

M Student: 안녕하세요, 여름 학기 수업에 어떻게 등록하는지 알고 싶어요.

W: 현재 이 학교의 학생인가요?

M: 네, 그래요.

W: 좋아요, 만약 아닌 경우에는 제가 등록부터 요청해야 하거든요. 학생은 이미 등록이 되어 있기 때문에 이 수업 시간표를 살펴보고 듣고 싶은 수업을 정하세요. 그런 다음에는 학교 홈페이지로 들어가거나 시간표에 있는 번호로 전화를 해서 등록을 하고요.

M: 그렇군요. 수업료는 어떻게 내죠?

W: 일반 학기의 경우와 같아요. 등록하면서 온라인으로 바로 납부해도 되고, 우편으로 납부해도 되고, 아니면 이곳 사무실에서 직접 납부해도 되죠.

M: 정말 감사합니다.

Exercise 2 1 ⓓ 2 ⓒ p.93

Script 🎧 04-10

M Professor: Melissa, do you know why I asked to see you today?

W Student: No, sir. I'm afraid that I don't.

M: It's about the paper you submitted. I regret to say that it isn't acceptable.

W: Are you sure? What's wrong with it?

M: You didn't follow the proper format. For instance, you were told to include an introduction and a conclusion. But the paper didn't have either.

W: Oh, I see.

M: In addition, you didn't properly defend the arguments you made in the essay. You're going to need to rewrite the paper.

W: Okay. I understand. When do you need me to return it by?

M: I'd like to have it by this Friday. So you have three extra days.

W: Okay, Professor Mellon. Thanks for giving me a second chance. I appreciate that.

해석

M Professor: Melissa, 오늘 제가 왜 보자고 했는지 알고 있나요?

W Student: 아니요, 교수님. 모르겠어요.

M: 학생이 제출한 보고서와 관련이 있어요. 유감이지만 보고서를 받아들일 수가 없어요.

W: 정말인가요? 무슨 문제가 있는 거죠?

M: 올바른 형식을 따르지 않았어요. 예를 들어 서론과 결론이 포함되어야 한다는 말을 들었잖아요. 하지만 이 보고서에는 둘 다 들어 있지 않더군요.

W: 오, 그래요.

M: 게다가 학생은 보고서에서 본인이 제기한 주장을 적절하게 뒷받침하지도 않았어요. 보고서를 다시 써야 할 거예요.

W: 그렇군요. 알겠습니다. 언제까지 제출하면 될까요?

M: 이번 주 금요일까지 받았으면 해요. 그러니 3일이 남은 셈이죠.

W: 알겠어요, Mellon 교수님. 두 번째 기회를 주셔서 고맙습니다. 정말 감사해요.

Exercise 3 1 ⓓ 2 ⓓ p.94

Script 🎧 04-11

W Professor: Hello, class. Welcome to Communications 101. Today, I will cover narrative speech. Each of you needs to give one. The topic is "Who Am I?" **You will provide this class with a general idea of who you are.** First, begin with your name, what it means, why your parents chose this name, and how you feel about it. Next, tell us your history. Where you were born, when you were born, where you grew up, and, if you like, how your parents met. Then, give us more personal information about yourself. Items should include your hobbies, talents, things you like, dislikes, your passion, goals, dreams, and so forth. Please turn in your outline by next week. The speeches will begin the week after you turn in your outline.

해석

W Professor: 안녕하세요, 여러분. 커뮤니케이션 101 수업에 오신 것을 환영합니다. 오늘은 서사적 화법을 다룰 거예요. 주제는 "나는 누구인가"입니다. 여러분은 이번 수업에서 자신이 누구인지에 관한 일반적인 아이디어를 말하게 될 거예요. 우선, 자신의 이름이 무엇인지, 그 이름이 어떤 의미인지, 왜 부모님께서 그런 이름을 선택했는지, 그리고 자기 이름에 대해 어떻게 생각하는지로 시작하세요. 그런 다음 여러분 자신에 관한 보다 개인적인 정보를 알려 주세요. 여기에는 취미, 재능, 좋아하는 것, 싫어하는 것, 열정, 목표, 꿈, 그리고 기타 등등의 항목이 포함되어야 합니다. 다음 주까지 개요를 제출해 주세요. 개요를 제출한 그 주부터 발표를 시작할 거예요.

Exercise 4 1 ⓐ 2 ⓑ p.95

Script 🎧 04-12

M Professor: Let's say that you are a designer that needs to create a rectangular TV or a swimming pool. Would you randomly select any ratio, or would you follow a certain rule? **If you know geometry, you will use the golden ratio.** This ratio has a length-to-width ratio of approximately 1.618. Since the early Greeks, it has been known as the most visually appealing ratio to the eye. Therefore, we can find many things around us that utilize this ratio. The Greek Parthenon and wide-screen TVs are two examples. The golden ratio appears in art, architecture, and even in natural structures. Why don't you find an example around you?

해석

M Professor: 여러분이 직사각형 TV나 수영장을 설계해야 하는 디자이너라고 합시다. 되는대로 아무 비율을 선택할까요, 아니면 어떤 규칙을 따르게 될까요? 여러분이 기하학을 안다면 황금 비율을 사용할 것입니다. 이 비율은 가로 대 세로의 비가 약 1.618입니다. 고대 그리스 시대부터 눈을 사로잡는 가장 매력적인 비율로 알려져 있죠. 그래서 우리 주변에서 이러한 비율을 활용한 것들을 많이 볼 수가 있습니다. 그리스의 파르테논 신전과 와이드 스크린 TV가 두 가지 예죠. 황금 비율은 미술, 건축, 그리고 심지어는 자연적인 구조에서도 찾을 수 있습니다. 여러분 주변에서 그 예를 찾아볼까요?

Exercises with Mid-Length Conversations & Lectures

Exercise 1 1 ⒟ 2 ⒝   p.96

Script 🎧 04-13

W Student: Professor Monroe, how are you? Do you have time to speak about my schedule for next semester now?

M Professor: I don't have anything scheduled for the rest of the day.

W: That's great news. Thanks.

M: So what's going on with your schedule?

W: I need one more class to take. I have already chosen four. They are an American history course, an algebra course, introduction to psychology, and organic chemistry.

M: Do you want to take an elective or a class in your major?

W: I'd prefer to take an elective.

M: Okay. What are your options?

W: I'm considering a class on Egyptian archaeology as well as an international relations class.

M: Professor Anderson is a fascinating lecturer. I highly recommend his course.

W: Great. Then I guess I'll be learning about ancient Egypt next semester. Thanks.

해석

W Student: Monroe 교수님, 안녕하세요? 다음 학기 시간표에 관해서 지금 이야기를 나눌 수 있으신가요?

M Professor: 남은 하루 동안에는 별다른 스케줄이 없어요.

W: 잘 되었군요. 고맙습니다.

M: 그러면 시간표에 어떤 문제가 있나요?

W: 한 과목을 더 들어야 해요. 이미 4개는 정했고요. 미국사, 대수학, 심리학 개론, 그리고 유기 화학이죠.

M: 선택 과목을 듣고 싶나요, 아니면 전공 과목을 듣고 싶나요?

W: 선택 과목을 듣고 싶어요.

M: 좋아요. 선택할 수 있는 것들이 어떤 것이죠?

W: 이집트 고고학 수업과 국제 관계 수업을 생각 중이에요.

M: Anderson 교수님께서는 정말로 강의를 잘 하세요. 그분 수업을 강력히 추천할게요.

W: 좋습니다. 그러면 다음 학기에 고대 이집트에 관해 배우게 되겠네요. 고맙습니다.

📝 **Summary Note** Ⓑ

The student asks to speak with the professor about her schedule for next semester. She already knows four of the classes she will take. She wants to take an elective for her fifth class. She is trying to decide between Egyptian archaeology and an international relations class. The professor recommends Professor Anderson, so the student decides to take the archaeology class.

Exercise 2 1 ⒝ 2 ⒟   p.98

Script 🎧 04-14

M Study Abroad Office Employee: Welcome to the study abroad office. What can I do for you?

W Student: Hello. I'm going to be a junior next year. I'm thinking of studying abroad for one semester.

M: Do you have a particular country in mind?

W: Well, I'd love to visit Italy and study there.

M: Do you speak Italian? That's a requirement if you want to study there.

W: What about Spain or Germany then? Those countries have some interest to me.

M: Sure. There are programs for students that speak those languages. But there are also programs for English speakers.

W: I'm not really good at any foreign languages. That's one reason I'd like to study abroad. I want to improve my skills.

M: That's a good attitude. Let me give you a couple of brochures. Why don't you look through them? I'll be right here if you have any questions.

W: Thanks a lot.

해석

M Study Abroad Office Employee: 유학 상담실에 오신 것을 환영합니다. 무엇을 도와 드릴까요?

W Student: 안녕하세요. 저는 내년에 3학년이 되는데요. 한 학기 동안 유학을 할까 생각 중이에요.

M: 특별히 생각하고 있는 국가가 있나요?

W: 음, 이탈리아에 가서 공부하면 정말 좋을 것 같아요.

M: 이탈리아어를 할 줄 아나요? 그곳에서 공부하려면 그것이 필수 조건이거든요.

W: 그러면 스페인이나 독일은 어떤가요? 이들 나라에도 관심이 있어요.

M: 그렇군요. 그곳 언어를 할 줄 아는 학생들을 위한 프로그램이 있어요. 하지만 영어 사용자들을 위한 프로그램들도 있죠.

W: 제가 외국어는 그다지 잘하는 편이 아니라서요. 그것이 바로 제가 유학을 가고 싶은 한 가지 이유이죠. 제 언어 능력을 향상시키고 싶어요.

M: 태도가 좋군요. 두어 개의 브로셔를 드릴게요. 한번 살펴보는 것이 어떨까요? 질문이 있는 경우에는 제가 여기에 있을 테니 오시고요.

W: 정말 고맙습니다.

✎ Summary Note Ⓑ

The student wants to study abroad for one semester during her junior year. She is interested in Italy but cannot speak Italian. Programs in Spain and Germany are for students that speak those languages and for English speakers. She wants to study abroad to improve her language skills. The man gives her some brochures so that she can look through them.

Exercise 3   1 ⓒ   2 Ⓑ   p.100

Script 🎧 04-15

W1 Professor: We will start on a new piece by Mozart today. Let's turn to page six for *Sonata Number 11*. This piece has three movements: andante grazioso, menuetto, and rondo alla turca.

W2 Student: Is the third movement from the famous Turkish Rondo?

W1: Yes, it is. Very good. Do you know why it is called Turkish Rondo?

W2: It's supposed to imitate the sound of Turkish bands.

W1: That's correct. The bands were called Janissary bands, and they were very popular.

W2: I did not know that the Turkish music was that popular back then. Things were sure different from now.

W1: Yes . . . Time changes. Now going back to the piece . . . The Andante grazioso is composed of a theme with six variations. Menuetto has a minuet and trio, and rondo alla turca is allegretto. Andante grazioso is known for its main melody. Menuetto should be played delicately. And the rondo alla turca should be played with fluctuating intensity but with accuracy. Since it is very fast paced, you have to be careful to play every note precisely. In addition, try not to get faster as you play. You need to keep a consistent pace.

해석

W1 Professor: 오늘은 모차르트의 새로운 곡으로 시작할 거예요. 6페이지에 있는 *소나타 11번*을 보세요. 이 곡은 세 개의 악장으로 되어 있어요. 안단테 그라지오소, 미뉴에토, 그리고 론도 알라 투르카입니다.

W2 Student: 세 번째 악장은 그 유명한 터키풍의 론도를 말하는 건가요?

W1: 네, 그래요. 훌륭하군요. 왜 터키풍의 론도라고 불리는지 아시나요?

W2: 터키 군악대의 소리를 흉내냈다고 들었어요.

W1: 맞아요. 예니체리 군악대라는 이름이었는데, 인기가 매우 좋았죠.

W2: 당시 터키 음악이 그렇게 인기가 좋았다는 점은 모르고 있었네요. 지금과는 확실히 달랐군요.

W1: 네… 세월은 변하죠. 이제 다시 곡으로 돌아가서… 안단테 그리지오소는 6개의 변주가 딸린 한 가지 주제로 이루어져 있어요. 미뉴에트는 미뉴에트와 트리오로 되어 있고, 론도 알라 투르카는 알레그레토예요. 안단테 그라지오소는 주선율로 유명하죠. 미뉴에트는 섬세하게 연주해야 해요. 그리고 론도 알라 투르카는 강약 조절을 하되 정확하게 연주해야 하죠. 리듬이 굉장히 빠르기 때문에 모든 음을 정확하게 연주하기 위해서는 주의해야 해요. 또한 연주를 하는 도중에 빨라지지 않도록 해야 하고요. 일정한 리듬을 유지해야 합니다.

✎ Summary Note Ⓑ

Sonata Number 11 by Mozart is a very famous piano piece. This piece has three movements that have very distinct sounds. The first movement starts with a well-known theme, and it is followed by six variations. The second movement is a minuet that should be played delicately. The third movement is known as the Turkish Rondo because it resembles the sounds of Turkish bands. This piece requires varying intensity, accuracy, and a consistent pace.

Exercise 4   1 ⓒ   2 ⓒ   p.102

Script 🎧 04-16

W Professor: The American Civil War occurred from 1861 to 1865 and was fought between the Union and the Confederacy. Although many people think that the Civil War's main objective was to free the slaves, the war began to preserve the authority and unity of the Union. **The Civil War also marked the beginning of a new generation of modern wars.** The Civil War introduced brand-new war plans, weapons, communications, and transportation.

M Student: I once heard that the war brought changes to the public as well.

W: That's correct. The war advanced hygiene, medicine, and social services. The war was modern not only because it involved a wide variety of resources but the public as well. The people behind the war front received much more detailed information and learned about the horrors of the war.

M: Why was that?

W: Photography had been recently invented. Therefore, for the first time in history, many aspects of the war, such as dead bodies and tensions, were witnessed by the general public. As the war came close to an end, the Confederacy suffered a great deal of economic difficulties, and those were chronicled by photographers as well.

M: How was the Union's condition?

W: The Union lost many of its people, but since they won the war, their ego and pride were sometimes viewed as conceited.

해석

W Professor: 남북 전쟁은 1861년부터 1865년까지 계속된 남군과 북군 사이의 전쟁이었습니다. 많은 사람들은 남북 전쟁의 주요 목적이 노예를 해방시키기 위한 것이었다고 생각하지만, 사실 전쟁은 북군의 권위와 통합을 유지하기 위해 시작되었어요. 남북 전쟁은 또한 새로운 세대의 현대전의 시작을 알렸습니다. 남북 전쟁에서 완전히 새로운 방식의 전투 계획, 무기, 커뮤니케이션, 그리고 운송이 등장을 했죠.

M Student: 전쟁으로 인해 대중들에게도 변화가 일어났다고 들었습니다.

W: 맞아요. 전쟁은 위생, 의학, 그리고 사회 서비스에 진보를 가져왔어요. 이 전쟁이 현대적이었던 이유는 다양한 자원뿐만 아니라 대중들과도 관련이 있었기 때문이었죠. 전선 뒤에 있던 사람들은 훨씬 더 자세한 정보를 전달받았고 전쟁의 끔찍함에 대해 알게 되었어요.

M: 어떻게 그런 일이 가능했나요?

W: 그 시기에 사진이 발명되었어요. 그래서 역사상 처음으로 전쟁의 여러 측면들, 예컨대 시신 및 긴장 상태 등을 일반 대중들도 목격하게 되었습니다. 전쟁이 막바지에 이르면서 남군은 경제적인 어려움을 겪었고, 이러한 점들 역시 사진 작가에 의해 시간 순으로 기록되었죠.

M: 북군의 상황은 어땠나요?

W: 북군은 많은 사상자를 냈지만 전쟁에서 승리했기 때문에 때로는 자신감과 긍지로 우쭐해 하는 모습을 보였어요.

📝 Summary Note B

The Civil War began to keep the Union together, but later freeing the slaves in the South became an important reason. The war was the first to introduce many modern technological features, thereby advancing social conditions. It also involved the public in the realities of war for the first time. The terrible aspects of the war hit home thanks to the photographs. As the Union won the war, the Confederates went through an economic downfall while the Union boasted about its victory.

Integrated Listening & Speaking
p.104

A

Script 🎧 04-17

W Professor: *Sonata Number 11* was written by Mozart. It has three movements, which are andante

grazioso, menuetto, and rondo alla turca. This piece is also called *Turkish Rondo*. The reason is that it's supposed to imitate the sound of Turkish bands. The andante grazioso is composed of a theme with six variations. Menuetto has a minuet and trio, and rondo alla turca is allegretto. Andante grazioso is known for its main melody. Menuetto should be played delicately. Finally, the rondo alla turca needs to be played with fluctuating intensity but also with accuracy. Since it is very fast paced, musicians have to be careful to play every note precisely. In addition, they should try to avoid getting faster as they play. The musicians need to keep a consistent pace.

1. a. The piece is called *Sonata Number 11* by Mozart, and it has three movements.
   b. *Sonata Number 11* has three movements, and it was composed by Mozart.

2. a. It has a well-known theme that is repeated in six variations.
   b. There are six variations of a single theme in the movement.

3. a. It should be played with varying intensity and accuracy.
   b. The third movement requires accuracy and varying intensity.

B

Script 🎧 04-18

W Professor: Although many people believe that the Civil War's main objective was to free the slaves, they are incorrect. In fact, the war began to preserve the authority and unity of the Union. It also marked the beginning of a new generation of modern wars. For instance, it introduced brand-new war plans, weapons, communications, and transportation methods. The war was modern not only because it involved a wide variety of resources but also the public. Many aspects of the war, such as dead bodies and tensions, were witnessed by the general public. This happened because photography had been invented. As the war began to end, the Confederacy suffered a great deal of economic difficulties. Those problems were recorded by photographers as well. The Union lost many of its people, but since they won the war, their ego and pride were sometimes viewed as conceited.

1. a. The objectives of the Civil War were to preserve the authority and unity of the Union and to free the slaves.
   b. Preserving the authority and unity of the Union and freeing the slaves were the main objectives of the Civil War.

2 **a.** The Civil War introduced many <u>advanced technologies and photographs.</u>

  b. The Civil War was the first war in the modern era to use <u>advanced technology and photographs.</u>

3 **a.** The Union <u>enjoyed a boost</u> to its ego, but the Confederacy <u>suffered.</u>

  b. The Confederacy <u>suffered many hardships,</u> but the Union's ego <u>was boosted.</u>

Mini TOEFL iBT Practice Test
p.106

1 ⓒ	2 ⓓ	3 ⓑ	4 ⒶＤ
5 ⓓ	6 ⓓ		

[1-3]

Script 🎧 04-19

M Student: Hi. I have a few questions about your camp program.

W Student Activities Office Employee: Sure. Which program are you interested in?

M: I am interested in the outdoor activity camp. I have never attended one, but I am athletic. Would your program suit me?

W: Do you like to camp and go hiking in general?

M: Yes, I do.

W: Then you should be fine since you are athletic and like hiking. It is an intermediate-level camp, so it can be a bit challenging.

M: That sounds good. I would rather deal with challenges than be bored.

W: That is a good attitude. We will present you with tasks that will keep you busy both mentally and physically.

M: What are the basic activities? Are there any elective activities?

W: The participants will backpack in the Angeles National Forest, go rock climbing, and visit Los Angeles College for a rope-teambuilding course. There are no elective activities.

M: I see. Besides the basic activities, how does the program bring together participants?

W: Students will work together as a team to prepare meals, to set up the camp, and to go hiking.

M: What is the level of competitiveness between teammates?

W: Everyone will be assigned to a team, and each team will compete against the others. There are no individual

competitions.

M: How much is the fee, and when is the registration due?

W: The fee is 400 dollars, and the registration is due on July 18. Oh, the camp is co-ed. Do you have any other questions?

M: No, that will do it. Thank you very much for your time.

W: My pleasure.

해석

M Student: 안녕하세요. 캠프 프로그램에 관해 몇 가지 질문이 있어서요.

W Student Activities Office Employee: 그래요. 어떤 프로그램에 관심이 있나요?

M: 야외 활동 캠프에 관심이 있어요. 한 번도 참가해 본 적은 없지만, 운동은 잘 하는 편이에요. 프로그램이 저한테 맞을까요?

W: 캠핑과 하이킹하는 걸 좋아하나요?

M: 네, 그래요.

W: 운동도 잘 하고 하이킹을 좋아한다니 괜찮을 거예요. 중급 캠프라서 약간 힘들 수는 있어요.

M: 잘 됐군요. 지루한 것보다는 힘든 걸 하는 것을 더 좋아하거든요.

W: 자세가 좋군요. 머리와 몸을 다 써야 하는 활동들이 주어질 거예요.

M: 기본 활동은 어떤 것들인가요? 그리고 선택할 수 있는 활동들도 있나요?

W: 참가자들은 앤젤레스 국유림에서 백패킹을 하고, 암벽 등반을 하고, 그리고 로스앤젤레스 대학을 방문해서 로프를 이용한 팀빌딩 수업을 받게 될 거예요. 선택할 수 있는 활동은 없고요.

M: 그렇군요. 기본 활동 외에 프로그램 참가자들은 어떤 팀 활동을 하나요?

W: 학생들은 팀을 짜서 식사를 준비하고, 야영 시설을 설치하고, 그리고 하이킹을 할 거예요.

M: 팀 동료간의 경쟁 수준은 어느 정도인가요?

W: 모두가 팀에 배정되어서 각 팀끼리 서로 경쟁을 하게 될 거예요. 개인 경쟁은 없어요.

M: 비용은 얼마이고, 등록 마감일은 언제인가요?

W: 비용은 400달러이고 등록 마감일은 7월 18일이에요. 참, 캠프는 혼성이에요. 다른 질문이 있나요?

M: 아니요, 그 정도면 됐어요. 시간을 내 주셔서 고맙습니다.

W: 천만에요.

[4-6]

Script 🎧 04-20

M Professor: As you know, an ecosystem includes all of the living and nonliving things in a certain area. The living things include plants, animals, bacteria, fungi, and everything else that's alive. The nonliving things include soil, rocks, and air. They all come together to form various ecosystems. There are a wide variety of ecosystems. On land, they include forests, plains, deserts, and tundra. Of course, there are varieties of these ecosystems. For example, regarding forests, there are rainforests, temperate forests, pine forests, mangrove forests, and so on. Water ecosystems include oceans, seas, rivers, lakes, streams, creeks, and ponds.

Some ecosystems are enormous. The Sahara Desert is a huge desert ecosystem that spans most of northern Africa. The Pacific Ocean is a massive ocean ecosystem, too. There are also some very, very small ecosystems. These are called microecosystems. Can any of you name a microecosystem? Stephanie, your hand is up.

W Student: Would that be something like a pond?

M: **Nice try.** But think smaller. For example, a puddle of water could be a microecosystem. Or how about the ground beneath a large rock? Have you ever lifted a rock and seen different animals living there? That was a microecosystem.

W: Why?

M: Basically, the conditions beneath that rock are different than in the area around it. For instance, beneath the rock is dark, but the land around it is light. Underneath the rock, it's cool. But the sun provides heat in the area around it. Worms or bugs may live under the rock. But they don't live around it. The conditions under the rock are different from the surrounding land. That makes it a microecosystem.

해석

M Professor: 아시다시피 생태계에는 일정 지역에 존재하는 모든 생물과 무생물이 포함됩니다. 생물에는 식물, 동물, 박테리아, 균류, 그리고 살아 있는 그 밖의 모든 것이 포함되죠. 무생물에는 토양, 암석, 그리고 공기가 포함됩니다. 이들이 모두 합쳐져 다양한 생태계가 만들어지는 것이에요. 매우 다양한 생태계가 존재합니다. 육지의 경우 숲, 평원, 사막, 그리고 툰드라가 있습니다. 물론 이들 생태계들도 다양한 형태로 존재해요. 예를 들어, 숲에 대해 말하자면, 우림, 온대림, 소나무림, 맹그로브림, 그리고 기타 등등이 있죠. 수생태계에는 대양, 바다, 강, 호수, 개울, 시내, 그리고 연못이 포함되고요.

몇몇 생태계는 크기가 엄청납니다. 사하라 사막은 거대한 사막 생태계로 북아프리카 대부분의 지역에 뻗어 있습니다. 태평양 역시 거대한 바다 생태계입니다. 또한 매우, 매우 작은 생태계들도 있어요. 이들은 미소 생태계라고 불립니다. 미소 생태계를 말해 볼 사람이 있나요? Stephanie, 손을 들었군요.

W Student: 연못 같은 곳이 될까요?

M: 시도는 좋았어요. 하지만 더 작은 것을 생각해 보세요. 예를 들면 물 웅덩이도 미소 생태계가 될 수 있어요. 혹은 커다란 바위 아래에 있는 땅은 어떤가요? 바위를 들쳐내서 그곳에 살고 있는 여러 동물들을 본 적이 있나요? 그것도 바로 미소 생태계였습니다.

W: 왜죠?

M: 기본적으로 바위 아래의 조건은 바위 주변 지역과 다릅니다. 예를 들어 바위 아래는 어둡지만 바위 주변은 밝아요. 바위 아래는 춥습니다. 하지만 바위 주변 지역에는 태양이 열을 공급해 주죠. 벌레나 곤충들이 바위 아래에서 살고 있을 수도 있습니다. 하지만 바위 주변에는 살지 않아요. 바위 밑의 조건은 주변 지역과 다릅니다. 이로써 미소 생태계가 만들어지는 것이죠.

Vocabulary Check-Up ——— p.109

A
1 ⓛ	2 ⒡	3 ⒤	4 ⒜	5 ⒢
6 ⓜ	7 ⓞ	8 ⒝	9 ⒞	10 ⓝ
11 ⒟	12 ⒥	13 ⒣	14 ⓚ	15 ⒠

B
| 1 ⒞ | 2 ⒠ | 3 ⒟ | 4 ⒜ | 5 ⒝ |

UNIT 05 Understanding the Speaker's Attitude

Skill & Tip ·············· p.112

Skill Practice

A

1 Why is the door locked?
2 Do you want coffee or tea?
3 It will look really nice when it is sitting on the table.
4 Now, when you read, don't just consider what the author thinks.
5 **W**: Which is more important, health or wealth?
   M: You need health and wealth together.

B

W Student: What are those workmen doing on the roof of the dorm?

M Resident Assistant: I was told that they're fitting some solar panels.

W: What are they for?

M: They're for heating water using just the heat of the sun. They can provide from thirty to seventy percent of an ordinary home's needs for hot water each year.

W: And for free! That's really worth having.

C

W Professor: Hurricanes' names are chosen from the list in your material. The Atlantic is assigned six lists of names, with one list used each year. Every sixth year, the first list begins again. Each name on the list starts with a different letter. For example, the name of the very first hurricane of the season starts with the letter A, the next starts with the letter B, and so on. The letters Q, U, X, Y, and Z, however, are not used. Is your name among the currently used or retired hurricane names?

Basic Drill

······· p.114

Drill 1 (D)

Script 🎧 05-05

W Student: I thought of two possible topics for the project. The first one is on how soil affects the pH of water, and the second one is on how soil changes with depth.

M Professor: They are both okay. Which one do you feel more comfortable with?

W: I like the second one, but it is more challenging.

M: Will you go with something that is easy or something that you can learn and accomplish more through putting in more of an effort?

W: It sounds like you are telling me to do the second one.

M: Well, it is up to you. I was just giving you a suggestion.

해석

W Student: 프로젝트에 대한 두 개의 가능한 주제를 생각해 봤어요. 첫 번째는 토양이 어떻게 물의 pH에 영향을 미치는가에 대한 것이고, 두 번째는 토양이 깊이에 따라 어떻게 변하는지에 관한 것이에요.

M Professor: 둘 다 괜찮군요. 어떤 주제가 더 편하게 생각되나요?

W: 두 번째 주제가 마음에 들지만 더 어려울 거예요.

M: 쉬운 쪽을 택하고 싶나요, 아니면 더 노력해서 보다 많은 것을 배우고 성취할 수 있는 것을 택하고 싶은가요?

W: 두 번째 것을 선택하라고 말씀하시는 것 같네요.

M: 음, 그건 학생한테 달려 있어요. 저는 제안을 하고 있을 뿐이고요.

Drill 2 (D)

Script 🎧 05-06

M Student: It's my first time here.

W Computer Lab Assistant: Okay. Just fill out this application, and you are registered.

M: Thank you. One more thing . . . Can you tell me how to use the lab?

W: You can just go to any computer or come to the help desk to reserve a computer. The time limit is two hours. If you want to print a document, it costs five cents per page. No food or drinks are allowed.

M: Thank you. It's pretty much the same as the old one I used to go to before.

해석

M Student: 이곳이 처음인데요.

W Computer Lab Assistant: 그렇군요. 이 신청서를 작성하면 등록이 될 거예요.

M: 고맙습니다. 한 가지가 더 있는데… 컴퓨터실 이용법을 알려 주실 수 있나요?

W: 아무 컴퓨터로 가도 되고, 아니면 안내 데스크로 가서 컴퓨터를 예약할 수도 있어요. 제한 시간은 2시간이에요. 만약 문서를 프린트하고자 한다면 장당 2센트의 비용이 들어요. 음식물이나 음료수 반입은 허용되지 않고요.

M: 고맙습니다. 제가 전에 다녔던 곳과 상당히 비슷하군요.

Drill 3 (D)

Script 🎧 05-07

W Professor: Vitamin A plays a vital role in your eyes. It helps your eyes adjust to light changes so that you can see during the day and night. Plus, it helps your eyes stay moist. Therefore, if you feel uncomfortable seeing at night or your eyes feel dry, your eyes need vitamin A. Of course, there can be other reasons, but studies show that vitamin A prevents those illnesses from happening.

해석

W Professor: 비타민 A는 눈에 매우 중요한 역할을 합니다. 눈이 빛의 변화에 적응하도록 만들기 때문에 우리가 낮과 밤에 볼 수 있는 것이죠. 또한 눈이 촉촉한 상태를 유지할 수 있도록 돕습니다. 따라서 밤에 잘 보이지 않거나 눈이 건조하다고 생각된다면 여러분 눈에 비타민 A가 필요한 때입니다. 물론 다른 이유들이 있을 수도 있지만, 연구에 따르면 비타민 A는 그러한 질병들이 발생하는 것을 예방해 줍니다.

Drill 4 (A)

Script 🎧 05-08

W Professor: The U.S. president is elected every four years. Everyone probably thinks that the qualifications for the candidates are very high. But once you find out the criteria, you will have a different idea. First, the candidate has to be a natural-born citizen of the U.S. Second, the person should be at least thirty-five years of age and a resident of the U.S. for at least fourteen years. Since gender and race are not mentioned, anyone here who is a natural-born citizen can dream of being the president.

해석

W Professor: 미국 대통령은 4년마다 선출됩니다. 아마도 모든 사람들은 대통령 후보의 자격 조건이 매우 까다로울 것이라고 생각할 거예요. 하지만 그 조건을 알게 되면 생각이 달라질 것입니다. 첫째, 대통령 후보는 미국에서 태어난 시민이어야 합니다. 둘째, 나이가 35세 이상이어야 하고, 미국에서 최소 14년 동안 거주한 사람이어야 합니다. 성별과 인종은 언급되어 있지 않기 때문에 미국에서 태어난 시민이라면 이곳 누구나 대통령이 되는 꿈을 가질 수 있어요.

Exercises with Short Conversations & Lectures

Exercise 1 1 ⒷB 2 ⒷB   p.116

Script 🎧 05-09

M Student: Hello. I wonder if you can help me.

W Student Activities Office Employee: I'll do my best. What do you need?

M: I heard there is a job fair coming up soon. Can you tell me about it?

W: Sure. It's going to take place this Saturday. Around 200 companies will be in attendance. They will be from all kinds of industries. So no matter what your major is, there should be something there for you.

M: That's great to hear. Do you have any advice for me?

W: Please bring some copies of your résumé to hand out. And be sure to wear a suit.

M: I don't actually own one.

W: **It's a worthwhile investment.** It will impress recruiters if you wear one.

M: Good point. I guess I need to go shopping soon.

해석

M Student: 안녕하세요. 저를 도와 주실 수 있는지 궁금해서요.

W Student Activities Office Employee: 최선을 다 할게요. 무엇이 필요한가요?

M: 곧 취업 박람회가 열린다고 들었어요. 그에 대해 말씀해 주실 수 있나요?

W: 물론이죠. 이번 주 토요일에 열릴 거예요. 약 200개의 기업이 참석할 예정이고요. 모든 산업 분야에서 올 거예요. 그러니 학생의 전공이 무엇이더라도 학생을 위한 곳이 있을 거예요.

M: 반가운 얘기군요. 저에게 해 주실 조언이 있을까요?

W: 제출할 이력서 사본을 몇 장 가지고 가세요. 그리고 꼭 정장을 입으시고요.

M: 사실 정장은 갖고 있는 것이 없는데요.

W: 정장은 투자할만한 가치가 있는 것이에요. 정장을 입으면 채용 담당자들에게 좋은 인상을 남길 거예요.

M: 좋은 지적이군요. 곧 쇼핑을 하러 가야 할 것 같네요.

Exercise 2 1 ⒹD 2 ⒸC   p.117

Script 🎧 05-10

W1 Librarian: Hi, Jennifer. What are you borrowing today? Wow! Are you sure you can finish all these in time?

W2 Student: Yes. I'm so into mysteries these days. I can read them all night long. It is so exciting to imagine and guess where the story is leading.

W1: Yes, it enhances your creativity and imagination. Do you have a favorite author?

W2: I kind of have one, but I'm trying to read one book by every author. I'll definitely have one soon. What are you reading these days?

W1: **I like mysteries, but I'm more into nonfiction that deals with politics and business.**

W2: That sounds interesting.

W1: Yes, it is. Well, you know your interests and thoughts change over time. I might get interested in mysteries like you someday. We will talk about those books when I do.

W2: That is a wonderful idea. I love talking about books with people.

해석

W1 Librarian: 안녕하세요, Jennifer. 오늘은 어떤 책을 빌릴 건가요? 와! 시간 내에 이걸 다 읽을 수 있을 것 같아요?

W2 Student: 네. 요즘 미스터리 소설에 푹 빠져 있거든요. 밤새워 읽을 수도 있어요. 이야기가 어떻게 흘러갈지 상상하고 추측하는 일이 너무 재미있어요.

W1: 네, 창의력과 상상력을 길러 주죠. 좋아하는 작가가 있나요?

W2: 한 명 정도 마음에 드는데, 모든 작가들의 책을 한 권씩 읽어보려고 해요. 곧 가장 좋아하는 작가가 분명 생길 거예요. 선생님은 요즘 어떤 책을 읽으세요?

W1: 저도 미스터리 소설을 좋아하지만, 정치와 비즈니스를 다루는 논픽션 작품들을 더 좋아해요.

W2: 재미있을 것 같네요.

W1: 네, 그래요. 음, 알겠지만 시간이 지나면서 관심사와 생각이 바뀌죠. 저도 언젠가 학생처럼 미스터리 소설에 빠질 수도 있을 거예요. 그렇게 되면 이 책들에 관한 이야기를 하게 될 테고요.

W2: 멋진 생각이네요. 저는 사람들과 책 얘기를 하는 것을 정말 좋아하거든요.

Exercise 3 1 ⒶA 2 ⒶA   p.118

Script 🎧 05-11

M Professor: Last week, we talked about food and its relation to health in general. Starting today, we will go into more details. We are going to spend six weeks studying food and health. We are going to start with fiber. I'm sure you have heard a lot about fiber in general. **I'm also sure you have heard the facts I'm going to talk about now.** First of all, fiber is good for the digestive system, and it lowers the body's cholesterol level. Foods with fiber are good sources of essential nutrients. This means that foods with fiber are good for our health. In addition, fiber should be consumed frequently and regularly to be effective.

해석

M Professor: 지난 주에는 음식 및 음식과 건강과의 관계에 대한 일반적인 이야기를 나누었습니다. 오늘부터는 보다 구체적인 이야기를 하려고 해요. 우리는 6주에 걸쳐 음식과 건강에 대해 공부할 것입니다. 섬유질부터 시작해 보죠. 섬유질에 대한 일반적인 이야기는 여러분들이 분명 많이 들어보셨을 것입니다. 지금 제가 말씀드리려는 사실 역시 분명 들어보셨을 것이고요. 무엇보다도 섬유질은 소화계에 좋고, 체내의 콜레스테롤 수치를 낮춰 줍니다. 섬유질이 들어 있는 식

품은 필수 영양소를 공급해 주죠. 섬유질이 들어 있는 식품은 건강에 좋다는 뜻이에요. 또한 섬유질의 효과를 보기 위해서는 이를 자주, 그리고 규칙적으로 섭취해야 합니다.

Exercise 4　1 ⓓ　2 ⓓ　　　　　　　　　p.119

Script 🎧 05-12

> **W Professor**: Let me ask you a question before I start. Do you love poetry or have a favorite poem? Some of you may answer yes, and some of you may answer no. **You might not have noticed, but we talk about poems and poetry a lot in our daily lives.** What is written in poetry is a topic of our daily lives. However, we don't have a clear idea of what poetry is. How would you define poetry? I believe most of you are not familiar with the meaning. Therefore, what I am going to do is define the word poetry for you. First of all, the word is of Greek origin and means to make or to create.

해석

W Professor: 시작하기 전에 질문을 하나 할게요. 여러분은 시를 좋아하나요, 혹은 좋아하는 시가 있나요? 여러분 중 일부는 그렇다고 답할 것이고 일부는 아니라고 답할 것 같군요. 여러분은 눈치채지 못했겠지만, 우리는 일상 생활 속에서 시와 시가에 대해 많이 이야기합니다. 시로 쓰여진 것들은 일상 생활의 주제이죠. 하지만 우리는 시가 무엇인지에 대해 명확한 아이디어를 가지고 있지 않습니다. 시를 어떻게 정의할 수 있을까요? 여러분 대부분이 그 의미를 잘 모르고 있을 것으로 생각해요. 그래서 제가 여러분들에게 시라는 단어의 정의를 내려 드리겠습니다. 먼저 이 단어는 그리스어에서 유래된 것으로 '만들다' 또는 '창조하다'의 뜻을 나타냅니다.

Exercises with Mid-Length Conversations & Lectures

Exercise 1　1 ⓓ　2 ⓓ　　　　　　　　　p.120

Script 🎧 05-13

> **M Student**: Hello. I got my schedule and found that I was enrolled in the wrong class.
>
> **W Registrar's Office Employee**: Let me see your schedule so I can find out what went wrong.
>
> **M**: Here you are.
>
> **W**: Thank you. What are the classes you requested, Jake?
>
> **M**: I requested biology, English, algebra, tennis, art, and American history.
>
> **W**: Hmm, you have chemistry instead of biology. I'll fix that now. Give me a second.
>
> **M**: Am I going to have the same schedule and just switch chemistry to biology? Or are you going to change the whole schedule?
>
> **W**: Let me check. Sometimes I have to switch classes around, but hopefully, that won't be the case for you.
>
> **M**: It wouldn't be a big deal even if you changed my classes around.
>
> **W**: Good. Some students don't like making changes.
>
> **M**: I'm flexible. I'm okay as long as I get to take all the classes I chose.
>
> **W**: You are an easygoing person with a great personality. I'm almost done here. Fortunately, there's a biology class during third period, so you get to keep your schedule as is.
>
> **M**: Great!

해석

M Student: 안녕하세요. 시간표를 받았는데 제가 엉뚱한 수업에 등록이 되어 있더군요.

W Registrar's Office Employee: 무엇이 잘못되었는지 확인하기 위해 학생의 시간표를 볼게요.

M: 여기 있어요.

W: 고마워요. 신청한 수업이 어떤 수업이었나요, 제이크?

M: 생물학, 영어, 대수학, 테니스, 미술, 그리고 미국사를 신청했어요.

W: 흠, 생물학 대신 화학이 들어가 있군요. 제가 지금 고쳐 줄게요. 잠시 기다려주세요.

M: 시간표는 그대로 있고 화학만 생물학으로 바뀌는 건가요? 아니면 시간표 전체를 바꾸시는 건가요?

W: 확인해 볼게요. 주변 수업들을 바꿔야 하는데, 아마도 학생의 경우는 안 그래도 될 것 같군요.

M: 주변 수업들을 바꾸셔도 크게 문제가 될 건 없을 거예요.

W: 잘 되었네요. 일부 학생들은 바뀌는 걸 좋아하지 않거든요.

M: 전 유연한 편이거든요. 제가 선택한 과목들을 다 들을 수만 있으면 상관없어요.

W: 무던한 좋은 성격을 가지고 있군요. 거의 다 되었어요. 다행히 3교시 생물 수업이 있어서 시간표는 그대로 두어도 되겠어요.

M: 잘 됐네요!

📝 Summary Note Ⓑ

The student found a mistake in his schedule. He went to see the employee to fix his schedule. Many students don't like their schedules being switched. However, the student doesn't mind changes in his schedule. The employee believes the student is a pleasure to deal with. Luckily, the student can keep his other classes in the same periods and switched chemistry to biology.

Exercise 2　1 Ⓑ　2 ⓓ　　　　　　　　　p.122

Script 🎧 05-14

> **M Professor**: Brenda, you aren't doing very well in this class. You got a C+ on the first test and a C- on the last one.

W Student: I'm trying my best, sir. This is just difficult material for me.

M: What are your study habits like?

W: Well, I usually study about two days before the exam.

M: Is that all?

W: My other classes keep me busy, so I don't have more time to study biology.

M: That's not good enough. That explains why you're doing so poorly.

W: What should I do then?

M: Review your notes after every class. In addition, be sure to do the reading for each lecture. If you do those two things, you should improve your grade.

W: I'll try, but I am pretty busy this semester. But I want to do well in this class.

M: Please spend more time on the material. It will definitely help your grade.

해석

M Professor: Brenda, 이번 수업에서 그다지 좋지가 못하네요. 첫 번째 시험에서는 C+를 받았고 지난 번 시험에서는 C−를 받았군요.

W Student: 저는 최선을 다하고 있어요, 교수님. 이번 수업 내용이 제게 어려워요.

M: 어떤 식으로 공부하고 있죠?

W: 음, 보통 시험 이틀 전에 공부를 해요.

M: 그것이 다인가요?

W: 다른 수업 때문에 바빠서 생물학을 공부할 수 있는 시간이 그 이상은 더 없어요.

M: 그렇게 하면 안되죠. 그래서 학생 성적이 그처럼 좋지 않은 것이군요.

W: 그러면 제가 어떻게 해야 할까요?

M: 수업이 끝날 때마다 필기한 것을 복습하세요. 그리고 강의가 있는 때에는 꼭 읽기 과제도 하고요. 이 두 가지 일을 하면 성적이 올라갈 거예요.

W: 노력해 보겠지만 이번 학기에 상당히 바빠서요. 하지만 이번 수업에서 좋은 성적을 받고 싶어요.

M: 시간을 더 내서 수업 내용을 공부하세요. 그러면 분명 성적에 도움이 될 거예요.

Summary Note B

The professor tells the student she got two low grades on her tests. He asks about her study habits. The student studies two days before the exam. The professor tells her that is not good enough and that she needs to review her notes daily and do the reading. The student says she is busy but will try.

Exercise 3 1 Ⓐ 2 Ⓒ   p.124

Script 🎧 05-15

M Professor: One social issue faced by the state of Alaska is the lack of mental and emotional well-being among native Alaskans. It is unfortunate that many Native Americans live in poor conditions throughout the country. In the cases of native Alaskans, virtually entire villages suffer from a lack of mental and emotional well-being, which includes poor physical and mental health. Alcohol abuse, domestic violence, homicides, and suicides are frequent in them, which, of course, lead to families falling apart. It is tragic to see that many children are abused and not educated properly. As a matter of fact, children themselves are abusing alcohol and other chemicals, and the rate is increasing over time. Since parents are suffering from mental illnesses and alcohol abuse, they can't take care of their children, so many children end up being taken care of by others or are simply neglected. Therefore, we can conclude that Alaskan natives are losing hold of their communities, cultural identities, and, most importantly, their childhoods. So you can see how serious the issue is. Plus, rather than making a living for themselves, many depend on public services and subsidies. They have lost control of their economy and governing institutions.

해석

M Professor: 알래스카주가 직면하고 있는 사회 문제 중 하나는 알래스카 원주민들 사이에 정신적인, 그리고 정서적인 안정이 부족하다는 점입니다. 전국에 걸쳐 많은 미 원주민들이 열악한 환경에서 생활하고 있다는 점은 안타까운 일이에요. 알래스카 원주민의 경우, 사실상 모든 마을에서 정신적인, 그리고 정서적인 안정과 관련된 문제를 겪고 있는데, 여기에는 신체 건강과 정신 건강 문제도 포함됩니다. 이들에게는 알코올 중독, 가정 폭력, 살인, 그리고 자살이 빈번한 일로, 이는 물론 가정의 붕괴로 이어집니다. 많은 아동들이 학대를 받으며 적절한 교육을 받지 못한다는 점은 비참한 일로 여겨집니다. 실제로 아동들은 알코올 및 기타 화학 약품에 중독되고 있으며, 그 비율은 시간이 지남에 따라 증가하고 있어요. 부모들이 정신 질환 및 알코올 중독을 겪고 있기 때문에 자식들을 돌보지 못해서 많은 아이들이 다른 사람들의 보살핌을 받거나 또는 방치되고 있죠. 따라서 알래스카 원주민들은 자신들의 공동체, 문화 정체성, 그리고 무엇보다 아동들을 잃고 있다고 결론지을 수 있어요. 그러니 여러분들은 문제가 얼마나 심각한지 알 수 있을 거예요. 게다가 많은 사람들이 스스로 생계를 이어나가지 못하고 공공 서비스 및 보조금에 의지하고 있습니다. 자신들의 경제 및 통치 기관들에 대한 통제력을 잃어버린 것이죠.

Summary Note B

Native Alaskans' lives are unprivileged. They lack mental and emotional well-being. Alcohol abuse, domestic violence, homicides, and suicides are some results. In addition, children are not properly taken care of by their parents. A lack of education leads to alcohol and other chemicals abuse. As native Alaskans lose control of themselves, they also lose control of their economy and governing institutions.

Script 🎧 05-16

W Professor: Class, we are going to distinguish the difference between fiction and nonfiction. Basically, fiction is storytelling of imagined events, and nonfiction is fact or reality. Specifically, fiction is imagined stories such as novels, fables, fairy tales, cartoons, and comics. These can contain some factual events that are revised with imaginary contents.

M Student: What about movies?

W: Excellent question. I'm pleased you asked that. What do you think?

M: Fiction.

W: Very good! Movies and video games—the ones you guys always play after school—are fiction. Most of them are made-up stories. Some are based on true stories, but they have added imaginary stories to grab people's attention. Fiction has the ability to stir people's emotions. It can give us hope and make us laugh or cry. I'm sure you have cried, laughed hard, or felt sorry for characters in fiction works you have read or seen. Finally, contrasted with fiction, nonfiction deals with facts. However, the facts could contain false information.

M: How?

W: Well, the author believes that what he or she has written is true, but that information could be proven false afterward. Common examples of nonfiction works are essays, journals, documentaries, photographs, and biographies.

해석

W Professor: 여러분, 픽션과 논픽션의 차이를 알아보도록 해요. 기본적으로 픽션은 지어낸 사건을 이야기하는 것이고, 논픽션은 사실 또는 실제 있었던 일입니다. 구체적으로 말하면 픽션은 소설, 우화, 동화, 시사 만화, 그리고 만화와 같은 가상의 이야기인 것이죠. 여기에는 실제 사건들이 상상 속 이야기들로 바뀌어져 있을 수도 있습니다.

M Student: 영화는 어떤가요?

W: 좋은 질문이군요. 물어봐 줘서 기분이 좋네요. 어떻게 생각하나요?

M: 픽션입니다.

W: 아주 잘 했어요! 영화와 여러분이 방과 후에 항상 하는 비디오 게임은 픽션입니다. 대부분이 지어낸 이야기죠. 일부는 실화에 바탕을 두고 있지만, 사람들의 관심을 끌기 위해 상상 속 이야기들이 포함되어 있어요. 픽션은 사람들의 감정을 움직일 수 있는 능력을 가지고 있습니다. 우리에게 희망을 줄 수도 있고, 우리를 웃거나 울게 만들 수도 있어요. 분명 여러분이 읽거나 본 픽션 작품의 등장 인물들 때문에 여러분들도 울거나, 웃거나, 혹은 안타까움을 느낀 적이 있을 거예요. 마지막으로, 픽션과 반대로 논픽션은 사실을 다룹니다. 하지만 그러한 사실에는 거짓 정보가 들어 있을 수 있어요.

M: 어떻게요?

W: 음, 작가는 자신이 쓴 것이 사실이라고 생각하지만, 이후에 그러한 정보가 잘못된 것으로 판명될 수 있죠. 논픽션의 흔한 예로는 에세이, 저널, 다큐멘터리, 사진, 그리고 전기를 들 수 있습니다.

📝 **Summary Note** Ⓑ

The difference between fiction and nonfiction is that fiction is based on created stories while nonfiction is based on facts. Fiction includes novels, fables, cartoons, comics, and movies that can touch people's emotions and which make people laugh and cry. Contrasted with fiction, nonfiction includes essays, journals, documentaries, and biographies and can be either true or false depending on the information the author has.

Integrated Listening & Speaking   p.128

A

Script 🎧 05-17

M Professor: One social issue faced by the state of Alaska is the lack of mental and emotional well-being among native Alaskans. Unfortunately, many Native Americans live in poor conditions all throughout the state. In the cases of native Alaskans, virtually entire villages do not have mental and emotional well-being. Alcohol abuse, domestic violence, homicides, and suicides are frequent in them. These problems often lead to families falling apart. It is tragic to see that many children are abused and not educated properly. As a matter of fact, Alaskan children themselves are abusing alcohol and other chemicals. The rate of abuse is even increasing over time. Since parents are suffering from mental illnesses and alcohol abuse, they can't take good care of their children. Thus, many children are being taken care of by others or are neglected. As a result, Alaskan natives are losing hold of their communities, cultural identities, and, most importantly, their childhoods.

1 a. Alaskan natives lack mental and emotional well-being.
   b. Alcohol abuse, domestic violence, child abuse, homicide, and suicide are the results that poor physical and mental health lead to.

2 a. Many children are taken care of by others or neglected.
   b. Parents cannot take care of their children sometimes.

3 a. The causes are long psychological and spiritual wounds.
   b. The causes are unsettled cultural and political deprivation.

B

Script 🎧 05-18

W Professor: Let's point out some of the differences between fiction and nonfiction. Basically, fiction is storytelling of imagined events whereas nonfiction is fact or reality. Specifically, fiction is imagined stories such as novels, fables, fairy tales, cartoons, and comics. Movies and video games are also fiction. Some may be based on true stories, but they have added imaginary stories to grab people's attention. One thing about fiction is that it has the ability to stir people's emotions. It can give us hope and make us laugh or cry. On the contrary, nonfiction deals with facts. However, these facts could contain false information. The author may believe that what he or she has written is true, but that information could be proven false afterward. Some common examples of nonfiction works are essays, journals, documentaries, photographs, and biographies.

1 a. Novels, fables, cartoons, and comics are fiction.
   b. Some fiction is based on factual events, but it is revised with imagination.

2 a. Fiction stirs people's emotions.
   b. Fiction makes people cry or laugh.

3 a. The author's false knowledge could contribute to false information in a book.
   b. Information could be proven false at a later time in the future.

Mini TOEFL iBT Practice Test   p.130

1 Ⓓ   2 Ⓑ   3 Ⓓ   4 Ⓒ   5 Ⓒ
6 Ⓑ

[1-3]

Script 🎧 05-19

W Student: Hello. My name is Denise Peterson. I'm supposed to report here for my first day of work.

M Economics Department Office Employee: It's nice to meet you, Denise. I've been expecting you. My name is Philip Peters.

W: It's a pleasure to meet you, sir. So, uh . . . what am I supposed to do here?

M: Basically, you'll do simple office work for the most part.

W: So I'll type and file papers?

M: Yes, that's some of the work that you'll do. There are other things, too.

W: Such as?

M: Hmm . . . Students often come into the office to ask questions. You'll need to answer those questions. Most of them are simple ones that you can answer easily.

W: What kinds of simple ones?

M: For instance, some might ask where a professor's office is.

W: I can handle that.

M: Sure you can. You'll get asked about office hours as well. And sometimes you might need to assist a professor. You might need to make photocopies or do other work.

W: This job sounds like it will be fun.

M: Most student employees like it. Just do your best and don't be afraid to ask for help. In a couple of weeks, you'll be able to do most of the work without getting assistance.

W: Okay. I'm really looking forward to this.

해석

W Student: 안녕하세요. 제 이름은 Denise Peterson이에요. 이곳에서 제 첫 근무를 보고하기로 되어 있죠.

M Economics Department Office Employee: 만나서 반가워요, Denise. 기다리고 있었어요. 제 이름은 Philp Peters예요.

W: 만나서 반갑습니다, 선생님. 그러면, 어… 제가 이곳에서 무엇을 하면 될까요?

M: 기본적으로는 주로 단순한 사무 작업을 하게 될 거예요.

W: 그러면 타이핑을 하고 서류들을 정리하게 될까요?

M: 네, 학생이 하게 될 일들 중 일부이죠. 다른 일들도 있고요.

W: 예를 들면요?

M: 흠… 종종 학생들이 질문을 하러 사무실을 방문하죠. 그런 질문에 답변해야 할 거예요. 대부분은 쉽게 답할 수 있는 쉬운 질문들이죠.

W: 어떤 종류의 쉬운 질문인가요?

M: 예를 들면 교수님의 사무실이 어디인지 물어볼 수도 있을 거예요.

W: 그건 처리할 수 있어요.

M: 물론 그렇겠죠. 또한 사무실 근무 시간에 관한 질문도 받게 될 거예요. 그리고 때로는 교수님을 도와야 하는 경우도 있을 수 있어요. 복사를 하는 것 등의 일을 해야 할 수도 있죠.

W: 이번 일은 재미있을 것 같군요.

M: 대부분의 학생 직원들이 일을 좋아해요. 최선을 다하고 도움을 청하는 것을 꺼리지 마세요. 두 주 후에는 학생이 도움을 받지 않고서도 대부분의 일을 해낼 수 있을 거예요.

W: 좋아요. 정말로 이번 일이 기대되네요.

[4-6]

Script 🎧 05-20

W1 Professor: We are going to review for the exam on chapter five tomorrow. Turn to page 107 and look at the review questions. Question number one: List the original thirteen colonies in order of the year in which they were established. Who can answer that?

W2 Student: I think I can name them but not in the order when they were established.

W1: **Try. You have nothing to lose.**

W2: I'm not one-hundred percent sure, but here we go. Virginia, Massachusetts, New Hampshire, Maryland, Connecticut, Rhode Island, Delaware, North Carolina, South Carolina, New Jersey, New York, Pennsylvania, and Georgia. Did I get it right?

W1: Indeed! Question number two: Who founded Virginia, and when was it founded?

W2: Virginia was founded by the London Company in 1607.

W1: Another correct answer. When was Massachusetts founded, and what was the motivation behind it? John, can you answer this question?

M1 Student: Sure. Massachusetts was founded in 1620. The motivation was to find refuge in America where the colonists could create a home for themselves. Oh, and they came over on the *Mayflower*.

W1: Nicely done. Name the New England colonies.

W2: New Hampshire, Rhode Island, Connecticut, and Massachusetts.

W1: Excellent. Which colony separated from Virginia?

W2: Carolina.

W1: Right. Carolina then divided into North and South Carolina. Which colony was founded as New Netherlands by the Dutch West India Company and seized by the English in June 1664. Justin, can you answer this?

M2 Student: Let me think. That's a tough one.

W1: You can do this, Justin . . . Come on . . . Give me the answer.

M2: Yes, I can do this. Give me a second. Is it New York?

W1: Bingo! Do you want to answer the next question?

M2: Go ahead.

W1: Which colony was chartered by King Charles II in 1663?

M2: You know I'm not good with names. That would be Rhode Island.

W1: Another correct answer. I'll stop picking on you. It seems like you all are ready for the exam tomorrow.

해석

W1 Professor: 내일 5장 시험을 위한 복습을 할 거예요. 107페이지 펴서 복습 문제를 보세요. 1번 문제, 최초 13개의 식민지를 설립된 연대순으로 나열하세요. 누가 대답해 볼까요?

W2 Student: 이름은 말할 수 있는데 설립된 순서는 잘 모르겠어요.

W1: 대답해 봐요. 손해 볼 건 없잖아요.

W2: 100% 확실하지는 않지만 해 볼게요. 버지니아, 매사추세츠, 뉴햄프셔, 메릴랜드, 코네티컷, 로드아일랜드, 델라웨어, 노스캐롤라이나, 사우스캐롤라이나, 뉴저지, 뉴욕, 펜실베이니아, 그리고 조지아입니다. 맞게 대답을 했나요?

W1: 잘했어요! 2번 문제, 버지니아를 세운 사람은 누구이며 언제 세워졌을까요?

W2: 버지니아는 1607년에 런던 회사에 의해 세워졌습니다.

W1: 또 정답이군요. 매사추세츠는 언제 세워졌고 그 목적은 무엇이었을까요? John, 이 질문에 답할 수 있겠어요?

M1 Student: 물론이죠. 매사추세츠는 1620년에 세워졌어요. 목적은 아메리카에서 식민지 주민들이 가정을 꾸릴 수 있는 안전한 장소를 마련하기 위해서였죠. 오, 그리고 이들은 *메이플라워*호를 타고 넘어 왔어요.

W1: 잘 대답했어요. 뉴잉글랜드 식민지의 이름을 말해 보세요.

W2: 뉴햄프셔, 로드아일랜드, 코네티컷, 그리고 매사추세츠입니다.

W1: 훌륭하군요. 어떤 주가 버지니아에서 떨어져 나왔나요?

W2: 캐롤라이나입니다.

W1: 맞아요. 그런 다음 캐롤라이나는 노스캐롤라이나와 사우스캐롤라이나로 분리됐죠. 네덜란드 서인도 회사에 의해 뉴네덜란드로 세워지고 1664년 6월에 영국이 차지했던 주는 어디일까요? Justin, 이 질문에는 학생이 대답해 볼까요?

M2 Student: 생각해 볼게요. 어려운 문제군요.

W1: Justin, 할 수 있어요… 자… 답을 말해 보세요.

M2: 네, 대답해 볼게요. 잠시만요. 뉴욕인가요?

W1: 빙고! 다음 질문에도 대답해 볼래요?

M2: 그럴게요.

W1: 1663년 찰스 2세에 의해 승인을 받은 주는 어디일까요?

M2: 아시다시피 제가 이름을 잘못 외우는 편인데요. 로드아일랜드인 것 같아요.

W1: 또 정답이네요. 질문은 그만하죠. 여러분 모두 내일 시험에 대한 준비가 잘 되어 있는 것 같군요.

Vocabulary Check-Up ————————— p.133

A

1 Ⓙ	2 Ⓔ	3 Ⓐ	4 Ⓜ	5 Ⓑ
6 Ⓗ	7 Ⓒ	8 Ⓞ	9 Ⓛ	10 Ⓓ
11 Ⓝ	12 Ⓖ	13 Ⓕ	14 Ⓘ	15 Ⓚ

B

1 Ⓑ	2 Ⓓ	3 Ⓐ	4 Ⓔ	5 Ⓒ

PART III Connecting Information

UNIT 06 Understanding Organization

Skill & Tip p.138

Skill Practice

1 Therefore
2 because
3 For example
4 On the contrary
5 the first thing

B

W Professor: Okay, class. Let's turn to chapter four. Chapter four is on organic chemistry.

M Student: Is it different from what we have dealt with so far?

W: Sure. There is a huge difference. Remember that organic means "coming from vitality." Let's start with carbon-carbon bonding.

C

W Professor: Now I would like to tell you the origin of waves. Most waves are formed as a result of wind passing over water. Wind speed and direction help determine the sizes of waves. Steady winds blowing over water for a long period produce larger waves. Furthermore, waves can be formed by moving something through the water, such as a boat or by underwater earthquakes that can create very large, long waves called tsunamis. These can reach heights of up to 200 feet.

Basic Drill p.140

Drill 1 Ⓒ

Script 🎧 06-05

M Student: Hello. I lost my ID card. What do I do to replace it?

W Registrar's Office Employee: Fill out your name and social security number on this form and stand behind that line. I will take your picture here.

M: I am ready.

W: Okay. You are all set. I will print your new ID in about a minute.

M: Great. Thank you.

W: You'll have to pay a fee of ten dollars.

M: That's not a problem at all.

해석

M Student: 안녕하세요. 제가 학생증을 잃어버렸어요. 재발급 받으려면 어떻게 해야 하나요?

W Registrar's Office Employee: 이 신청서에 이름과 사회 보장 번호를 쓰시고 선 뒤에 서 주세요. 여기에서 제가 사진을 찍어 드릴게요.

M: 준비 됐어요.

W: 좋아요. 끝났습니다. 약 1분 후에 새 학생증이 나올 거예요.

M: 잘 되었군요. 감사합니다.

W: 10달러의 요금을 내셔야 해요.

M: 물론 그럴게요.

Drill 2 Ⓓ

Script 🎧 06-06

W Student: Hello. My laptop computer died on me. Can you fix it?

M Computer Lab Assistant: Let me take a look. When did this happen?

W: This morning while I was working on my homework. I didn't even get to save it.

M: Oh . . . That's not good. Let me see if I can recover your file.

W: Do you know why it crashed?

M: It looks like the hard drive just gave up. But your file has been stored in the backup.

W: Oh, thank you so much. You have saved my day!

해석

W Student: 안녕하세요. 제 노트북 컴퓨터가 멈춰버렸어요. 고칠 수 있으신가요?

M Computer Lab Assistant: 한번 볼게요. 언제 이런 일이 일어났죠?

W: 오늘 아침에 숙제를 하고 있을 때였어요. 심지어 저장도 할 수 없었죠.

M: 오… 안됐군요. 파일을 복구할 수 있는지 볼게요.

W: 왜 고장이 났는지 아시나요?

M: 하드 드라이브가 멈춰버린 것 같아요. 하지만 파일은 백업 파일에 저장되어 있군요.

W: 오, 정말 고맙습니다. 덕분에 살았어요!

Drill 3 Ⓑ

W Professor: An earthquake happens when two adjacent blocks of earth suddenly move. The surface of the movement is called the fault or fault plane. There are several enormous faults in the state of California alone. The hypocenter, the location where the earthquake starts, sits below the Earth's surface whereas the epicenter sits on the Earth's surface directly above the hypocenter.

해석

W Professor: 인접해 있는 지구의 두 판이 갑자기 움직이면 지진이 발생합니다. 이동면을 단층 또는 단층면이라고 부르죠. 캘리포니아주에서만 여러 개의 거대한 단층이 존재합니다. 지진이 시작되는 지점인 진원은 지표면 아래에 있는 반면, 진앙은 진원 바로 위의 지표면에 있어요.

Drill 4 Ⓓ

Script 🎧 06-08

M Professor: The genetic information of a higher organism is contained in large molecules called chromosomes. These chromosomes are a package of a very long, continuous, double helix DNA. One strand of the helix is a long chain of molecules called nucleotides, and the other helix has the pairing nucleotides of the opposite helix. There are four types of nucleotides. Each nucleotide has only one possible match.

해석

M Professor: 고등 생물의 유전적 정보는 염색체라는 커다란 분자 안에 들어 있습니다. 이 염색체는 매우 길고 연속적으로 이어져 있는 이중 나선 구조의 DNA로 이루어져 있어요. 나선 구조의 한 가닥은 뉴클레오타이드라고 불리는 분자들로 길게 연결되어 있는데, 다른 한 가닥에는 반대편 나선과 짝을 이루는 뉴클레오타이드들이 있습니다. 네 종류의 뉴클레오타이드가 존재해요. 각각의 뉴클레오타이드는 단 하나의 짝하고만 어울릴 수 있습니다.

Exercises with Short Conversations & Lectures

Exercise 1 1 Ⓑ 2 Ⓐ p.142

Script 🎧 06-09

M Student: Professor Campbell, I'm trying to decide if I should attend summer school or not.

W Professor: Do you need to make up some extra credits?

M: No, I don't. But I have a summer job on campus. So I thought I might take a class or two as well.

W: Hmm . . . In that case, why don't you take an elective? Did you know Professor Morrisson is teaching a class this summer?

M: He's really popular, isn't he? I tried to get in his English literature class last year, but it was full.

W: That's right. He's teaching a course on English literature about King Arthur. You might try registering for it.

M: That's a great idea. I think I'll do that.

해석

M Student: Campbell 교수님, 제가 여름 학기 수업을 들어야 하는지 듣지 말아야하는지에 대해 결정을 내리려고 해요.

W Professor: 추가로 학점을 따야 하나요?

M: 아니요, 그건 아니에요. 하지만 여름에 교내에서 아르바이트를 하게 되었어요. 그래서 수업 한두 개를 들 수도 있겠다고 생각했죠.

W: 흠… 그런 경우라면 선택 과목을 듣는 것이 어떨까요? Morrison 교수님께서 이번 여름에 수업을 맡으실 것이라는 점을 알고 있었나요?

M: 그분은 정말로 인기가 많으시죠, 그렇지 않아요? 작년에 그분의 영문학 수업을 들으려고 했는데, 수업이 꽉 찼어요.

W: 맞아요. 그분께서는 아서왕에 관한 영문학 수업을 맡으실 거예요. 그 수업에 등록하면 될 것 같아요.

M: 좋은 아이디어로군요. 그렇게 할게요.

Exercise 2 1 Ⓒ 2 Ⓓ p.143

Script 🎧 06-10

W Student: Professor Robinson, I have a couple of questions about the exam.

M Professor: Sure, Penelope. What do you want to know?

W: Um . . . What exactly do I need to study for the test?

M: Just study all of the pages I assigned in the textbook. Be sure to read your notes as well.

W: What about the lecture we just had today? Will that be on the test?

M: You should definitely know about the events that happened in the Revolution of 1848.

W: Ah, okay. I wasn't sure about that.

M: Study those things, and I'm sure you'll do quite well.

해석

W Student: Robinson 교수님, 시험에 관해서 두어 개의 질문이 있어요.

M Professor: 그래요, Penelope. 무엇이 알고 싶나요?

W: 음… 시험에 대비해서 정확히 무엇을 공부해야 하나요?

M: 교재에서 제가 지정한 모든 페이지를 공부하세요. 잊지 말고 필기한 것들도 읽어 보고요.

W: 오늘 들은 강의는 어떤가요? 그 내용도 시험에 나오나요?

M: 1848년 혁명에서 일어났던 사건들은 반드시 알고 있어야 해요.

W: 아, 그렇군요. 그 점이 확실하지가 않았거든요.

M: 그 부분도 공부해 두면 분명 좋은 성적을 받게 될 거예요.

Exercise 3 1 Ⓑ 2 Ⓒ p.144

Script 🎧 06-11

> **W Professor**: Bacteria are a <u>major group</u> of living organisms. The term "bacteria" is <u>applied</u> to such a wide variety of single-cell <u>organisms</u> that it is difficult to define. However, bacteria have many <u>characteristics</u> that set them apart from other organisms. Bacteria are found nearly <u>everywhere</u> in soil, water, and other organisms with symbiotic relationships. Most are <u>tiny</u>, being only about 0.5 to 5.0 μm in <u>length</u>. They usually have cell walls like <u>plants</u> and fungus, but bacteria walls are made of <u>protein</u>. On the other hand, plants have fiber-based cell walls, and fungus has cell walls <u>similar to</u> insects' bodies. Many bacteria <u>reproduce</u> by simply dividing; thus, their colonies <u>multiply</u> explosively under the right <u>conditions</u>.

해석

W Professor: 박테리아는 주요한 생물 중 하나입니다. "박테리아"라는 용어는 다양한 종류의 단세포 동물에 적용되기 때문에 정의를 내리기가 어려워요. 하지만 박테리아는 다른 생물들과는 구별되는 여러 가지 특징을 지니고 있습니다. 박테리아는 토양, 물, 그리고 공생 관계에 있는 다른 생물의 거의 모든 곳에서 찾아볼 수 있어요. 대부분은 크기가 매우 작아서 길이가 0.5에서 5.0μm 정도에 불과합니다. 이들은 보통 식물이나 균류처럼 세포벽을 가지고 있지만 박테리아의 세포벽은 단백질로 이루어져 있어요. 반면에 식물은 섬유질로 된 세포벽을 가지고 있고, 균류의 세포벽은 곤충의 신체와 비슷하죠. 많은 박테리아는 단순히 분열해서 번식하기 때문에 적절한 조건 하에서는 박테리아 무리가 폭발적으로 증가하게 됩니다.

Exercise 4 1 Ⓒ 2 Ⓒ p.145

Script 🎧 06-12

> **W Professor**: Submarine volcanoes are <u>rather common</u> on the ocean floor. In <u>shallow</u> water, some produce the same <u>effects</u> as land volcanoes. However, many will not show any <u>signs</u> above water due to their <u>depth</u>. Submarine volcanoes produce <u>different</u> lava rocks than land volcanoes. One type of rock is pillar rock. These pillars can be so <u>steep</u> that they could become islands. One <u>famous</u> example is Hawaii. Lava can also <u>form</u> rocks called pillow lava. These rocks are called pillow lava because they <u>look like</u> round blobs or pillows. They are <u>formed</u> as hot lava oozes out of a solidified lava crust. These pillow types are the <u>most common</u> type of lava rocks.

해석

W Professor: 해저 화산은 해저에서 다소 흔한 편이에요. 얕은 수역에 있는 해저 화산들은 육지의 화산과 동일한 영향을 끼칩니다. 하지만 많은 해저 화산들의 경우, 그 깊이 때문에 수면 위로는 어떠한 징후도 나타나지 않죠. 해저 화산에서는 육지의 화산과 다른 화산암이 만들어집니다. 그러한 화산암 중 하나가 암석 기둥이에요. 이 기둥들의 경사가 너무 가파르면 섬이 형성될 수도 있습니다.

한 가지 유명한 예가 하와이죠. 또한 용암으로 인해 베개 용암이라고 불리는 암석이 만들어질 수도 있어요. 이러한 암석들은 동그란 방울 모양이나 베개 모양을 나타내기 때문에 베개 용암이라고 불립니다. 이들은 용암의 굳은 용암 껍질로부터 뜨거운 용암이 스며 나올 때 형성되죠. 이러한 베개 유형의 암석이 화산암 중에서 가장 흔한 유형이에요.

Exercises with Mid-Length Conversations & Lectures

Exercise 1 1 Ⓐ 2 Ⓓ p.146

Script 🎧 06-13

> **W Professor**: What are you <u>planning</u> to do for your <u>class project</u>, Jason?
>
> **M Student**: I'm not really sure, Professor Campbell. That's <u>why</u> I came here to see you.
>
> **W**: Well, tell me something . . . What about this class <u>interests</u> you?
>
> **M**: Let me think for a moment . . . Hmm . . . I really <u>enjoyed</u> the lectures you gave on <u>marine creatures</u>. The talk you gave about <u>pond ecosystems</u> was particularly interesting.
>
> **W**: Okay. Perhaps you could do some kind of experiment <u>related to</u> one of those topics.
>
> **M**: That <u>sounds</u> great. But, uh, my problem is . . . I just don't know <u>what kinds</u> of experiments to do. I mean, uh, I have <u>never taken</u> a biology class before. So I'm a bit <u>lost</u>.
>
> **W**: Ah, I <u>understand</u> your problem now. Here, uh, take this <u>folder</u>.
>
> **M**: What is it?
>
> **W**: It has <u>descriptions</u> of <u>various projects</u> that students have done for this class. It <u>goes back</u> about ten years.
>
> **M**: Wow. I should be able to get some <u>good ideas</u> by reading everything then.
>
> **W**: That's right. Why don't you <u>take</u> the folder with you and read the <u>contents</u> tonight? Then, come back tomorrow, and we can <u>figure out</u> what you can do.
>
> **M**: I really appreciate your <u>assistance</u>. I'll see you tomorrow around three.

해석

W Professor: 수업 프로젝트로 어떤 것을 할 계획인가요, Jason?

M Student: 사실 잘 모르겠어요, Campbell 교수님. 제가 교수님을 뵈러 여기에 온 것도 바로 그 때문이에요.

W: 음, 이야기해 보세요… 이번 수업의 어떤 부분에서 흥미를 느끼나요?

M: 잠깐 생각 좀 해 볼게요… 흠… 해양 생물에 관한 교수님의 강의가 정말로 재미있었어요. 연못 생태계에 관한 내용이 특히 흥미로웠죠.

W: 좋아요. 아마도 그러한 주제 중 하나와 관련이 있는 실험을 하면 될 것 같군요.

M: 좋은 생각이에요. 하지만, 어, 제 문제는⋯ 제거 어떤 실험을 해야 할지 모르겠어요. 제 말은, 어, 저는 전에 생물학 수업을 들어본 적이 없거든요. 그래서 어떻게 해야 할지 모르겠어요.

W: 아, 이제 문제가 이해가 가네요. 자, 어, 이 폴더를 받으세요.

M: 이것이 무엇인가요?

W: 이 수업에서 학생들이 했던 다양한 프로젝트가 여기에 설명되어 있어요. 약 10년 동안의 기록이죠.

M: 와. 그럼 전부 읽어보면 좋은 아이디어가 떠오를 수도 있겠군요.

W: 맞아요. 폴더를 가지고 가서 오늘밤에 그 내용들을 읽어보는 것이 어떨까요? 그런 다음 내일 다시 오면 학생이 무엇을 할 수 있을지 알 수 있을 거예요.

M: 도와 주셔서 정말로 고맙습니다. 내일 3시쯤 뵙겠습니다.

📝 Summary Note B

The student visits the professor to talk about a class project. The professor asks what lectures interested him. He enjoyed the ones on marine creatures and pond ecosystems. The student says he does not know what kind of experiment to do since he has never taken a biology class. The professor gives him a folder with descriptions of past projects. She tells the student to read the contents and to come back later to discuss them.

Exercise 2 1 Ⓑ 2 Ⓒ p.148

Script 🎧 06-14

M Student: Hi. I would like to find out how to be a tutor here. Can you tell me what the requirements are?

W Student Services Office Employee: Sure. You can only tutor classes you have already taken, and you must have passed them with an A- or better. Which classes are you interested in tutoring?

M: I would like to tutor Biology 1A, Calculus 1B, and Organic Chemistry 1A. I passed all these classes with A's.

W: Okay. We need tutors for those classes. We also offer workshops in science and study sessions. Would you be interested in leading these workshops, too?

M: Can you give me more information on them?

W: These workshops teach students effective ways to study and provide reviews on certain science classes. You, as a leader, will be given topics and materials before the workshop.

M: Will leaders meet together to study the material before the workshops?

W: Yes. You will be fully prepared before the workshop.

M: In that case, I will give it a try.

W: Great! Here is an application form.

해석

M Student: 안녕하세요. 어떻게 개인 지도 교사가 될 수 있는지 알고 싶어서

왔는데요. 자격 조건이 어떻게 되는지 말씀해 주실 수 있나요?

W Student Services Office Employee: 그럼요. 이미 들은 적이 있는 수업에 대해서만 개인 지도가 가능하고, 그 수업을 A- 이상의 성적으로 통과했어야 해요. 어떤 과목을 지도하고자 하나요?

M: 생물학1A, 미적분1B, 그리고 유기 화학1A에 대한 개인 지도를 하고 싶어요. 이 수업들은 모두 A로 통과했죠.

W: 좋아요. 그 수업들에 대해서는 개인 지도 교사가 필요해요. 저희는 또한 과학 워크숍과 스터디 모임도 제공하고 있어요. 워크숍을 이끄는 것에도 관심이 있나요?

M: 좀 더 자세히 말씀해 주시겠어요?

W: 이 워크숍들은 학생들에게 효율적인 공부 방법을 가르쳐 주고 특정 과학 과목에 대한 복습을 할 수 있도록 해 주죠. 리더가 되면 워크숍 전에 주제와 자료를 받게 될 거예요.

M: 리더들이 워크숍 전에 미리 만나서 자료에 대해 공부해야 하나요?

W: 네. 워크숍 전에 완벽한 준비가 되어 있어야 할 거예요.

M: 그러면 한번 해 볼게요.

W: 잘 되었군요! 여기 신청서가 있어요.

📝 Summary Note B

A student goes to the school student services office to register as a tutor. He talks to a counselor to find out the requirements to join. He wants to tutor three classes that he passed with A's. The employee asks the student if he would like to lead the workshops that teach students how to study efficiently and also review science classes. After learning that the center will provide training, the student decides to tutor and to lead the workshops.

Exercise 3 1 Ⓒ 2 Ⓐ, Ⓒ p.150

Script 🎧 06-15

M Professor: We will start on opera today. The first opera we will study is *La Traviata*. The opera was written by Verdi and was based on a novel by Dumas called *La Dame Aux Camélias*. Alfredo, the main character, falls in love with a famous Paris courtesan named Violetta. Their whirlwind romance is not welcomed by Alfredo's father. The romance ends, and Violetta becomes terribly ill, which leads to her tragic death. Both Verdi and Dumas lived in the same era and shared similar backgrounds. Dumas wrote the novel based on his own affair with a notorious courtesan. Verdi lived with an opera singer who had a history like Violetta. Both Verdi and Dumas had relationships with women who lived fast and died young. Although the story does not seem scandalous in our times, it was a socially controversial and daring topic back then. These men experienced the dark, troublesome side of their era and expressed it in art.

M Professor: 오늘은 오페라로 시작해 보죠. 우리가 공부할 첫 번째 오페라는 *라트라비아타*입니다. 이 오페라는 베르디가 쓴 것으로, 뒤마가 쓴 *춘희*라는 소설에 기초해 있습니다. 주인공인 알프레도는 파리의 유명한 매춘부인 비올레타와 사랑에 빠집니다. 그들의 폭풍 같은 로맨스를 알프레도의 아버지는 못마땅해하죠. 로맨스가 끝나고 비올레타는 큰 병을 앓게 되어 비극적인 죽음을 맞이합니다. 베르디와 뒤마 모두 동시대에 살았고 비슷한 배경을 가지고 있었어요. 뒤마는 악명 높은 매춘부와의 연애 경험에 기초해서 소설을 썼죠. 베르디는 비올레타와 같은 인생사를 살아 온 오페라 가수와 함께 지냈고요. 베르디와 뒤마 모두 짧은 생을 살고 이른 나이에 사망한 여인들과 관계가 있었습니다. 요즘에는 이런 이야기가 스캔들로 보이지 않지만 당시에는 사회적인 논란의 대상이자 대담한 주제였어요. 이들은 자신의 시대의 암울하고 문제가 되는 측면을 경험하고 그것을 예술로 표현했습니다.

📝 Summary Note ⓑ

The opera *La Traviata* was written by Verdi and was based on a novel by Dumas. The main character, Violetta, is a Paris courtesan that falls in love with a man named Alfredo. However, their romance meets a heartbreaking ending. Verdi and Dumas had similar relationships with women just like in the novel and the opera they wrote, respectively. Even though this story was based on fairly common practices, publicly writing about it was a bold thing to do. They used art to express social issues.

Exercise 4   1 ⓐ   2 ⓑ   p.152

Script 🎧 06-16

> **W Professor**: There was an amazing animal friendship story a few years ago. You all remember the tsunami disaster in Indonesia, right? Well, the same tsunami stranded a group of hippos near Kenya. Unfortunately, only a baby hippo survived, and people rescued the hippo.
>
> **M Student**: What happened to the hippo after it was rescued?
>
> **W**: It was brought to an animal park. They named him Owen for the person who rescued him.
>
> **M**: How did Owen handle his new home?
>
> **W**: Well, he was really scared, obviously. But when he saw a giant tortoise named Mzee, Owen ran behind him and hid there. Mzee was really surprised, but he accepted the situation and became friends with Owen. Their friendship has grown ever since, and now they eat, sleep, and play together all the time. Mzee, the tortoise, is more than 140 years old, and he was larger than Owen in the beginning.
>
> **M**: What a remarkable story of friendship.

W Professor: 몇 년 전 동물들의 놀라운 우정에 관한 일이 있었습니다. 여러분 모두 인도네시아에서 일어났던 재해인 쓰나미를 기억할 거예요, 그렇죠? 음,

그 쓰나미 때문에 케냐 근처에서 한 하마 무리가 고립되었습니다. 안타깝게도 새끼 하마 한 마리만 살아남았는데, 사람들이 이 하마를 구조했어요.

M Student: 구조된 다음에 하마에게 어떤 일이 일어났나요?

W: 동물원으로 가게 되었어요. 하마를 구조한 사람의 이름을 따서 오웬이라는 이름이 붙여졌고요.

M: 오웬이 새 보금자리에 어떻게 반응했나요?

W: 음, 정말로 두려워하는 모습이 명백했어요. 하지만 음지라는 이름의 코끼리 거북을 보자 그 뒤로 가서 몸을 숨겼죠. 음지는 크게 놀랐지만, 상황을 인지하고 오웬과 친구가 되었습니다. 그 이후로는 둘의 우정이 깊어져서 지금은 항상 둘이 함께 식사를 하고, 잠도 자고, 그리고 놀기도 하죠. 음지의 나이는 140살이 넘는데, 처음에는 오웬보다 덩치도 컸어요.

M: 우정에 관한 정말 인상적인 이야기군요.

📝 Summary Note ⓑ

When a tsunami hit Kenya, a baby hippo lost his family and was rescued by people. The hippo was brought to an animal park, and the park named him Owen. Terrified, Owen ran to a giant tortoise named Mzee for safety. Owen's action caught Mzee by surprise, but he soon befriended Owen. They spend most of their time together now. They have overcome the age and species difference and have developed an incredible friendship.

Integrated Listening & Speaking   p.154

A

Script 🎧 06-17

> **M Professor**: The opera we are studying today is *La Traviata*. The opera was written by Verdi. It was based on a novel written by Dumas called *La Dame Aux Camélias*. Alfredo, the main character, falls in love with a famous Paris courtesan named Violetta. However, their romance is not welcomed by Alfredo's father. The romance ends, and Violetta becomes terribly ill. This results in her tragic death. Both Verdi and Dumas lived in the same era and shared similar backgrounds. Dumas wrote the novel based on his own affair with a notorious courtesan. Verdi lived with an opera singer who had a history similar to that of Violetta. Both Verdi and Dumas had relationships with women who lived fast and died young. Although the story does not seem scandalous in modern times, it was a socially controversial and daring topic in the past. These men experienced the dark, troublesome side of their era and expressed it in art.

1   a. Violetta is a courtesan who falls in love with a social elite named Alfredo.

   b. The main characters are Violetta and Alfredo, who fall in love with each other despite their difference in status.

2   a. Verdi wrote the opera *La Traviata* based on a novel by Dumas.

b. The composer Verdi based his opera *La Traviata* on Dumas's novel.

3 a. They both had relationships with women like Violetta, and they daringly wrote about them.

b. They shared similar experiences with women with shady pasts, and they chose to write about this controversial topic.

B

Script 🎧 06-18

W Professor: There was an amazing animal friendship story that happened a few years ago. Well, the same tsunami stranded a group of hippos near Kenya. Unfortunately, of that group, only a baby hippo survived. Some people managed to rescue that hippo. After that, it was brought to an animal park. The hippo was named Owen for the person who rescued him. Owen was really scared when he arrived at the park. But when he saw a giant tortoise named Mzee, Owen ran behind him and hid there. Mzee was really surprised, but he accepted the situation. The two animals then became friends. Their friendship has grown ever since. Nowadays, they eat, sleep, and play together all the time. Mzee, the tortoise, is more than 130 years old, and he was larger than Owen in the beginning.

1 a. When the baby hippo was stranded, people brought the hippo to the park where the tortoise lived.

b. The giant tortoise lived in the park where the baby hippo came after getting stranded.

2 a. The baby hippo is named Owen, and the giant tortoise is named Mzee.

b. The hippo and the tortoise are called Owen and Mzee, respectively.

3 a. Owen and Mzee became friends, and they are inseparable now.

b. Their relationship blossomed into an inseparable friendship.

Mini TOEFL iBT Practice Test

p.156

1 Ⓐ   2 Ⓓ   3 Ⓑ   4 Ⓑ   5 Ⓐ
6 Ⓒ

[1-3]

Script 🎧 06-19

W Professor: George, are you still looking for an internship?

M Student: Yes, ma'am. I have applied for a few of them, and I got a couple of interviews.

W: And . . . ?

M: And nobody called me back. I guess the companies offered the positions to other students.

W: I'm sorry to hear that. You are interested in interning at a bank, right?

M: That's correct. I'd love to go into banking after I graduate.

W: Well, I may have some good news for you. One of my old students called me up last night. He happens to work at a local bank. His bank is starting an internship program.

M: Really? What bank is it?

W: The name is Ravenwood Bank. Have you heard of it?

M: Oh, sure. There's a branch near my home.

W: That's good to know. Anyway, he's a school alumnus, so he prefers to take on student interns from our school. Are you interested?

M: For sure.

W: Okay, uh, I'll email you a link to the application form. I'll also put in a good word for you. You're one of my best students, so I hope you can get a position there.

M: Thanks so much, Professor. I appreciate it.

W: Try to complete the application today or tomorrow. He indicated that he wants to make a quick decision.

해석

W Professor: George, 아직도 인턴쉽 자리를 찾고 있나요?

M Student: 네, 교수님. 몇 군데 지원을 해서 두 차례 면접을 보았어요.

W: 그리고는…?

M: 그리고는 답이 없었어요. 기업들이 다른 학생들에게 일자리를 준 것 같아요.

W: 그런 말을 들으니 유감이네요. 은행에서 인턴으로 근무하는 것에 관심이 있죠, 그렇죠?

M: 맞아요. 졸업한 후 은행에 취직하고 싶거든요.

W: 음, 학생에게 좋은 소식이 있는 것 같네요. 제 예전 학생들 중 한 명이 어젯밤에 전화를 했어요. 공교롭게도 인근 은행에서 근무를 하더군요. 그 은행에서 인턴쉽 프로그램이 시작될 거예요.

M: 정말인가요? 어느 은행이죠?

W: 이름이 Ravenwood 은행이에요. 들어본 적이 있나요?

M: 오, 물론이죠. 저희 집에서 가까운 곳에 지점이 있어요.

W: 다행이네요. 어쨌든, 그가 학교 동문이기 때문에 우리 학교 출신의 인턴 사원을 고용하고 싶어해요. 관심이 있나요?

M: 그럼요.

W: 다행이군요. 지원서로 연결되는 링크를 이메일로 보내 줄게요. 학생을 추천하는 말도 전할 것이고요. 학생이 가장 우수한 학생 중 한 명이기 때문에 그곳에서 일자리를 얻기를 바랄게요.

M: 정말 고맙습니다. 교수님. 감사해요.

W: 오늘이나 내일 지원서 작성을 완료하세요. 그가 빨리 결정을 내리고 싶다는 점을 내비쳤거든요.

W Professor: Animals and plants all adapt to their environment for survival. We will talk about how desert animals and plants adapt to their harsh environment. First of all, what are the conditions they have to endure?

M1 Student: Extreme heat and lack of water.

W: That's right. They need to fight these conditions that are brutal to other animals and plants. There are three ways to beat the lack of water: store water, conserve water, and tolerate dehydration. Animals store water in fat, and plants store water in roots, stems, and leaves. Does anyone know an example?

M2 Student: Camels' humps.

W: Yes, camels store fat on their backs that indirectly stores water. Some animals conserve water by minimizing water loss through skin, producing dry or highly concentrated urine and feces, and reducing water loss during breathing. Kangaroo rats hardly drink any water during their lifetimes because their water-efficient bodies produce enough water. The third way is to tolerate dehydration.

M1: Do you mean they actually endure the loss of water?

W: Exactly. Many desert plants like cacti and some animals like desert toads can bear a huge water loss. Now, what about that awful heat? How do they beat the heat? Well, one way is to avoid the sun all together. Any ideas how they do this?

M2: Many animals sleep during the day and become active at night.

W: Right. That's called nocturnal behavior. Very good. Other ways include creating shade, positioning leaves to reduce sun exposure, insulation, and having shiny surfaces. Another way is to get rid of body heat. Some do that by evaporation, having long body parts, or having small bodies to increase their surface area.

M1: Is that why some desert rabbits have huge ears?

W: Precisely. Those ears have lots of blood vessels to let the body heat out. The third method is simply to tolerate the heat. Some animals' body temperatures can rise much higher than human. Nature gets pretty creative.

해석

W Professor: 동물과 식물 모두 생존을 위해 환경에 적응합니다. 사막의 동물과 식물들이 가혹한 환경에 적응하는 방법에 대해 논의해 보도록 하죠. 우선, 그들이 견뎌야 하는 조건은 무엇일까요?

M1 Student: 극심한 더위와 물 부족입니다.

W: 맞아요. 다른 동물과 식물들한테는 혹독한 그런 조건들에 맞서야 하죠. 물 부족을 극복할 수 있는 세 가지 방법이 있습니다. 물을 저장하고, 물을 보존하고, 그리고 탈수를 견디는 것이에요. 동물은 지방에, 그리고 식물은 뿌리, 줄기, 그리고 잎에 물을 저장합니다. 예를 들어볼 사람이 있나요?

M2 Student: 낙타의 혹입니다.

W: 네, 낙타는 등에 지방을 저장함으로써 간접적으로 물을 저장해요. 몇몇 동물들은 피부를 통한 수분 손실을 최소화함으로써, 건조하거나 대단히 진한 대소변을 배출함으로써, 그리고 호흡을 하는 동안 수분 손실을 줄임으로써 수분을 보존합니다. 캥거루쥐는 평생 동안 거의 물을 마시지 않는데, 수분 효율적인 신체에서 충분한 양의 물이 만들어지기 때문이에요. 세 번째 방법은 탈수를 견디는 것입니다.

M1: 수분 손실을 그냥 견딘다는 말씀이신가요?

W: 그래요. 선인장 같은 여러 사막 식물들과 사막두꺼비 같은 일부 동물들은 엄청난 수분 손실을 견딜 수가 있어요. 자, 그 지독한 더위는 어떨까요? 어떻게 더위에 맞설까요? 음, 한 가지 방법은 태양을 완전히 피하는 것입니다. 어떻게 그렇게 하는지 아는 사람이 있나요?

M2: 많은 동물들이 낮에 잠을 자고 밤에 활동을 해요.

W: 맞아요. 그것을 야행성이라고 하죠. 잘 맞췄어요. 다른 방법은 태양에 노출되는 것을 막기 위해 잎을 이동시켜 그늘을 만들고, 열을 차단하고, 그리고 반짝이는 표면을 지니는 것이죠. 또 다른 방법은 체열을 없애는 것이에요. 어떤 생물은 증발을 통해 그렇게 하는데, 이들의 경우 신체 일부가 기다랗거나, 또는 몸통이 작아서 표면적을 넓히게 되죠.

M1: 사막에 사는 토끼들이 거대한 귀를 가지고 있는 이유가 바로 그러한 점 때문인가요?

W: 정확히 그래요. 토끼의 귀에는 많은 혈관이 분포되어 있는데, 여기에서 체열이 밖으로 빠져 나갑니다. 세 번째 방법은 그냥 더위를 참는 것이에요. 일부 동물의 경우 체온이 사람보다 훨씬 높은 온도까지 올라갈 수 있습니다. 자연은 상당히 창의적이죠.

Vocabulary Check-Up — p.159

A 1 Ⓚ   2 Ⓜ   3 Ⓗ   4 Ⓔ   5 Ⓑ
　6 Ⓐ   7 Ⓞ   8 Ⓕ   9 Ⓙ   10 Ⓒ
　11 Ⓘ   12 Ⓓ   13 Ⓖ   14 Ⓛ   15 Ⓝ

B 1 Ⓐ   2 Ⓔ   3 Ⓑ   4 Ⓒ   5 Ⓓ

UNIT
07 **Connecting Content**

Skill & Tip ····· p.162

Skill Practice

A

W Student: Let's review for the test. How big is Saturn? Mark, can you answer?

M Student: How big? Well, its diameter is about 110,000 kilometers, and it weighs 100 times more than Earth. Actually, it is the second largest planet in size.

W: Well done. And how far from the sun is it?

M: It is 1.4 billion kilometers away from the sun, and it moves at a speed of ten kilometers per second.

B

1	joule	**6**	kilogram
2	Newton	**7**	hertz
3	hectare	**8**	meter
4	Kelvin	**9**	Pascal
5	lux	**10**	ampere

C

W Professor: The Nile River is about 6,695 kilometers, or 4,160 miles, in length and is the longest river both in Africa and in the world. The river begins in the mountains of Africa and flows north to the Mediterranean Sea. The Nile originates in Burundi, south of the equator, and flows northward through northeastern Africa. It eventually flows through Egypt and finally drains into the Mediterranean Sea. The construction of the Aswan Dam in the 1960s meant that from 1970, the annual floods were controlled. Its average discharge is 3,100,000 liters, or 680,000 gallons, per second.

Basic Drill ·········· p.164

Drill 1 ⓑ

Script 🎧 07-05

M Professor: I am a little concerned that you didn't turn in your homework today.

W Student: I'm sorry. I promise I'll make it up.

M: Is everything okay? We've been in school for four months now, and this is the first time you haven't done your homework.

W: I've been a little stressed by my parents' divorce. I'll turn this work in tomorrow. I promise.

해석

M Professor: 학생이 오늘 과제물을 제출하지 않아서 약간 걱정이 되는군요.

W Student: 죄송합니다. 반드시 제출하도록 할게요.

M: 아무 문제 없나요? 학기가 시작되고 4개월이 지났는데, 학생이 과제물을 제출하지 않은 건 이번이 처음이잖아요.

W: 부모님 이혼 때문에 약간 스트레스를 받고 있어요. 이번 과제는 내일까지 제출할게요. 약속드려요.

Drill 2 Sedimentary Rocks: ①, ④ Metamorphic Rocks: ②, ③

Script 🎧 07-06

M Student: I get confused between sedimentary rocks and metamorphic rocks at times.

W Professor: You shouldn't. Sedimentary rocks form in layers. And metamorphic rocks are those that have undergone changes from other types of rocks.

M: Ah, heat and pressure can make them do that, right?

W: Correct. Quartz, marble, and slate are examples of metamorphic rocks. Do you know any sedimentary rocks?

M: I know limestone is one. I don't know any others.

해석

M Student: 저는 때때로 퇴적암과 변성암이 헷갈려요.

W Professor: 헷갈리면 안되죠. 퇴적암은 층을 형성해요. 그리고 변성암은 다른 종류의 암석이 변해서 만들어진 암석이고요.

M: 아, 열과 압력으로 인해 그렇게 되는 것이죠, 그렇죠?

W: 맞아요. 석영, 대리석, 그리고 점판암이 변성암에 속해요. 퇴적암에 속하는 암석들도 아나요?

M: 석회암이 퇴적암인 것은 알고 있어요. 다른 건 모르겠고요.

Drill 3 Fact: ①, ④ Not a Fact: ②, ③

Script 🎧 07-07

W Professor: Another ancient civilization is the Indus Valley Civilization. It was located in the area that is now Pakistan and the northwest part of India. The majority of its ruins are found between two rivers. These rivers are the Indus River and Ghaggar-Hakra River. Scholars believe that the Indus Valley Civilization flourished from 3300 B.C. to 1700 B.C. Its ruins were first found by a British man in the early 1920s.

해석

W Professor: 또 다른 고대 문명은 인더스 강 문명입니다. 이 문명은 현재 파키스탄과 인도 북서부에 해당되는 지역에 위치해 있었죠. 대부분의 유적들은 두 개의 강 사이에서 찾아볼 수 있어요. 바로 인더스강과 각가르-하크라강입니다. 학자들은 인더스 강 문명이 기원전 3300년에서 기원전 1700년까지 번성했다고 생각해요. 이곳 유적은 1920년대 초반 한 영국인에 의해서 최초로 발견되었습니다.

Drill 4 ⓑ

Script 🎧 07-08

M Professor: Hot springs are a natural, wonder of the world. They are found worldwide. Hot springs are places where hot water comes out of the ground and forms a pool or pond. At some hot springs, the water is hot because it is heated by the Earth's inner heat. Other hot springs happen because the water is near a volcano. This water is heated because it comes in contact with molten rocks.

M Professor: 온천은 불가사의한 자연 현상입니다. 전 세계에서 찾아볼 수 있죠. 온천은 땅에서 뜨거운 물이 나와 연못이나 웅덩이를 형성하는 곳입니다. 일부 온천의 물이 뜨거운 이유는 지구 내부의 열기로 인해 물이 뜨거워지기 때문이에요. 화산 근처에 물이 있어서 온천이 생기는 경우도 있습니다. 이러한 물은 용융된 암석과 접해 있기 때문에 뜨거워지는 것이죠.

Exercises with Short Conversations & Lectures

Exercise 1 1 Ⓑ 2 Ⓓ p.166

Script 🎧 07-09

W Student: Hi, Mr. Jones. May I ask you a question?

M Campus Orchestra Conductor: Of course.

W: I just picked up the music we're playing for graduation, and I have some questions about it.

M: Okay.

W: Well, I play the violin in the orchestra, and I got the sheet music for the first violin part and the second violin part. So I'm a little confused because I can't play both parts at the same time.

M: Of course, you can't. Everyone got both parts. We'll be picking our parts during practice today.

W: Oh, okay. That makes sense. I feel kind of silly now that I've asked about it.

M: Don't worry about it. It was a valid question. Just make sure you look over both parts before practice.

W Student: 안녕하세요. Jones 선생님. 질문 하나 해도 될까요?

M Campus Orchestra Conductor: 물론이죠.

W: 방금 졸업식에서 연주할 곡을 받았는데요. 그에 대해서 몇 가지 질문이 있어요.

M: 그렇군요.

W: 음, 저는 오케스트라에서 바이올린을 연주하는데, 제1바이올린과 제2바이올린을 위한 악보를 받았어요. 양쪽 파트를 동시에 연주할 수가 없기 때문에 약간 당황스러워요.

M: 물론 그럴 수는 없죠. 모두가 두 파트를 받았어요. 오늘 연습 시간에 파트를 정할 거예요.

W: 오, 그렇군요. 이해가 가네요. 이런 질문을 하다니 제가 약간 바보 같은 기분이 드는군요.

M: 그런 생각 말아요. 마땅한 질문이었어요. 잊지 말고 연습 전에 두 파트 모두 훑어보세요.

Exercise 2 1 Ⓑ 2 Ⓑ p.167

Script 🎧 07-10

M Student: Professor Folsom, I could use some advice, please.

W Professor: Of course. What do you want to talk about?

M: I'm considering studying abroad for a year, but I don't know if I should.

W: Hmm . . . You'd get to experience a foreign culture, but study abroad programs can be a bit pricey.

M: That's true. Would it affect my major negatively?

W: I don't think so. You're an art history major. Go to Europe, and you'll be able to see many works of art in person.

M: Ah, that's a good point. But I don't speak any foreign languages.

W: You'll learn quickly if you go abroad. If you can afford it, you should try it.

M Student: Folsom 교수님, 조언을 좀 해 주셨으면 해요.

W Professor: 그래요. 무엇에 대해 이야기하고 싶나요?

M: 1년 동안 해외 유행을 할까 생각 중인데, 어떻게 해야 할지 모르겠어요.

W: 흠… 외국의 문화를 경험할 수 있겠지만, 해외 유학 프로그램에는 상당한 비용이 들 수 있어요.

M: 맞는 말씀이세요. 제 전공에 부정적인 영향을 끼치게 될까요?

W: 그렇게 생각하지는 않아요. 학생은 역사를 전공하고 있잖아요. 유럽을 가게 된다면 많은 예술 작품들을 직접 볼 수가 있을 거예요.

M: 아, 좋은 지적이군요. 하지만 저는 외국어를 전혀 하지 못하는데요.

W: 해외에 나가면 빨리 배우게 될 거예요. 여유가 되면 시도해 보세요.

Exercise 3 1 Ⓒ 2 Ⓓ p.168

Script 🎧 07-11

W Professor: All right, guys, it's almost the end of the year, and I know you're all a little restless. So I think we should talk about something interesting today. I'd like to discuss endangered animals. A species qualifies as endangered for two reasons. The first is that there are so few of them that they may become extinct. The second reason is that environmental factors may cause them to become extinct. Environmental factors include things that people do to the environment that end up killing these animals. For example, when people cut down entire forests, they cause a lot of different animals to lose their homes and to die.

W Professor: 좋아요, 여러분, 한 해가 거의 다 끝나가고 있고, 여러분 모두에

게 약간 휴식이 필요한 것으로 알고 있어요. 그래서 오늘은 흥미로운 이야기를 하고자 합니다. 멸종 위기 동물에 대해 논의해 보고 싶어요. 두 가지 이유 때문에 하나의 종이 멸종 위기종으로 분류됩니다. 첫 번째는 그 수가 너무 적어서 종이 멸종할 수 있는 경우예요. 두 번째는 환경적 요인 때문에 멸종할 수 있는 경우이죠. 환경적 요인에는 이 동물들을 결국 멸종시키게 만드는, 인간이 환경에 가하는 행위들도 포함됩니다. 예를 들어 인간이 숲 전체를 베어버리면 다양한 동물들이 보금자리를 잃고 죽게 됩니다.

Exercise 4 1 (D) 2 (A)   p.169

Script 🎧 07-12

> **M Professor**: I'm sure you have wondered why there are so few Native Americans in America. We can trace one answer to that question all the way back to Christopher Columbus. What happened was that the Native Americans had been living on this continent for centuries. Then, the Europeans, starting with Columbus, began to explore and settle in the New World. When they came over, the Europeans brought all kinds of diseases, such as smallpox. These diseases didn't affect the Europeans because they had built up immunity to them. But the Native Americans weren't immune. So these diseases ended up killing large numbers of Native Americans.

해석

M Professor: 미국에는 왜 극소수의 원주민들만이 있는지에 대해 틀림없이 궁금했던 적이 있었을 것입니다. 이 질문에 대한 한 가지 답은 크리스토퍼 콜럼버스 시대에서 찾을 수 있어요. 그 당시만 해도 원주민들이 수 세기 동안 이 대륙에서 살고 있었죠. 그런데 콜럼버스를 시작으로 유럽인들이 신세계를 개척하고 이곳에 정착하기 시작했어요. 유럽인들은 넘어 오면서 천연두와 같은 온갖 종류의 질병을 가지고 왔습니다. 이 질병들은 그에 대한 면역력을 갖춘 유럽인들에게는 영향을 미치지 않았죠. 그러나 미 원주민들은 면역력을 가지고 있지 않았어요. 그래서 이러한 질병 때문에 결국 수많은 원주민들이 목숨을 잃었습니다.

Exercises with Mid-Length Conversations & Lectures

Exercise 1 1 Anthropology Course: [1], [2]   p.170
                  International Relations Course: [3], [4]

                  2 (C)

Script 🎧 07-13

> **M Student**: I can't decide between taking an anthropology course and an international relations course next semester.
>
> **W Professor**: The anthropology course would be an elective, right?
>
> **M**: Yes. I'm sort of interested in it. The instructor will be Professor Kensley.
>
> **W**: He's an excellent lecturer. You'd probably enjoy his class.

> **M**: I wasn't aware of that.
>
> **W**: What about the international relations class?
>
> **M**: I need that class for my major. It's only offered once a year, uh, during the fall semester.
>
> **W**: I see. Who is the professor?
>
> **M**: It's Professor Chamberlain. I've taken two of her classes in the past.
>
> **W**: Then you should know her style. Which one do you think you should take?
>
> **M**: I should probably take Professor Chamberlain's class.
>
> **W**: That's a good decision. You can take the other class in summer. I know you like staying around campus each summer vacation.

해석

M Student: 다음 학기에 인류학 수업과 국제 관계학 수업 중 무엇을 택해야 할지 모르겠어요.

W Professor: 인류학 수업은 선택 과목이죠, 그렇죠?

M: 네. 그 수업에 관심이 있어서요. Kensley 교수님께서 맡으실 거예요.

W: 강의를 매우 잘하는 분이시죠. 아마 그분 수업을 좋아하게 될 거예요.

M: 그 점은 제가 몰랐네요.

W: 국제 관계학 수업은 어떤가요?

M: 전공 때문에 그 수업을 들어야 해요. 1년에 한 번만, 어, 가을 학기에만 개설이 되거든요.

W: 알겠어요. 교수님이 누구신가요?

M: Chamberlain 교수님이세요. 전에 그분 수업을 두 차례 들어보았어요.

W: 그러면 그분 스타일을 알고 있겠군요. 어떤 수업을 들어야 한다고 생각하나요?

M: 아마도 Chamberlain 교수님 수업을 들어야 할 것 같아요.

W: 좋은 선택이에요. 다른 수업은 여름에 들을 수도 있어요. 학생이 여름 방학마다 캠퍼스 근처에서 지내는 것을 좋아한다고 알고 있어요.

📝 **Summary Note** B

The student is trying to decide which class to take next semester. The anthropology class is an elective, but the lecturer is excellent. The international relations class is needed for the student's major. It's also offered just one time a year. The student says he should probably take the international relations class. The professor agrees and recommends taking the other class in summer.

Exercise 2 1 (A) 2 (B)   p.172

Script 🎧 07-14

> **M Student**: Hello, Ms. Sanderson. How are you doing today?
>
> **W Sociology Department Office Employee**: I'm all right, Keith. But what are you doing here? You're not assigned to work any hours here today.

M: Actually, I need to talk to you about my shift tomorrow.

W: What's up?

M: My biology teacher just told me I need to do a lab for the class. The only time I can do it is tomorrow morning. So . . .

W: I see. Well, you should obviously put your studies ahead of your part-time position.

M: Thanks for understanding. I appreciate that.

W: No problem.

M: Um . . . You know, Stacy Blair doesn't have anything to do tomorrow morning. If you want, I could call her and ask if she can cover my shift.

W: I didn't realize that you knew her.

M: Oh, yeah. We've been friends for a couple of years.

W: That's interesting. Well, don't worry about contacting her. I'll give her a call and ask her if she's interested in making a few extra dollars tomorrow.

M: Thanks so much, Ms. Sanderson. I'm glad that you're an understanding boss.

해석

M Student: 안녕하세요, Sanderson 선생님. 오늘 어떠신가요?

W Sociology Department Office Employee: 좋아요, Keith. 하지만 학생은 여기에서 무엇을 하고 있나요? 오늘은 이곳에서 근무하는 날이 아니잖아요.

M: 실은 내일 제 근무 시간에 대해 선생님과 이야기를 해야 해서요.

W: 무슨 일이죠?

M: 생물학 교수님께서 제가 수업에 관한 실험을 해야 한다고 말씀해 주셨어요. 제가 실험할 수 있는 시간은 내일 오전뿐이에요. 그래서…

W: 알겠어요. 음, 분명 아르바이트보다는 학업을 우선시해야 하죠.

M: 이해해 주셔서 고마워요. 감사합니다.

W: 괜찮아요.

M: 음… 아시겠지만, Stacy Blair가 내일 오전에 아무 일도 없어서요. 괜찮으시면 제가 그녀에게 전화를 걸어서 제 근무를 대신할 수 있는지 물어볼 수 있어요.

W: 학생이 그녀를 알고 있다는 점은 제가 몰랐네요.

M: 오, 그러셨군요. 저희는 2년 동안 친구로 지내왔어요.

W: 흥미롭군요. 음, 그녀와 연락하는 일은 걱정하지 마세요. 제가 그녀에게 전화를 해서 내일 추가로 몇 달러를 더 벌 생각이 있는지 물어볼게요.

M: 정말 고맙습니다, Sanderson 선생님. 제 상사가 이해심이 많은 분이라서 기쁘군요.

Summary Note B

The student visits the office to tell the woman that he cannot work his shift tomorrow. He has to do a lab, and the only time available is tomorrow morning. The woman agrees to let the student not work. The student mentions that Stacy Blair is not busy tomorrow. He states that he could call her, but the woman says that she will call Stacy and ask her to work.

Exercise 3 1 Ⓐ 2 Fact: [1], [2] Not a Fact: [3], [4] p.174

Script 🎧 07-15

W Professor: Yesterday, we started talking about how geological formations take a long time to be created. One formation is called the glacier. Does anyone know what a glacier is?

M Student: It's a lot of ice!

W: Well, kind of. It's certainly a lot of ice, but it's more than just that. A glacier is like a river of ice that moves slowly. The way a glacier moves depends on the slope of the land. A glacier moves with gravity. I need to talk about how these glaciers are formed. What happens is that snowfall covers mountainous regions. This snow never completely melts. It might thaw a little and then refreeze a bit though. So you have this thawing and refreezing, which changes the snow to granules. Then, more snow accumulates. Can anyone guess what happens to the snow that's at the bottom of this pile?

M: Wouldn't it get really firm from all the pressure?

W: Exactly. So over thousands of years, from lots and lots of pressure, these huge sheets of slow-moving ice form. That's how a glacier is made. The cool thing about these glaciers is that they leave imprints in the ground kind of like fossils. So scientists can tell what the world was like when it was covered by glaciers back during the last ice age.

해석

W Professor: 어제는 오랜 시간에 걸쳐 지질학적 지형이 형성되는 과정에 대한 이야기로 시작했어요. 지형 중 하나는 빙하라는 것입니다. 빙하가 무엇인지 아는 사람이 있나요?

M Student: 거대한 얼음이요!

W: 음, 그런 셈이죠. 분명 거대한 얼음이지만, 그 이상이에요. 빙하는 천천히 움직이는 얼음의 강이라고 할 수 있어요. 빙하가 움직이는 방식은 땅의 경사에 따라 달라집니다. 빙하는 중력 때문에 움직이죠. 이러한 빙하가 어떻게 만들어지는지에 대한 이야기를 해야 할 것 같군요. 눈이 내려서 산악 지대가 눈으로 덮입니다. 이 눈은 결코 완전히 녹지 않아요. 하지만 약간 녹았다가 다시 얼 수는 있죠. 이러한 해빙과 재결빙의 과정으로 인해 눈이 작은 알갱이들로 바뀝니다. 그런 다음 더 많은 눈이 쌓이게 되죠. 이러한 눈 더미 아래에 있는 눈에 어떤 일이 일어나는지 말해볼 사람이 있나요?

M: 큰 압력을 받아서 정말로 단단해지지 않을까요?

W: 정확해요. 그래서 수천 년에 걸쳐 엄청나고 엄청난 압력을 받아 이처럼 천천히 움직이는 거대한 얼음판이 만들어진 것이죠. 이것이 바로 빙하가 만들어지는 방식이에요. 빙하에 있어서 흥미로운 점은 이들이 일종의 화석 같은 흔적을 지면에 남긴다는 것이에요. 그래서 과학자들이 마지막 빙하기 당시 빙하로 덮여 있던 세상이 어떠했는지 알 수가 있습니다.

Summary Note B

Glaciers are rivers of ice that move slowly with gravity. The way a glacier moves depends on the slope of the land.

They are created over many thousands of years. Snow falls and accumulates. But it never completely melts. Instead, it thaws a bit and then refreezes. Years and years of snowfall create pressure. This pressure forms sheets of ice. Over time, glaciers leave imprints in the ground like fossils. This way, scientists can tell what the world was like during the last ice age.

Exercise 4 1 ⓓ 2 ⓑ   p.176

Script 🎧 07-16

W1 Professor: All right, class, so we've been talking about famous inventors this week. One of the most famous inventors of the Renaissance was Leonardo da Vinci. Who knows what else Leonardo was famous for?

W2 Student: Paintings! He did the *Mona Lisa*!

W1: That's absolutely right. Leonardo was the artist who painted the famous *Mona Lisa*. He also painted *The Last Supper* and was famous for architecture, sculptures, and so many different art forms. In addition to all this, he was a very famous inventor. He drew sketches of airplanes 400 years before the first plane took flight. The thing was, though, that most of these inventions were way ahead of his time. So they didn't help people much during his time. Yes?

M Student: What do you mean by "way ahead of his time?"

W1: Well, he thought these things up, but the technology back then wasn't good enough to create most of these inventions. Anyway, some of his inventions were created. For example, Leonardo created the anemoscope. An anemoscope is a device that tells you which direction the wind is blowing. It also is supposed to tell you what direction the wind is going to change to before it even does.

W2: So does the anemoscope still exist?

W1: No one really uses it anymore. But they did a long time ago.

해석

W1 Professor: 좋아요, 여러분, 이번 주에는 유명한 발명가들에 대해 이야기를 하고 있습니다. 르네상스 시대의 가장 유명한 발명가 중 한 명은 레오나르도 다빈치였어요. 다빈치가 그 외에 무엇으로 유명했는지 아는 사람이 있나요?

W2 Student: 그림이요! *모나리자*를 그렸어요.

W1: 맞아요. 다빈치는 그 유명한 *모나리자*를 그린 화가였어요. *최후의 만찬*도 그렸고, 건축, 조각, 그리고 여러 가지 다양한 형태의 예술로도 유명했죠. 그 외에도 매우 유명한 발명가이기도 했어요. 그는 최초의 비행기가 하늘을 난 때보다 400년 앞서 비행기 그림을 그렸습니다. 그런데 중요한 것은 이러한 발명품들이 대부분 그가 살았던 시대보다 앞서 있었다는 점이었어요. 그래서 그가 살아 있는 동안에는 사람들에게 도움이 되지 못했습니다. 네?

M Student: "시대보다 앞서 있었다"는 말씀은 무슨 뜻인가요?

W1: 음, 그가 그러한 것들을 생각해 내기는 했지만, 당시의 기술 수준은 그러한 대부분의 발명품들을 만들 수 있을 정도로 높지가 않았어요. 어쨌든 그의 발명품 중 일부는 제작이 되었습니다. 예를 들어 다빈치는 풍향계를 제작했어요. 풍향계는 바람이 부는 방향을 알려 주는 도구죠. 또한 바람의 방향이 바뀌기 전에 어떤 방향으로 바뀔지를 알려 주기도 하고요.

W2: 그러면 그 풍향계가 아직도 존재하나요?

W1: 지금은 더 이상 사용되지 않아요. 하지만 오래 전에는 사용되었죠.

📝 **Summary Note** Ⓑ

Leonardo da Vinci was a famous inventor. He lived during the Renaissance. Aside from inventing things, Leonardo also created many famous pieces of art. The *Mona Lisa* is his most famous painting. Leonardo's inventions were way ahead of his time. This is why he rarely made the things he invented. Some of his inventions were created though. One of them is called the anemoscope. This is a device that tells which direction the wind is blowing. It also tells how the wind is going to change to before it ever does. People do not use anemoscopes anymore, but they did a long time ago.

Integrated Listening & Speaking   p.178

A

Script 🎧 07-17

W Professor: Yesterday, we started talking about how it takes thousands of years for geological formations to form. One such formation is called the glacier. A glacier is kind of like a river of ice that moves slowly. It moves due to gravity. Let me tell you how a glacier is formed. What happens is that snowfall covers mountainous regions. This snow never completely melts. It might thaw a little. But then it refreezes. So there are both thawing and refreezing, which changes the snow to granules. Then, more snow accumulates. Over thousands of years, because of great amounts of pressure, these huge sheets of slow-moving ice form. That's how a glacier is made. The cool thing about glaciers is that they leave imprints in the ground, which makes them kind of like fossils. So scientists are able to tell what the world was like when it was covered by glaciers back during the last ice age.

1 a. It takes a glacier thousands of years to form.
    b. Glaciers take thousands of years to form.

2 a. Glaciers move because of gravity.
    b. The thing that makes glaciers move is gravity.

3 a. Glacier imprints can tell scientists what the world was like during the last ice age.
    b. Reading glacier imprints lets scientists know what the world was like long ago.

B

Script 🎧 07-18

W Professor: One of the most famous inventors of the Renaissance was Leonardo da Vinci. Leonardo was, of course, the artist who painted the famous *Mona Lisa*. He also painted *The Last Supper* and was famous for his work in architecture, sculpture, and other art forms. Leonardo was also a famous inventor. He drew sketches of airplanes 400 years before the first plane took flight. However, most of the inventions he came up with were way before his time. So they didn't help people much while he was alive. However, some of his inventions actually were created. For example, Leonardo created the anemoscope. That is a device that tells which direction the wind is blowing. It also is supposed to tell what direction the wind is going to change to before that happens.

1 a. He was good at painting and inventing things.
   b. His talents included painting and inventing.

2 a. His most famous painting was the *Mona Lisa*.
   b. He painted the famous *Mona Lisa*.

3 a. The anemoscope was actually created.
   b. One invention that was created was the anemoscope.

Mini TOEFL iBT Practice Test
p.180

1 ⓒ   2 Ⓑ   3 ⓒ   4 ⓒ   5 The Center
of the Lake: [1]   Along the Lakeshore: [4]   The Deepest Part
of the Lake: [2], [3]   6 ⓒ

[1-3]

Script 🎧 07-19

M Cafeteria Assistant: Excuse me. Can I have a moment of your time, please?

W Student: Okay.

M: Right now, the managers at the cafeteria are thinking about some of the changes they've made to the menu. They're considering making even more changes. They want some students' opinions about the changes. Do you have a couple of minutes to answer some questions?

W: Sure. What do you need to know?

M: So what is your favorite food that the cafeteria serves?

W: Um . . . I really like the spaghetti. It's very tasty.

M: Okay, great. And what's your least favorite food?

W: Well, I had a burger the last time you guys made them. I'm pretty sure it was the worst burger I've ever had.

M: Ugh, gross. Yeah, I didn't like them either. Okay, so now I need to know what you think of some of the new items. Do you like the new salad bar?

W: Yeah, I think it's great. There definitely weren't enough fresh vegetables before.

M: And what about the taco bar?

W: Um . . . I like that less. I mean, the idea is cool, but the stuff you have to make the tacos with is not very good. I mean, the refried beans are always dry and mealy. The rice has no flavor. I think the meat actually upset my stomach recently.

M: Yeah, that's not good at all. That's kind of what other students were saying about it, too. So if we keep the taco bar, we need better ingredients, right?

W: Yeah, definitely.

M: Is there anything that you'd like to see at the cafeteria?

W: Um . . . Yeah, actually. I think it would be great if we had a sandwich bar. You know, where students could just pick whatever they wanted and make their own sandwiches. I'm kind of surprised that we don't have one already since we have a taco bar and all.

M: That's a great suggestion. A sandwich station seems like a much more practical idea than a taco bar. Thanks for your time. I'll pass on this information to the managers.

W: No problem.

해석

M Cafeteria Assistant: 실례합니다. 잠깐 시간을 내실 수 있나요?

W Student: 그래요.

M: 지금 교내 식당의 매니저들이 메뉴에 준 변화에 대해 생각 중이에요. 더 많은 변화를 주는 것도 고려 중이죠. 매니저들은 그러한 변화에 대한 학생들의 의견을 듣고 싶어해요. 일이 분 정도 시간을 내서 질문에 답해 주실 수 있으세요?

W: 그러죠. 어떤 것을 알고 싶나요?

M: 그러면 교내 식당에서 제공하는 음식 중에서 무엇이 가장 마음에 드시나요?

W: 음… 저는 정말로 스파게티를 좋아해요. 무척 맛있어요.

M: 그렇군요. 좋아요. 그러면 가장 싫어하는 음식은 무엇인가요?

W: 음, 지난 번에 당신네들이 만든 버거를 먹었어요. 이제까지 먹어본 버거 중에서 분명 최악이었죠.

M: 이런, 그랬군요. 네, 저도 마음에 들지가 않았어요. 좋아요, 그러면 새로 생긴 것들에 대해 어떻게 생각하는지 알고 싶군요. 새로 생긴 샐러드 바는 마음에 드시나요?

W: 그래요, 좋은 것 같아요. 전에는 분명히 신선한 야채가 별로 없었거든요.

M: 그러면 타코 바는 어떤가요?

W: 음… 별로 좋아하지 않아요. 제 말은, 아이디어는 신선했지만 타코를 만드는 재료가 그다지 좋지 않다는 뜻이에요. 다시 튀긴 콩이 항상 말라 있고 퍼석퍼석한 편이에요. 밥도 아무런 맛이 없어요. 최근에는 고기 때문에 제 속이 뒤집어지는 줄 알았어요.

M: 그래요, 결코 좋지가 않네요. 다른 학생들도 그 점에 대한 이야기를 하더군요. 만약 타코 바를 그대로 둔다면 더 나은 재료가 필요하겠죠, 그렇죠?

W: 그래요, 물론이죠.

M: 그러면 교내 식당에 있었으면 하는 것이 있을까요?

W: 음… 그래요, 있어요. 샌드위치 바가 있으면 정말 좋을 것 같아요. 아시다시피 학생들이 먹고 싶은 것을 선택해서 자신만의 샌드위치를 만들 수 있는 곳이죠. 이미 타코 바와 다른 것들은 다 있는데, 샌드위치 바가 없다는 점은 약간 의외에요.

M: 좋은 제안이군요. 샌드위치 바가 타코 바보다 훨씬 더 실용적인 아이디어인 것 같네요. 시간을 내 주셔서 고마워요. 이 정보는 매니저들에게 전달할게요.

W: 천만에요.

[4-6]

Script 🎧 07-20

W1 Professor: All right, we're going to start talking about lake ecology today. I hope everyone did their homework last night. It's going to be very important in understanding what we talk about today. First of all, who can tell me what lake ecology is? Yes?

W2 Student: Um . . . the study of lakes and their organism and surroundings.

W1: Absolutely. Good job. Now, when we talk about lake ecology, the first thing we should probably talk about is lake zones. Can anyone tell me how many zones a lake has?

M Student: Three!

W1: That's right. And what are they? You don't have to tell me their specific names, but just tell me how a lake is divided.

M: Um . . . the first zone is the part of the lake along the shore where the land slopes down. The second zone is the middle of the lake but just along the surface. And the third zone is . . . um . . . the deepest part of the lake, where no light can get to.

W1: Very good! You're absolutely right. Now, it's very important to understand what these different zones are. The plants and animals, and even the bacteria and other microscopic organisms, are very different from zone to zone. Sometimes, the deepest water . . . the third zone . . . doesn't have any types of plant or animal life at all. It's so vital to understand the differences between these zones for that reason. Are there any questions so far? Yes?

W2: Why does the deep-water zone sometimes not have any life?

W1: That's a very good question. **This is something we will go into in much more detail in a bit.** But for now, let's just say that sometimes this deep water doesn't get any oxygen. All life requires oxygen to exist, so if there's no oxygen in the water, life can't happen there. We'll talk about what prevents some water from having oxygen a little later.

해석

W1 Professor: 좋아요, 오늘은 호수 환경 생태학에 대해서 공부할 거예요. 모두들 지난 밤에 과제를 했기 바랍니다. 오늘 이야기하는 내용은 반드시 이해하고 계셔야 해요. 우선 호수 환경 생태학이 무엇인지 말해볼 사람이 있나요? 네?

W2 Student: 음… 호수와 호수에 사는 생물 및 그 주변 환경에 대한 연구입니다.

W1: 정확해요. 잘 했어요. 자, 호수 환경 생태학에 대해 이야기를 할 때 아마도 제일 먼저 이야기해야 할 것이 호수의 지대입니다. 호수에 몇 개의 지대가 있는지 누가 말해볼까요?

M Student: 세 개입니다!

W1: 맞았어요. 그러면 그 세 개는 무엇일까요? 정확한 이름은 말하지 않아도 되지만, 호수가 어떻게 구분되는지는 밝혀야 해요.

M: 음… 첫 번째 지대는 땅이 경사져 있는 호수의 가장자리 부분입니다. 두 번째 지대는 호수의 가운데 부분이지만, 수면을 따라 있는 부분만 해당되고요. 그리고 세 번째 지대는… 음… 호수에서 가장 깊은 부분으로 빛이 도달할 수 없는 곳입니다.

W1: 아주 잘했어요! 맞습니다. 자, 이 서로 다른 지대들이 무엇인지 반드시 이해해야 해요. 식물, 동물, 그리고 심지어 박테리아 및 기타 미생물들이 지대에 따라 달라집니다. 때로는 가장 깊은 수역인… 세 번째 지대에는… 어떤 종류의 식물 혹은 동물도 존재하지가 않습니다. 그러한 이유에서 이 지대들 간의 차이점을 이해하는 것이 매우 중요해요. 여기까지 질문이 있나요? 네?

W2: 왜 가장 깊은 곳에 때때로 생명체가 존재하지 않나요?

W1: 아주 좋은 질문이에요. 잠시 후에 이에 대해서 보다 자세히 다룰 예정입니다. 하지만 지금으로서는 이처럼 깊은 물속에는 산소가 없다는 점만 얘기해 두죠. 모든 생명체의 생존에는 산소가 필요하기 때문에 물속에 산소가 없다면 생명체는 존재할 수 없을 거예요. 잠시 후 무엇 때문에 일부 수역에 산소가 존재하지 않는지 이야기하도록 하겠습니다.

Vocabulary Check-Up ———— p.183

A　1 ⓓ　　2 ⓚ　　3 ⓘ　　4 ⓒ　　5 ⓛ
　　　6 ⓑ　　7 ⓝ　　8 ⓞ　　9 ⓙ　　10 ⓔ
　　　11 ⓕ　　12 ⓖ　　13 ⓐ　　14 ⓜ　　15 ⓗ

B　1 ⓒ　　2 ⓐ　　3 ⓔ　　4 ⓑ　　5 ⓓ

UNIT
08 Making Inferences

Skill & Tip ·· p.186

Skill Practice

1 We <u>can</u> get the magazine to write something.

2 I can believe you're right, and I feel much better about the past progress.

3 Really good professors won't bring the sense of wonder in a direct way.

4 His parents plan to move to their new home next week.

B

> **W Professor**: Come in and have a seat. How are you?
>
> **M Student**: I'm fine. Thanks. Have you had a chance to look at my proposal?
>
> **W**: Yes, I have. That's what I mainly want to talk about.
>
> **M**: I wasn't sure whether it was exactly the kind of thing you wanted.
>
> **W**: Oh, have no worries. It's precisely what we need, and you did really good work.
>
> **M**: Well, I must say that's a great relief.

C

> **W Professor**: You'd think Mars would be easier to understand. Like Earth, Mars has polar ice caps and clouds in its atmosphere, seasonal weather patterns, volcanoes, canyons, and other recognizable features. However, conditions on Mars vary wildly from what we experience on our own planet. Over the past three decades, spacecraft have shown us that Mars is rocky, cold, and sterile beneath its hazy pink sky.

Basic Drill p.188

Drill 1 Ⓑ

Script 🎧 08-05

> **M Student Affairs Office Employee**: We always tell new students a bit about the school before they start class. One thing you need to know is that you have ten minutes between classes to get to your next class.
>
> **W Student**: But this school's so big! What if ten minutes isn't enough? I mean, how can it be if we have to go all the way across campus?
>
> **M**: Most students carry books for a couple of classes at a time. That makes it a little easier.
>
> **W**: I think I might have to make a couple of practice runs. I don't want to be late for class.

해석

M Student Affairs Office Employee: 저희는 신입생들이 수업을 시작하기 전에 항상 학교에 대한 이야기를 해 주죠. 한 가지 알고 있어야 할 것은 수업 사이에 10분간의 휴식 시간이 있는데, 그때 다음 수업에 가야 한다는 것이에요.

> **W Student**: 하지만 이 학교는 너무 넓잖아요! 10분으로 충분하지 않으면요? 제 말은, 캠퍼스 전체를 가로질러서 가야 하는 경우에는 어떻게 그럴 수 있죠?
>
> **M**: 대부분의 학생들이 한 번에 두 수업의 교재들을 들고 다녀요. 그러면 좀 더 편하죠.
>
> **W**: 두어 번 정도 모의 테스트를 해 봐야 것 같군요. 수업에 늦고 싶지는 않으니까요.

Drill 2 Ⓑ

Script 🎧 08-06

> **M Student**: Can you help me find a book I need?
>
> **W Librarian**: Sure. What are you looking for?
>
> **M**: I need a book about volcanoes for a report that I'm writing for one of my classes.
>
> **W**: Good luck with your report. You will find our books on volcanoes in the science section on the second floor. Just go up the stairs and make a left.
>
> **M**: Thank you so much!

해석

> **M Student**: 제게 필요한 책을 찾아 주실 수 있으신가요?
>
> **W Librarian**: 물론이죠. 무슨 책을 찾고 있나요?
>
> **M**: 제가 듣는 수업에서 작성 중인 보고서에 화산과 관련된 책이 필요해요.
>
> **W**: 보고서가 잘 되기를 빌게요. 화산에 관한 책은 2층 과학 섹션에서 찾을 수 있어요. 계단을 올라가서 왼쪽으로 가세요.
>
> **M**: 정말 고맙습니다!

Drill 3 Ⓑ

Script 🎧 08-07

> **W Professor**: Today, we're going to start talking about nutrition. It is really important to eat healthy foods so that we get the nutrients our bodies need to function. An easy way to make sure we get the nutrients we need is to follow the food pyramid. The food pyramid is a chart that tells us how much of which kinds of foods we should eat every day. The groups on the food pyramid include grains, fruits, vegetables, dairy products, meat, and fats.

해석

W Professor: 오늘은 영양에 대한 이야기로 시작할게요. 건강에 좋은 음식을 먹어서 우리 신체가 기능하는데 필요한 영양분을 얻는 것이 정말로 중요합니다. 우리에게 필요한 영양소를 얻을 수 있는 손쉬운 방법 중 하나는 음식 피라미드를 따르는 것이에요. 음식 피라미드는 매일 우리가 어떤 종류의 음식을 얼마나 먹어야 하는지를 알려 주는 표입니다. 음식 피라미드에 있는 식품군에는 곡류, 과일, 야채, 유제품, 육류, 그리고 지방이 포함되어 있습니다.

Drill 4 Ⓒ

Script 🎧 08-08

> **M Professor**: One of the most common psychiatric disorders is depression. Depression affects as much as ten percent of the population at any given time. The most common symptoms of depression are half moons and lack of pleasure from previously enjoyable activities. Other symptoms include changes in appetite, changes in sleep, feelings of guilt, and loss of energy. People who suffer from depression aren't able to function well on a day-to-day basis.

해석

M Professor: 가장 흔한 정신 질환 중 하나가 우울증입니다. 어떤 때라도 우울증은 인구의 10퍼센트에 영향을 미치죠. 우울증의 가장 일반적 증상은 슬픈 기분을 느끼고 이전에는 재미있었던 활동에서 즐거움을 찾지 못하는 것이에요. 또 다른 증상으로는 식욕 감퇴, 수면 변화, 죄의식, 기력 상실을 들 수 있습니다. 우울증을 겪는 사람들은 일상 생활을 유지하기가 힘들 수도 있습니다.

Exercises with Short Conversations & Lectures

Exercise 1 1 Ⓐ 2 Ⓓ p.190

Script 🎧 08-09

> **M Student**: Hi, Ms. Olson. May I ask you a question?
>
> **W Registrar's Office Employee**: Of course. What can I do for you?
>
> **M**: I was wondering about our yearbooks. I know we have to order them in advance, but I don't know when the deadline is, how much they cost, when to pick them up, or anything.
>
> **W**: I can give you all that information. You can preorder your yearbook, or you can just buy one when they come in. The preorder deadline is in a week. You just have to drop off your order form and check here. The yearbooks are fifty dollars. They'll be here in two months, and you can pick yours up here.
>
> **M**: So I still have some time to decide whether or not I want to preorder?
>
> **W**: Absolutely. But if you know you definitely want a yearbook, I would recommend preordering. That way, everything will be set for you just to pick it up when it gets here.
>
> **M**: You know, I think I'll go ahead and do that.

해석

M Student: 안녕하세요, Olson 선생님. 질문을 하나 해도 될까요?

W Registrar's Office Employee: 그럼요. 무엇을 도와 드릴까요?

M: 졸업 앨범에 관해 궁금했거든요. 미리 주문해야 한다는 점은 알고 있는데, 마감일이 언제인지, 비용은 얼마인지, 언제 받으러 와야 하는지 등은 모르겠어요.

W: 모두 알려 줄 수 있어요. 졸업 앨범은 선주문을 할 수도 있고 입고된 때 구입도 가능해요. 선주문의 마감일은 일주일 후예요. 주문서를 제출하고 이곳에서 확인하면 되죠. 앨범 가격은 50달러예요. 두 달 후 이곳에 도착하면 여기에서 받아 가실 수 있어요.

M: 그러면 선주문 여부를 결정할 시간이 아직 있는 것이죠?

W: 그럼요. 하지만 앨범을 꼭 원하는 경우라면 선주문을 추천할게요. 그렇게 해야 앨범이 도착할 때 학생이 받아갈 수 있는 모든 준비가 끝나 있을 테니까요.

M: 그럼 그렇게 해야 할 것 같군요.

Exercise 2 1 Ⓑ 2 Ⓓ p.191

Script 🎧 08-10

> **W Student**: Professor Andrews?
>
> **M Professor**: Yes, Catherine?
>
> **W**: I have a question about class today.
>
> **M**: What can I help you with?
>
> **W**: Well, we went over the different Excel functions today, but some of the stuff didn't make sense to me. I think the reason is that this is only my second class. I believe I missed something from an earlier class.
>
> **M**: All right. We did cover some of the groundwork for this lesson last week.
>
> **W**: That makes sense. I didn't understand how everyone already knew which formulas to enter.
>
> **M**: Of course. If you take a look at chapter two in your book, I think it will help you a lot. Then, if you're still having trouble, we can tackle that later.
>
> **W**: Thanks, Mr. Andrews!

해석

W Student: Andrews 교수님?

M Professor: 네, 캐서린?

W: 오늘 수업에 관해 질문이 있어서요.

M: 어떤 도움이 필요한가요?

W: 음, 오늘 여러 가지 엑셀 기능을 공부했는데, 공부한 내용 중 몇 가지는 이해가 가지 않아서요. 그 이유는 이번이 제 두 번째 수업이기 때문이라고 생각해요. 이전 수업에서 제가 듣지 못한 부분이 있는 것 같아요.

M: 그래요. 지난주에 오늘 배운 내용에 대한 기초를 다루었죠.

W: 이해가 가는군요. 어떻게 모두들 어떤 공식을 입력해야 하는지 이미 알고 있었다는 점이 이해가 가지 않았거든요.

M: 그래요. 교재 2장을 보면 많은 도움이 될 것으로 생각해요. 그리고도 여전히 문제가 있으면 나중에 이야기할 수 있을 거예요.

W: 감사합니다, Andrews 교수님!

Exercise 3 1 Ⓒ 2 Ⓓ p.192

Script 08-11

> **M Professor**: I'm sure many of you have heard about the <u>importance</u> of drinking water. You know, you're supposed to drink several cups of water <u>each day</u>. Have you ever asked why? The <u>reason</u> is not just that the body is around sixty percent water. There are <u>several benefits</u> to drinking it. It <u>prevents</u> the dehydration of the body. It also helps <u>carry</u> oxygen through the body. Water makes the skin <u>healthy</u> and improves how it looks. It <u>removes</u> waste from the body and also helps you maintain regular <u>blood pressure</u>. I'd say that drinking water is <u>pretty important</u>, wouldn't you?

해석

M Professor: 여러분 중 다수는 분명 물을 마시는 것의 중요성에 대해 들어본 적이 있을 것입니다. 아시겠지만 여러분은 매일 여러 컵의 물을 마셔야 해요. 왜 그래야 하는지 물어본 적이 있나요? 그 이유는 신체의 약 60%가 물로 이루어져 있기 때문만은 아니에요. 물을 마시는 것에는 여러 가지 이점이 있습니다. 신체의 탈수를 예방해 줍니다. 또한 신체에 산소가 돌아다니는 것을 도와 주죠. 물은 피부를 건강하게 만들고 피부가 좋아 보이도록 만듭니다. 신체에서 노폐물을 제거해 주고, 정상적인 혈압 유지에도 도움을 줍니다. 물을 마시는 것은 매우 중요하다고 말씀드리고 싶군요, 그렇지 않나요?

Exercise 4 1 Ⓓ 2 Ⓓ p.193

Script 08-12

> **W Professor**: Today, we're going to talk about <u>ancient</u> Greek theater. The ancient Greeks mostly did comedies and <u>tragedies</u>. The first <u>part</u> we're going to talk about is comedy. Greek comedy is <u>separated</u> into three divisions. They are old comedy, <u>middle</u> comedy, and new comedy. One of the ways that those <u>types</u> of comedy are <u>different</u> is in the topics they covered. Old comedy poked <u>fun</u> at real people from that time. Middle comedy mostly <u>focused on</u> reviewing the way society was. It made fun of the <u>way</u> people lived. New comedy covered <u>similar issues</u> as middle comedy. But it also started to add aspects of <u>love</u>.

해석

W Professor: 오늘은 고대 그리스의 연극에 대해 이야기할 거예요. 고대 그리스인들은 주로 희극과 비극을 공연했어요. 먼저 다룰 부분은 희극입니다. 그리스 희극은 세 가지로 나누어져요. 구희극, 중희극, 그리고 신희극이죠. 이러한 형태의 희극들이 차이를 보이는 한 가지 측면은 다루어지는 주제입니다. 구희극은 당시의 실제 인물들을 풍자했어요. 중희극은 사회의 현실을 비판하는데 주로 초점을 맞췄고요. 사람들이 사는 방식을 풍자했죠. 신희극은 중희극과 유사한 주제를 다루었습니다. 하지만 사랑의 요소를 추가하기 시작했어요.

Exercises with Mid-Length Conversations & Lectures

Exercise 1 1 Ⓐ 2 Ⓓ p.194

Script 08-13

> **W Student**: Hello, Professor Adams. You <u>wanted</u> to see me?
>
> **M Professor**: Hi, Sara. Yes, I want to talk about your zoology <u>report</u>. I'm making <u>appointments</u> with everyone to talk about their papers.
>
> **W**: Oh, okay.
>
> **M**: What are you <u>writing</u> your report on now?
>
> **W**: I'm looking at <u>bird migrations</u>.
>
> **M**: That's a great topic. Are you focusing on <u>anything specific</u>?
>
> **W**: I think I've <u>narrowed it down</u> to birds that do short-distance migrations. You know, geese and other <u>similar birds</u>.
>
> **M**: Was there a reason you chose that <u>particular</u> topic?
>
> **W**: Actually, a <u>big part</u> of the decision just came from the <u>fact</u> that I found the most information on short-distance migration. I also found a lot of <u>information</u> on geese.
>
> **M**: That's a pretty <u>good reason</u> to go with that. So what <u>direction</u> are you taking this report?
>
> **W**: I thought I'd write about goose migration <u>in general</u>. I found out that all geese have the <u>same</u> general migration pattern. So I'm going to <u>discuss</u> that first. Then, I'm going to talk about the <u>patterns</u> of specific geese. I thought I'd <u>compare</u> a few different species, like the Canadian goose and the Hawaiian goose.
>
> **M**: That sounds good. I'm <u>looking forward</u> to reading your paper.

해석

W Student: 안녕하세요, Adams 교수님. 저를 보자고 하셨나요?

M Professor: 안녕하세요, Sara. 학생의 동물학 보고서에 관해서 얘기를 하고 싶어서요. 보고서에 관해 이야기하기 위해 모든 학생들과 약속을 잡고 있는 중이죠.

W: 오, 그렇군요.

M: 현재 무엇에 관한 보고서를 쓰고 있나요?

W: 철새 이동을 살펴보고 있어요.

M: 좋은 주제로군요. 특정한 점에 초점을 맞추고 있나요?

W: 짧은 거리를 이동하는 철새로 범위를 좁히고 있어요. 아시겠지만, 기러기와 그와 비슷한 새들이요.

M: 특별히 그 주제를 선택한 이유가 있었나요?

W: 사실 그러한 결정을 내린 큰 이유는 단거리 이동에 관한 정보를 많이 찾을 수 있다는 사실 때문이었어요. 또한 기러기에 관한 정보도 많이 찾았고요.

M: 상당히 좋은 이유로 주제를 선택했군요. 그러면 이번 보고서는 어떤 식으로 전개하고 있나요?

W: 기러기의 이동에 관한 일반적인 내용을 쓸 생각이었어요. 모든 기러기들의 일반적인 이동 패턴이 동일하다는 점을 알게 되었죠. 그래서 그러한 점에 대해 먼저 논의할 거예요. 그런 다음 특정 기러기들의 패턴에 대해 언급할 생각이에요. 캐나다기러기와 하와이기러기와 같은 몇 가지 종들을 비교할 생각이었어요.

M: 좋은 생각이에요. 보고서를 기대하고 있을게요.

📝 **Summary Note** Ⓑ

The professor is speaking with a student about her zoology report. The student tells the professor that she will focus the report on short-distance bird migrations. The main reason she chose this topic is that she found a lot of information about it. The student will begin her report by talking about goose migration in general. She states that most geese have the same general migration pattern. She will then compare different species of geese.

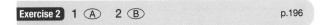

Exercise 2 1 Ⓐ   2 Ⓑ   p.196

Script 🎧 08-14

> **W Student Activities Office Employee**: Hi, Steve. What can I help you with?
>
> **M Student**: I'm looking into some after-school activities, and I was wondering if I could get some information about them.
>
> **W**: Definitely. Is there anything in particular you're interested in?
>
> **M**: I really want to do the after-school swimming lessons. I mean, I never learned how to swim properly when I was younger.
>
> **W**: That's an admirable goal. Let me grab the information about the swimming, and we'll figure out what you need to know.
>
> **M**: Great!
>
> **W**: Okay, swimming lessons occur twice a week on Tuesdays and Thursdays. Can you make those days?
>
> **M**: Yeah, I've got those days free.
>
> **W**: There's a small fee involved. You get lessons for the whole semester for fifteen dollars.
>
> **M**: That's really reasonable.
>
> **W**: Okay, great. Well, I don't know if there are still any openings available for the lessons. So what you should do right away is see one of the gym teachers. Let him know you want to sign up. It would help if you could take the fifteen dollars with you so that your spot will be reserved.
>
> **M**: Do you think there will still be spots left?
>
> **W**: There should be. It's still pretty early in the semester. Just make sure you get to the gym at once.
>
> **M**: All right, I'll do that. Thanks for your help!

해석

W Student Activities Office Employee: 안녕하세요, Steve. 무엇을 도와 줄까요?

M Student: 방과 후 활동을 찾고 있는데, 그에 대한 정보를 얻을 수 있는지 궁금해서요.

W: 그럼요. 특별히 관심이 가는 것이 있나요?

M: 방과 후 수영 강습을 꼭 받고 싶어요. 제 말은, 어렸을 때 수영하는 법을 제대로 배운 적이 없었거든요.

W: 멋진 목표군요. 수영에 관한 정보를 찾아보면 학생이 알아야 할 것이 무엇인지 알게 될 거예요.

M: 좋습니다!

W: 그래요, 수영 강습은 주 2회, 화요일과 목요일에 있군요. 그날 가능한가요?

M: 네, 그날 다 시간이 돼요.

W: 약간의 강습비가 있어요. 15달러를 내면 한 학기 동안 강습을 들을 수 있죠.

M: 정말 저렴하군요.

W: 좋아요, 잘 되었군요. 음, 강습에 아직 빈 자리가 있는지 잘 모르겠네요. 그러니 당장 가서 체육 선생님 한 분을 만나 보세요. 그분께 학생이 등록을 원한다는 점을 알려 주세요. 자리를 예약할 수 있도록 15달러를 가지고 가면 도움이 될 거예요.

M: 아직 남아 있는 자리가 있을까요?

W: 그럴 거예요. 아직 학기 초반이니까요. 지금 바로 체육관에 가 보세요.

M: 좋아요, 그렇게 할게요. 도와 주셔서 감사합니다!

📝 **Summary Note** Ⓑ

The student is asking about certain after-school activities. He would like to take swimming lessons because he never learned how to swim properly as a kid. The employee tells him that swimming lessons are on Tuesdays and Thursdays after school. They will cost fifteen dollars. The employee tells the student to see the gym teacher and to ask if there are any available spots open for the lessons. He is grateful for the woman's help.

Exercise 3 1 Ⓐ   2 Ⓓ   p.198

Script 🎧 08-15

> **W Professor**: Yesterday, I told you that we were going to start learning about a field of psychology called developmental psychology. This branch of psychology looks at the many ways people's minds and bodies develop from before they're even born until they die. So we should just start at the beginning. Let's start with infants. When a baby is born up until he or she starts talking, the baby is referred to as an infant. Infants can't do a lot of things that older children can do.
>
>   Let's look at the physical side of things. Babies are born with really poor vision. Actually, they're legally blind when born. Infants can mostly make out large shapes and stuff, but they can't tell detail. Their sense of color also isn't very good. For a long time, psychologists

thought infants were colorblind right after birth. As it turns out, research has shown that most babies can, in fact, make out bright colors. For example, an infant can tell the difference between a bright red ball and a bright blue ball. But it would be much harder for an infant to tell the difference between a light blue ball and a dark blue ball. As infants get older, their sense of sight improves. Some psychologists think that by the age of six months, an infant's vision is almost the same as an adult's.

해석

W Professor: 어제 제가 발달 심리학이라는 심리학 분야에 대해 배우게 될 것이라고 말씀을 드렸어요. 이 심리학 분야는 사람이 태어나기 전부터 죽을 때까지 사람들의 정신과 신체가 발달하는 여러 측면들을 살펴봅니다. 그러면 처음부터 시작하도록 할게요. 유아들로 시작해 보죠. 아기가 태어나서 말을 하기 시작할 때까지, 이 아기는 유아라고 불립니다. 유아들은 좀 더 큰 아이들이 할 수 있는 많은 일들을 할 수가 없어요.

신체적인 측면을 살펴보죠. 아기들은 시력이 정말 나쁜 상태로 태어납니다. 실제로 태어났을 때 법적으로는 눈이 안 보이는 상태예요. 유아들은 주로 커다란 형태 및 물건들만 알아보고 세부적인 것은 보지 못합니다. 또한 색채 감각도 그다지 좋지가 않아요. 오랫동안 심리학자들은 출생 직후의 유아들이 색맹이라고 생각했어요. 하지만 연구 결과 대부분의 아기들이 실제로는 밝은 색깔은 알아볼 수 있는 것으로 밝혀졌죠. 예를 들어 유아는 밝은 빨간색 공과 밝은 파란색 공은 구별할 수 있습니다. 하지만 유아에게 밝은 파란색 공과 어두운 파란색 공을 구별하는 일은 훨씬 더 어려울 거예요. 유아가 자라면서 시력은 좋아집니다. 일부 심리학자들은 유아가 6개월이 되면 유아의 시력이 성인의 시력과 거의 같아진다고 생각하죠.

📝 **Summary Note B**

Developmental psychology is a field of psychology that looks at how people grow. One thing this field looks at is infants and their growth. For example, when a baby is born, the child has very poor vision. The baby cannot make out detail, only large shapes. Infants can also only make out differences in bright colors. Vision improves as infants get older. At six months, an infant's vision is almost the same as an adult's.

Exercise 4 1 Ⓑ 2 Ⓐ   p.200

Script 🎧 08-16

M Professor: We're going to spend the rest of the month writing different kinds of essays. First though, we need to talk about what makes an essay good. There are certain things that every essay, despite what you'll be writing about, needs to have. Who can tell me one thing that an essay must have?

W Student: Um, doesn't every essay need an introduction?

M: Of course. Every essay must have an introduction. In the intro, you'll talk about the focus of your essay. You might also talk about some of your arguments or

subtopics. But if you do, you have to make sure that you're very brief about them. Your introduction shouldn't be more than a paragraph. What else does an essay need to have?

W: A conclusion?

M: Absolutely! If you're introducing your topic at the beginning, you must conclude your argument at the end. The conclusion talks about similar things as the introduction, but it's not exactly the same. Here, you have to wrap up your topic. You have to make sure that the reader is convinced that your point of view is right. Yes, do you have a question?

W: So what happens in the middle?

M: The middle's the most important part. That's where you tell your readers all the reasons that they should agree with you. **That's where you really get to show off what you know.**

해석

M Professor: 이번 달 나머지 시간에는 다양한 종류의 에세이를 작성하게 될 거예요. 하지만 먼저 무엇이 좋은 에세이를 만드는가에 대한 이야기를 해야겠어요. 어떤 것에 대한 에세이를 쓰더라도, 모든 에세이에 들어가야 하는 특정 요소들이 있습니다. 에세이에 반드시 들어 있어야 하는 것 중 하나를 누가 얘기해 볼까요?

W Student: 음, 모든 에세이에는 서론이 있어야 하지 않나요?

M: 그렇습니다. 모든 에세이에는 반드시 서론이 있어야 해요. 서론에서는 에세이의 초점에 대해 이야기를 하게 됩니다. 일부 주장이나 부주제들에 대해서 이야기할 수도 있고요. 하지만 그렇게 하는 경우, 그에 대해 아주 간단하게만 언급해야 한다는 점을 잊어서는 안됩니다. 서론이 한 문단이 넘어서는 안돼요. 그 밖에 에세이에 무엇이 있어야 할까요?

W: 결론이요?

M: 그렇죠! 시작 부분에서 주제를 소개했다면 끝 부분에서는 반드시 결론을 내려야 해요. 결론에서는 서론과 비슷한 이야기를 하지만, 정확하게 똑같지는 않습니다. 여기에서는 주제를 마무리지어야 해요. 여러분의 견해가 맞다는 점을 독자에게 확신시켜야 합니다. 그래요, 질문이 있나요?

W: 그러면 본론에서는 무엇을 하나요?

M: 본론이 가장 중요한 부분이에요. 독자가 여러분의 의견에 동의하도록 모든 근거들을 독자에게 제시해야 하는 부분입니다. 여러분이 가진 지식을 정말로 뽐낼 수 있는 곳이 바로 이 부분이에요.

📝 **Summary Note B**

A professor is teaching his class how to write a good essay. The three main parts of an essay are the introduction, the middle, and the conclusion. The introduction is the beginning of the essay. In this part, the writer first brings up his topic and arguments. He might begin to talk briefly about his arguments. The conclusion is the part of the essay that comes at the end. The writer wraps up his argument in the conclusion. The middle of the essay is the most important part. This is where the writer convinces the readers that his point of view is correct.

A

Script 🎧 08-17

W Professor: When a baby is born until the time that he or she begins talking, the baby is referred to as an infant. Infants can't do many of the activities that older children can. Let's look at the physical side of things. Babies are born with very poor vision. Actually, they're considered legally blind when born. Infants can mostly make out large shapes, but they can't see any details. Their sense of color also isn't particularly good either. For many years, psychologists thought infants were colorblind right after birth. As it turns out, research has shown that most babies can, in fact, make out bright colors. For example, an infant can tell the difference between a bright red ball and a bright blue ball. But it would be much harder for an infant to determine how a light blue ball and a dark blue ball are different. As infants get older, their sense of sight improves. Some psychologists believe that by the age of six months, an infant's vision is almost the same as an adult's.

1 a. The focus of developmental psychology is how people grow.
   b. Developmental psychology focuses on how people grow.

2 a. At birth, an infant's vision is very poor.
   b. An infant has very poor vision at birth.

3 a. An infant's vision is almost the same as an adult's by six months.
   b. By six months, an infant can see as well as an adult.

B

Script 🎧 08-18

M Professor: Now, let me talk about what makes an essay good. There are certain things that every essay, no matter what you are writing about, must have. First, every essay needs an introduction. In the intro, you should mention the focus of your essay. You might also write about some of your arguments or subtopics. But if you do that, be very brief about them. Your introduction shouldn't be more than a single paragraph. Next, if you introduce your topic at the beginning, you must conclude your argument at the end. The conclusion describes similar things as the introduction, but it's not exactly the same. Here, you have to wrap up your topic. You must make sure that the reader is convinced that your point of view is the right one. Lastly, the most important part is the middle. That's where you tell your readers all the reasons they should agree with you. That's where you really get to show off what you know.

1 a. The three main parts of an essay are the introduction, the middle, and the conclusion.
   b. The introduction, the middle, and the conclusion are the three main parts of an essay.

2 a. In the introduction, the writer first brings up his topic and arguments.
   b. The writer first brings up his topic and arguments in the introduction.

3 a. The purpose of the conclusion is to wrap up the argument.
   b. The writer wraps up the argument in the conclusion.

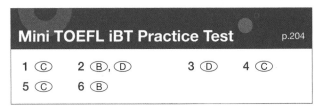

Mini TOEFL iBT Practice Test p.204

1 Ⓒ   2 Ⓑ, Ⓓ   3 Ⓓ   4 Ⓒ
5 Ⓒ   6 Ⓑ

[1-3]

Script 🎧 08-19

W Student Housing Office Employee: Hello. How may I help you?

M Student: Hello. I have a problem with my dorm room.

W: I'm sorry to hear that. What exactly is wrong with it?

M: Well, uh, it's not really my room. It's my roommate. We just don't get along at all.

W: In what ways?

M: Hmm . . . A lot of it is that he's very inconsiderate of me. For instance, he stays up really late at night, but I go to bed early.

W: Does he leave the lights on or something?

M: He'll come into the room when I'm sleeping and turn the lights on at two or three AM. He always wakes me up.

W: That's not good.

M: He plays a lot of loud music, too. I wonder if it's possible to change rooms.

W: Which dorm do you live in?

M: I live in Tyler Hall. I've got a room on the fourth floor there.

W: It looks like you're in luck. There's an empty room on the sixth floor. You'd have to pay a bit more because it's a single room though. Are you interested?

M: Definitely.

해석

W Student Housing Office Employee: 안녕하세요. 어떻게 도와 드릴까요?

M Student: 안녕하세요. 제 기숙사 방에 문제가 있어서요.

W: 그런 말을 들으니 유감이군요. 정확히 어떤 문제가 있나요?

M: 음, 어, 사실 방 때문이 아니에요. 제 룸메이트 때문이죠. 서로 전혀 맞지가 않아요.

W: 어떤 식으로요?

M: 흠… 주로 그가 저를 거의 배려하지 않기 때문이에요. 예를 들어 그는 매우 늦은 밤 시간까지 잠을 자지 않는데, 저는 일찍 잠자리에 들어요.

W: 그가 불을 켜 두거나 하나요?

M: 제가 자고 있을 때 방에 들어와서 오전 2시나 3시에 불을 키려고 하죠. 항상 저를 깨우고 있어요.

W: 좋지 않군요.

M: 게다가 음악을 정말 크게 틀어요. 방을 바꿀 수 있는지 궁금하군요.

W: 어떤 기숙사에서 지내죠?

M: Tyler 홀에서 지내고 있어요. 그곳 4층에 방이 있죠.

W: 운이 좋은 것 같네요. 6층에 빈 방이 하나 있어요. 하지만 1인실이기 때문에 기숙사비를 약간 더 내야 할 거예요. 관심이 있나요?

M: 그럼요.

[4-6]

Script 🎧 08-20

W1 Professor: Let's continue our discussion of personality disorders today. Yesterday, we talked about dependent personality disorder. Today, we're going to discuss narcissistic personality disorder. To understand this disorder better, let's break down what its name means. Who can tell me what narcissistic means? Yes?

M Student: Um . . . well, I think it means egotistic. You know, people are narcissistic if they are full of themselves.

W1: Right. When people are narcissistic, they generally think everything they do is perfect and that they're perfect people. Every now and then, everyone behaves in a way that's a little narcissistic. What do you think narcissistic personality disorder is about?

W2 Student: Well, I'm not really sure, but I think narcissistic personality disorder happens when people are that way all the time. And since it's a disorder, doesn't it have to be so much that it's disruptive to other people?

W1: Excellent. That's exactly right. People with narcissistic personality disorder are egotistic so often that it's very disruptive. But we have to remember something about personality disorders. While all psychiatric disorders are disruptive, personality disorders are disruptive in another way. See, uh, most disorders are a bother to the people who have the disorder. The thing with personality disorders is that they are a bother to the people who have to be around the individuals with the disorder. Can someone tell me what this would mean with someone who has narcissistic personality disorder?

W2: I think it means that someone with narcissistic personality disorder doesn't really care that she has that

disorder. But instead, everyone that that person interacts with is really bothered by the person's ego.

W1: That's absolutely right. This is all part of the reason that narcissistic personality disorder is hard to treat. The people with the disorder don't think anything is wrong with them. So they're very stubborn when it comes to treatment. It's very hard to treat people for a disorder if they don't think anything is wrong with themselves.

해석

W1 Professor: 오늘은 인격 장애에 관한 논의를 계속하도록 할게요. 어제는 의존성 인격 장애에 대해 이야기했어요. 오늘은 자기애성 인격 장애에 관해 논의하도록 할게요. 이 질환을 보다 잘 이해하기 위해, 그 이름의 의미를 분석해 보죠. 자기애성이 무엇을 의미하는지 말해 볼 사람이 있나요?

M Student: 음… 어, 제 생각에는 자기 중심적이라는 뜻 같은데요. 아시다시피 자만심에 차 있을 때 자기애가 있다고 하잖아요.

W1: 맞아요. 사람들이 자기애를 가지고 있는 경우에는 자신이 하는 모든 일들이 완벽하고 자신이 완벽한 사람이라고 보통 생각을 하죠. 가끔씩은 누구나가 약간 자기애적인 방식으로 행동을 해요. 자기애성 인격 장애는 어떤 질환이라고 생각하나요?

W2 Student: 음, 확실하지는 않지만, 자기애성 인격 장애는 사람들이 항상 자기애적인 경우에 나타난다고 생각해요. 그리고 질환이니까 정도가 너무 심해서 다른 사람에게 피해를 주지 않을까요?

W1: 훌륭해요. 정확하게 맞췄어요. 자기애성 인격 장애를 가진 사람들은 자기 중심적인 경우가 너무 많아서 문제를 일으킵니다. 하지만 인격 장애에 관해 기억해야 할 점이 있어요. 모든 정신 질환이 문제를 일으키지만, 인격 장애는 다른 방식으로 문제를 일으켜요. 그러니까, 어, 대부분의 질환은 그 병을 가진 사람에게 피해를 줍니다. 인격 장애의 특징은 그 질환을 가진 사람의 주변 사람들에게 피해를 준다는 것이에요. 자기애성 인격 장애를 가진 사람에게 이것이 무엇을 뜻하는지 말해 볼 사람이 있나요?

W2: 자기애성 인격 장애를 가진 사람은 자신이 그러한 장애를 가지고 있다는 점을 실제로 신경 쓰지 않는다는 의미인 것 같아요. 하지만 그 대신 그 사람과 관계를 맺고 있는 모든 사람들이 실제로 그 사람의 자아 때문에 피해를 입는 것이고요.

W1: 바로 그렇습니다. 그렇기 때문에 자기애성 인격 장애는 치료하기가 어려워요. 이 질환을 지닌 사람들은 자기한테 아무런 문제가 없다고 생각하죠. 그래서 치료에 대해 말하자면, 치료가 아주 힘들어요. 자신에게 아무런 문제가 없다고 생각하는 사람들의 장애를 치료하는 일은 매우 어렵습니다.

Vocabulary Check-Up ———— p.207

A | 1 ⓖ | 2 ⓓ | 3 ⓛ | 4 ⓕ | 5 ⓗ |
| 6 ⓐ | 7 ⓙ | 8 ⓑ | 9 ⓝ | 10 ⓜ |
| 11 ⓒ | 12 ⓞ | 13 ⓔ | 14 ⓘ | 15 ⓚ |

B | 1 ⓒ | 2 ⓐ | 3 ⓓ | 4 ⓑ | 5 ⓔ |

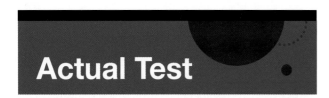

Actual Test

Actual Test   p.210

PART 1

1 Ⓑ	2 Ⓑ	3 Ⓑ	4 Ⓓ	5 Ⓐ
6 Ⓑ	7 Ⓑ	8 Ⓓ	9 Ⓐ	10 Ⓑ

11 Fact: ②   Not a Fact: ①, ③, ④

PART 2

1 Ⓒ	2 Ⓓ	3 Ⓑ	4 Ⓐ	5 Ⓐ
6 Ⓒ	7 Ⓓ	8 Ⓒ	9 Ⓒ	10 Fact:

②, ④   Not a Fact: ①, ③   11 Ⓓ

12 Ⓑ	13 Ⓒ	14 Ⓒ	15 Ⓒ	16 Ⓑ
17 Ⓑ				

PART 1

[1-5]

Script 🎧 09-03

> **W Student**: Good afternoon. I wonder if you can help me with one of my classes.
>
> **M Registrar's Office Employee**: I'll do my best. Why don't you tell me exactly what you need help with? Then, uh, I can try to fix your problem.
>
> **W**: Sure thing. Thanks. I'm a freshman, and this is my second semester. It's a requirement that I sign up for an English writing class.
>
> **M**: That's correct. All freshmen have to take English 1 and English 2 during the first and second semester, respectively. However, if you got an A in English 1, you don't have to take English 2.
>
> **W**: Yeah . . . I still need to take English 2.
>
> **M**: I see. So . . . what's the problem?
>
> **W**: I signed up to take English 2 at 9:30 AM every Monday, Wednesday, and Friday. The course is scheduled to be held in room 304 in Greenbrier Hall. However, when I went there this morning, nobody was in the room. I waited for twenty minutes, but nobody showed up.
>
> **M**: Who's the professor?
>
> **W**: Um . . . let me check . . . It's being taught by Professor Merredith Watson.
>
> **M**: Ah, I understand the problem now. Professor Watson had a personal issue that came up right before the semester started. All of her classes have been canceled. You should have received an email from the school about that. Didn't you get one?

> **W**: I'm afraid not.
>
> **M**: Hmm . . . I'm sorry about that. These kinds of things happen sometimes.
>
> **W**: So . . . What am I supposed to do?
>
> **M**: Well, you have two choices. First, you can wait until the fall semester of your sophomore year to take English 2. Or you can find another English 2 course that fits your schedule this semester.
>
> **W**: I prefer the latter choice.
>
> **M**: Okay. When do you have time available in your schedule? The English 2 courses are limited to fifteen students in each one. Unfortunately, there are not any spaces left in most of the classes.
>
> **W**: Let me guess . . . There are spaces available in the classes that start at 8:30, but there's no room left in any of the others.
>
> **M**: Not quite. You are correct about the 8:30 classes. There are several openings in them. However . . . according to the computer, there is an open slot from 11:30 to 1:00 on Tuesday and Thursday. Does that happen to fit your schedule?
>
> **W**: Hmm . . . Tuesday and Thursday? Ah, yes. I do have an opening then. I've already got several classes on both days. So I guess I won't have much time for lunch, but that's better than an early-morning class.
>
> **M**: Great. Shall I go ahead and sign you up then? I'll need to see your student ID card in order to do that. What do you think?

해석

W Student: 안녕하세요. 제 수업 중 하나와 관련해서 도움을 주실 수 있는지 궁금해요.

M Registrar's Office Employee: 최선을 다할게요. 정확히 무엇에 관한 도움이 필요한지 말씀해 주실래요? 그러면, 어, 제가 문제를 해결하도록 노력할게요.

W: 그럴게요. 고맙습니다. 저는 신입생이고 이번이 두 번째 학기에요. 필수 과목인 영작문 수업에 등록을 해야 하죠.

M: 맞아요. 모든 신입생들이 첫 번째와 두 번째 학기에 각각 영어1과 영어2 수업을 들어야 해요. 하지만 영어1 수업에서 A를 받았다면 영어2 수업은 듣지 않아도 되고요.

W: 네… 제 경우에는 영어2 수업을 들어야 해요.

M: 그렇군요. 그러면… 무엇이 문제인가요?

W: 저는 매주 월요일, 수요일, 그리고 금요일 오전 9시 30분에 있는 영어2 수업에 등록을 했어요. 이 수업은 Greenbrier 홀 304호실에서 진행될 예정이죠. 하지만 제가 오늘 아침에 그곳에 가보니 아무도 강의실에 없더군요. 20분 동안 기다렸지만 아무도 나타나지 않았어요.

M: 교수님이 누구신가요?

W: 음… 확인해 볼게요… Merredith Watson 교수님께서 맡고 계시는군요.

M: 아, 이제 문제를 알겠어요. 학기가 시작하기 전 Watson 교수님에게 개인적인 문제가 생겼어요. 그분의 모든 수업이 취소가 되었죠. 그에 대해 학교로부터 학생이 이메일을 받았어야 하는데요. 받지 못했나요?

W: 못 받은 것 같아요.

M: 흠… 그에 대해서는 유감이에요. 때때로 그런 일들이 일어나죠.

W: 그러면… 제가 어떻게 해야 하나요?

M: 음, 두 가지 선택이 가능해요. 먼저 2학년 가을 학기까지 기다렸다가 영어2 수업을 들을 수 있어요. 아니면 이번 학기에 학생 시간표에 맞는 다른 영어2 수업을 찾아볼 수도 있고요.

W: 후자가 더 낫겠어요.

M: 좋아요. 시간표상 비어 있는 시간이 언제인가요? 영어2의 각 수업은 수강 인원이 15명으로 제한되어 있어요. 안타깝게도 대부분의 수업에 남아 있는 자리가 없군요.

W: 제가 맞춰보죠… 8시 30분에 시작하는 수업에는 남아 있는 자리가 있지만, 다른 수업에는 남아 있는 자리가 없군요.

M: 꼭 그렇지는 않아요. 8시 30분 수업에 대해서는 학생 말이 맞아요. 몇 자리가 남아 있죠. 하지만… 컴퓨터에 의하면 화요일과 목요일 11시 30분에서 1시 사이 수업에 한 자리가 비어 있어요. 학생 시간표에 맞나요?

W: 흠… 화요일과 목요일이요? 아, 네. 그때 빈 시간이 있어요. 두 날 모두 수업이 몇 개 있기는 해요. 그래서 점심을 먹을 수 있는 시간은 많지 않겠지만, 이른 오전 수업보다는 그게 더 나을 것 같아요.

M: 잘 되었군요. 그럼 제가 등록을 해 드릴까요? 그렇게 하기 위해서는 학생의 학생증을 확인해야 해요. 어떻게 생각하나요?

[6-11]

Script 🎧 09-04

W Professor: If everyone is ready, I'll begin today's lecture. Make sure you pay special attention to the diagrams on page 125 of your textbook. I'll try to make this as concise as possible. Here we go. Today, we will discuss the role of fish fins. As is quite apparent, um, the fins are the most distinctive features of fish and certain marine mammals. Let's start with the most visible fin on a fish: the dorsal fin. As we know, dorsal fins are located on the backs of fish, whales, dolphins, and porpoises. Its main purpose is to, ah, stabilize the animal against rolling and to assist in sudden turns. Some animals have developed dorsal fins with protective functions, such as spines and even venom. We also know that dorsal fins come in a variety of shapes and sizes. A fish can have up to three of them depending on the species.

There are two types of dorsal fin rays: spiny and soft. A fin can contain only spiny rays, only soft rays, or a, um, combination. Nearly all types of fish have at least one dorsal fin although there are some exceptions, such as the knife-fish. Many have two or even three fins, or the fin may be a long one that merges with the caudal fin. Now here's a little more about the dorsal fin. In relation to the size of the creature, the dorsal fins of, say, whales, like a male orca, are quite large, as much as 1.8 meters high. The dorsal fins of most other whales are relatively small. The bowhead whale, however, has no dorsal fin at all, as an evolutionary adaptation to its, um, life spent cruising under

icepacks. The dorsal fins of whales develop distinctive nicks and wear patterns with time, and this fact is used by wildlife biologists to identify individuals in the field.

Next we have the tails, or, um, caudal fins of . . . let's use sharks as an example here. These vary considerably between species and are adapted to the lifestyle of the shark. The tail provides thrust, so speed and acceleration are dependent on tail shape. Different tail shapes have evolved in sharks adapted for different environments. The tiger shark's tail has a, how should I put this, yes, a large upper lobe which delivers the maximum amount of power for slow cruising or sudden bursts of speed. The tiger shark has a varied diet, and because of this, it must be able to, um, twist and turn in the water easily when hunting. In general, sharks swim at an average speed of, um, five miles per hour, but when feeding or attacking, the average shark can reach speeds upward of twelve miles per hour. The mako may range up to an incredible thirty-one miles per hour, making the mako one of the fastest fish. That's pretty fast in water by the way. The great white shark is also capable of considerable bursts of speed. Is everyone getting this? I hope so.

On the other hand, some fish may have one or more types of fins missing. An example of a missing fin on many fish is the, ah, right, the adipose fin, which is a soft, fleshy fin found on the back behind the dorsal fin and just forward of the caudal fin. It is absent in many fish families but is found in characins and catfish. Additionally, some types of fast-swimming fish have a, um, horizontal caudal keel just forward of the tail fin that provides stability and support to the caudal fin. Another one of these missing fins is, um, finlets. These are small, rayless, nonretractable fins between the anal fin and the caudal fin. They are found on, ah, fast-swimming fish such as tuna. Anyway, to close this, for every fin, there are a number of fish species in which these particular fins have been lost during evolution. Well, that pretty much wraps up the general uses of fins. Did everyone get that?

해석

W Professor: 모두들 준비가 되었으면 오늘 강의를 시작하도록 할게요. 여러분 교재 125페이지에 있는 도표를 특히 잘 살펴봐 주세요. 최대한 간략하게 설명할게요. 시작합니다. 오늘은 어류의 지느러미의 역할에 대해 논의할 거예요. 당연하게도, 음, 지느러미는 어류와 특정 해양 포유류의 가장 독특한 특징입니다. 어류에서 가장 잘 눈에 띄는 지느러미로 시작해 보죠. 바로 등지느러미입니다. 여러분도 알다시피 등지느러미는 어류, 고래, 돌고래, 그리고 참돌고래의 등에 위치해 있습니다. 등지느러미의 주요 역할은, 어, 물고기가 옆으로 기울어지지 않도록 균형을 잡는 것과 갑작스러운 방향 전환을 돕는 것이에요. 일부 동물들의 경우 가시나 심지어 독선과 같은 보호 장치가 있는 등지느러미가 발달해 있어요. 또한 우리는 등지느러미의 모양과 크기가 다양하다는 점을 알고 있습니다. 어류는 종에 따라 최대 세 개의 등지느러미를 가지고 있을 수 있어요.

등지느러미의 기조로는 두 가지 종류, 즉 극조와 연조가 있습니다. 지느러미에는 극조만 있을 수도 있고, 연조만 있을 수도 있으며, 혹은, 음, 두 개가 함께 있을 수도 있어요. 뒷날개고기와 같은 몇 가지 예외가 있기는 하지만, 거의 모든 어류는 적어도 하나 이상의 등지느러미를 가지고 있습니다. 많은 어류들이 두 개 또는 심지어 세 개의 등지느러미를 가지고 있으며, 혹은 등지느러미와 꼬리지느러미가 합쳐진 하나의 기다란 지느러미를 가지고 있을 수도 있어요. 이제 등지느러미에 관해 조금 더 알려 드리죠. 생물의 몸 크기에 비해, 예컨대 수컷 범고래와 같은 고래의 등지느러미는 크기가 상당히 커서 그 높이가 1.8미터에 이릅니다. 다른 대부분의 고래들의 등지느러미는 비교적 작습니다. 하지만 수염 고래의 경우, 유빙 아래를 유유히 돌아다니는 삶에 진화적 적응이 일어나서 이들에게는 등지느러미가 존재하지 않아요. 고래의 등지느러미에는 시간이 지남에 따라 독특한 자국과 마모 패턴이 생기는데, 야생 생물학자들은 이러한 사실을 이용해 현장의 고래들을 식별합니다.

다음으로는 꼬리, 또는, 음, 꼬리지느러미에 대해… 여기에서는 상어를 예로 들어 보죠. 꼬리지느러미는 종에 따라 매우 다양하며, 상어의 생활 방식에 맞게 발달해 왔습니다. 꼬리가 추진력을 제공해 주기 때문에 속도와 가속은 꼬리의 형태에 달려 있어요. 다양한 환경에 적합하도록 상어의 꼬리 형태는 다양하게 진화해 왔습니다. 뱀상어의 꼬리에는, 어떻게 얘기해야 할까요, 그래요, 느린 순항이나 빠른 가속을 위해 최대한의 힘을 전달해 주는 커다란 상엽이 있어요. 뱀상어는 다양한 먹이를 섭취하며, 이러한 점 때문에, 사냥을 하는 경우, 음, 물속에서 쉽게 몸을 비틀고 방향을 전환할 수 있어야 하죠. 보통 상어는 평균적으로, 음, 시속 5마일의 속도를 내지만, 먹이를 잡거나 공격을 할 때에는 평균적인 상어의 경우 시속 12마일 이상의 속도를 낼 수가 있어요. 청상아리는 최대 시속 31마일이라는 놀라운 속도를 낼 수도 있는데, 이러한 점 때문에 청상아리는 가장 빠른 어류에 속합니다. 물속에서는 상당히 빠른 속도죠. 백상어 역시 엄청난 속도를 낼 수 있어요. 모두 이해되시죠? 그렇기를 바랍니다.

반면에 일부 어류들의 경우 한 개 혹은 그 이상의 지느러미가 사라져 있는 경우도 있습니다. 많은 어류에서 사라진 지느러미의 예로, 아, 그래요, 기름지느러미가 있는데, 이 지느러미는 부드러우며, 살로 이루어져 있고, 등지느러미 뒤쪽과 꼬리지느러미 바로 앞에서 있습니다. 많은 어류 과에는 없지만 카라신과 메기에서 이를 찾아볼 수 있어요. 또한 헤엄치는 속도가 빠른 일부 어류들은, 음, 꼬리지느러미 바로 앞쪽에 수평용골돌기를 가지고 있는데, 이 수평용골돌기는 꼬리지느러미에 안정성을 가져다 주고 이를 지탱해 줍니다. 사라진 지느러미의 또 다른 예는, 음, 부지느러미입니다. 이들은 작고, 기조를 가지고 있지 않으며, 안으로 접히지 않는 지느러미로, 뒷지느러미와 꼬리지느러미 사이에 있습니다. 이는, 아, 참치처럼 빠르게 헤엄치는 어류에서 찾아볼 수 있어요. 어쨌든, 마무리하자면, 많은 어류 종들의 이러한 지느러미들은 진화 과정에서 사라졌습니다. 음, 지느러미의 일반적인 역할에 대해서는 이 정도로 마무리할게요. 다들 이해하셨나요?

PART 2

[1-5]

Script 🎧 09-06

M Professor: Hello, Candice. You're just the person I wanted to see. Do you have a few moments to talk to me?

W Student: Uh, sure, Professor Rodriguez. Is there something I can do for you?

M: As a matter of fact, there may be.

W: Okay.

M: Are you very busy this semester? What are your classes like, and are you doing any part-time work?

W: Hmm . . . I'm taking five classes this semester. But I arranged my schedule so that I only have class from

---

Monday to Thursday. And all of my classes end by three in the afternoon.

M: What about work?

W: This will be the third straight year that I work at the circulation desk at the library. I'm working twelve hours a week this semester. I've got shifts on Thursday evening as well as on Saturday and Sunday afternoon.

M: It sounds like you're keeping yourself busy, but, uh, you're not totally overworked.

W: I guess you could say that. I got all A's on my midterm exams, so the semester is going pretty well so far.

M: I'm very pleased to hear that. Do you remember my introduction to astronomy class that you took one year ago?

W: Of course, I do. That was one of my favorite classes.

M: Thanks for saying that. I recall that your grade in the class was a ninety-nine. That was the best grade in that class in more than a decade. I was extremely pleased with your performance in that class.

W: Thank you for saying that, sir. I really enjoyed the class. I wish that the school had more astronomy classes for me to take. As far as I know, that's the only one available.

M: You're right about that. But I'm glad that you are interested in astronomy because I have a proposal for you. You see, uh, many of the students in my class this semester did poorly on the midterm exam. I'd say around half of the class got a C or worse on the exam. They just don't seem to understand the material.

W: I'm really sorry to hear that.

M: So am I. So, uh, I wonder if you would be interested in leading a study group for the students. Basically, you could meet with them for one hour two times a week. You would go over the material that I cover in the class. And you would answer their questions. This is, of course, a paid position. I can give you twenty dollars an hour. The department authorized me to spend that amount.

W: Wow. That's a really appealing offer. And the payment is extremely generous. I would be pleased to do that for you.

M: Thank you so much for saying yes. Now, uh, why don't we look at your schedule? Then, we can figure out which two days are the best to have the study sessions.

해석

M Professor: 안녕하세요, Candice. 만나고 싶었어요. 잠시 저하고 이야기할 시간이 있나요?

W Student: 어, 그럼요, Rodriguez 교수님. 제가 도와 드릴 일이라도 있나요?

M: 실은 그런 것 같아요.

W: 좋습니다.

M: 이번 학기에 많이 바쁜가요? 수업은 어떻고, 혹시 아르바이트를 하고 있나요?

W: 흠… 저는 이번 학기에 5개의 수업을 듣고 있어요. 하지만 월요일부터 목요일

까지만 수업이 있도록 시간표를 짰죠. 그리고 제 수업은 모두 오후 3시에 끝나요.

M: 아르바이트는요?

W: 3년 연속으로 도서관의 대출대에서 일하게 될 거예요. 이번 학기에는 일주일에 12시간을 근무하고 있죠. 근무 시간은 목요일 저녁과 토요일 및 일요일 오후에 잡혀 있고요.

M: 바쁘지만, 어, 일이 완전히 많은 것처럼 들리지는 않군요.

W: 그런 것 같아요. 전과목 중간고사에서 A를 받았기 때문에 지금까지는 학기를 잘 보내고 있죠.

M: 그런 이야기를 들으니 기분이 매우 좋군요. 학생이 1년 전에 들었던 제 천문학 개론 수업을 기억하나요?

W: 물론 기억하죠. 제가 가장 좋아하는 수업 중 하나였어요.

M: 그렇게 말해 주니 고맙네요. 그 수업에서 학생의 성적이 99점이었던 것으로 기억해요. 10년 이상에 걸쳐 해당 수업에서의 최고 성적이었죠. 학생의 수업 성적 때문에 정말로 기분이 좋았어요.

W: 그렇게 말씀해 주시니 고맙습니다, 교수님. 정말로 그 수업이 좋았거든요. 학교에서 제가 들을 수 있는 천문학 수업을 더 많이 제공해 주면 좋을 것 같아요. 제가 알기로는 들을 수 있는 수업이 하나뿐이라서요.

M: 맞아요. 하지만 학생이 천문학에 관심이 있다니 다행인데, 학생에게 제안할 것이 하나 있어요. 그러니까, 어, 제 이번 학기 수업의 많은 학생들이 중간고사를 잘 보지 못했어요. 약 절반 정도의 학생들이 시험에서 C 이하의 성적을 받았다고 말해야 할 것 같군요. 수업 내용을 이해하지 못하는 것처럼 보여요.

W: 그런 말을 들으니 정말 유감이에요.

M: 저도 그래요. 그래서, 어, 학생이 학생들의 스터디 그룹을 맡는데 관심이 있을지 궁금해요. 기본적으로 학생은 일주일에 두번씩 한 시간 동안 학생들과 만나게 될 거예요. 제가 수업에서 다루는 내용을 학습하게 될 것이고요. 그리고 그들의 질문에도 답을 해 줘야 하죠. 이 일은, 물론, 보수가 지급되는 일이에요. 시간당 20달러를 지급할 수 있어요. 학과에서 그 정도 비용을 쓸 수 있도록 허가해 주었어요.

W: 와. 정말로 매력적인 제안이군요. 그리고 보수도 정말 많은 편이고요. 기꺼이 그렇게 하도록 하겠습니다.

M: 수락해 줘서 고마워요. 자, 어, 학생의 시간표를 볼까요? 그러면 스터디 날짜로 어떤 2일이 가장 적합할지 알 수 있을 거예요.

[6-11]

Script 🎧 09-07

W Professor: Good morning, everyone. It's good to see you all wide awake. Please remember to skim over those notes on bald eagle habitats because I'm really going to rack your brains on that topic on the midterm exam. Okay. In this lecture, I will complete our section on migratory birds with a rundown of the hummingbird's migratory traits.

To begin, the migratory habits of hummingbirds are not well documented by large numbers of banding records, but we do know a few facts, and we can draw logical conclusions about some of the, um, unknown areas. For those of you that may have forgotten, um, banding means the trapping of a bird and the wrapping of a tiny numbered strip of aluminum around one leg. This is currently the only way to identify individual hummingbirds.

Species are studied by, ah, gathering data on large numbers of individuals. So this lecture will focus on ruby-throated hummingbird migration because it's likely that more people see this species than all the others in North America combined. As I mentioned in the last class, hummingbirds are found only in the Americas from southern Alaska and Canada to Tierra del Fuego in South America as well as in the West Indies. The majority of species reside in tropical Central and South America, but several species also breed in temperate areas.

Well, um, let me give you a little more background here. Most hummingbirds in the U.S. and Canada migrate to warmer climates in the northern winter, but some remain in the warmest coastal regions. Some southern South American species also move to the tropics. These amazing birds, the world's smallest, have a heartbeat that can beat as high as 1,260 times per minute. That's fast! They also typically consume more than their own weight in food each day, and to do that they have to visit hundreds of flowers daily. And if that isn't enough, they also enter a hibernation-like state known as torpor. During torpor, the heart rate and the rate of breathing are both slowed dramatically. In fact, the heart rate drops to roughly fifty from one hundred eighty beats per minute, reducing their need for food. So as you can see, these birds are very good at conserving energy when they need to.

Now, recent banding studies suggest that individual birds may follow a set route year after year. It's not known if any, um, individual bird follows the same route in both directions, and there are some indications that they do not. Other studies, including a study of the hummingbird's metabolism, are highly relevant to the question of whether a migrating ruby-throated hummingbird can cross 500 miles of the Gulf of Mexico on a nonstop flight, as field observations suggest it does.

Most ruby-throated hummingbirds winter between southern Mexico and northern Panama. Since hummingbirds lead solitary lives, they neither live nor migrate in flocks. For example, an individual bird may spend the winter anywhere in this range where the habitat is favorable, and, um, it probably returns to the same location each winter. Ruby-throated hummingbirds begin moving north as early as January, and by the end of February, they are at the northern coast of the Yucatan Peninsula, gorging on insects and spiders to add a thick layer of fat in preparation for flying to the U.S. Some skirt the Gulf of Mexico and follow the Texas coast north while most, um, apparently cross the gulf, typically leaving at dusk for a nonstop flight of up to 500 miles, which takes eighteen to twenty-two hours depending on the weather.

Interestingly, hummingbirds may fly over water in company of mixed flocks of other bird species. It's also possible that a few of them island-hop across the Caribbean and enter the U.S. through the Florida Keys. Males depart the Yucatan first, followed about ten days later by the first females. Since the migration is spread over a three-month period, this prevents catastrophic weather events from wiping out the entire species. Once in North America, migration proceeds at an average rate of about twenty miles per day, generally following the earliest blooming flowers that hummingbirds prefer.

Hummingbirds really do travel great distances. For example, they travel as far as Canada, where ruby-throated hummingbirds are seen on a regular basis from central and southern Alberta to Nova Scotia. They arrive in May or early June and depart in August or early September. Additionally, the migratory ruby-throated hummingbird is the only hummingbird that breeds in the eastern part of North America. Let me close this by saying that, um, we still have many more questions than answers about hummingbird migration. Until technology provides radio transmitters small enough for a three-gram hummingbird to carry safely, banding is the best tool to collect data on individual birds.

해석

W Professor: 좋은 아침이에요, 여러분. 모두들 잠에서 완전히 깨어 있는 모습을 보니 좋군요. 중간고사 때 해당 주제에 대해 여러분들의 머리를 쥐어짜내게 될 테니 흰머리독수리의 서식지에 대한 필기를 잊지 말고 살펴보시길 바랍니다. 좋아요. 이번 수업에서는 이동과 관련된 벌새의 특성을 설명함으로써 철새와 관련된 부분을 마무리하도록 하죠.

우선, 벌새의 이동 습성이 다수의 밴딩 기록에 의해 잘 문서화되어 있지는 않지만, 우리는 몇 가지 사실을 알고 있으며, 음, 일부 미지의 영역에 대해서는 논리적인 결론을 도출해 낼 수가 있어요. 어, 혹시 잊어 버린 학생들을 위해 이야기하면, 음, 밴딩이란 새를 잡아서 새 다리에 숫자가 적힌 작고 가느다란 알루미늄 띠를 두르는 것입니다. 현재로서는 이것이 각각의 벌새를 식별할 수 있는 유일한 방법이에요. 여러 개체들의 데이터를, 어, 수집함으로써 종에 대한 연구가 이루어집니다. 따라서 이번 강의는 붉은가슴벌새의 이동에 초점을 맞출 것인데, 그 이유는 북아메리카에서 많은 사람들이 다른 모든 종을 합친 것보다 이 종을 보게 될 가능성이 더 높기 때문입니다. 지난 수업에서 언급한 것처럼, 벌새는 알래스카 남부와 캐나다에서부터 남아메리카의 티에라 델 푸에고 및 서인도 제도까지의 아메리카 대륙에서만 찾아볼 수 있어요. 대다수의 종은 열대의 중앙아메리카와 남아메리카에서 서식하지만, 몇몇 종은 온대 지역에서 번식을 합니다.

그럼, 음, 약간의 배경 지식을 알려 드릴게요. 미국과 캐나다에 사는 대부분의 벌새는 북쪽에 겨울이 찾아보면 보다 따뜻한 곳으로 이동하지만, 가장 따뜻한 해안가 지역에서 계속 지내는 벌새들도 있습니다. 또한 남쪽의 남아메리카에 사는 일부 종들은 열대 지방으로 이동을 해요. 세상에서 가장 작은 이 놀라운 새들의 심박수는 분당 1,260회에 이를 수도 있습니다. 정말 빠르죠! 또한 하루에 자신의 몸무게를 뛰어넘는 양의 먹이를 섭취하는데, 그렇게 하기 위해서는 매일 수백 송이의 꽃을 찾아 다녀야 합니다. 이것으로도 충분하지 않은 경우에는 휴면 상태라고 알려진 동면과 비슷한 상태에 들어갑니다. 휴면 상태에서는 심박수와 호흡률 모두가 급격히 줄어들어요. 실제로 심박수가 분당 50회에서 180회까지 떨어지는데, 이로써 음식을 섭취할 필요성이 줄어듭니다. 따라서 여러분도 알 수 있듯

이 이 새들은 필요한 경우에 매우 효과적으로 에너지를 보존합니다.

자, 최근의 밴딩 연구에 따르면 각 개체들은 해마다 정해진 경로를 따릅니다. 갈 때와 올 때 모두 같은 경로를 따라 이동하는 개체가 있는지는 밝혀지지 않았으며, 이들이 같은 경로를 따르지 않는다는 증거들은 있습니다. 벌새의 신진대사에 관한 연구를 포함하여, 이동 중인 붉은가슴벌새들이 500킬로미터에 이르는 멕시코만을 쉬지 않고 비행할 수 있는지와 관련된 연구들도 있는데, 현장 관측의 결과 이는 가능한 일로 생각됩니다.

대부분의 붉은가슴벌새는 멕시코 남부와 파나마 북부 사이의 지역에서 겨울을 납니다. 벌새는 혼자서 지내기 때문에 무리를 지어 살거나 이동하지 않죠. 예를 들어 벌새 한 마리는 환경이 좋은 그러한 지역 중 한곳에서 겨울을 날 수도 있는데, 음, 그러면 아마도 겨울마다 같은 장소로 돌아오게 될 것입니다. 붉은가슴벌새는 1월에 북쪽으로 이동하기 시작해서 2월 말쯤 유카탄 반도의 북쪽 해안가에 도달하게 되는데, 이때 곤충과 거미를 잡아먹고 두꺼운 지방층을 형성하면서 미국으로 가기 위한 준비를 합니다. 일부는 멕시코만을 돌아서 북쪽으로 텍사스 해안을 따라가지만, 음, 대부분은 분명 멕시코만을 가로질러 가는데, 이들은 보통 황혼 무렵에 출발을 해서 최고 800킬로미터에 이르는 무착륙 비행을 하고, 이러한 비행에는 날씨에 따라 18일에서 22일까지의 시간이 소요되죠.

흥미롭게도 벌새들은 다른 종의 새들과 섞여 떼를 이루면서 물 위를 비행할 수도 있어요. 또한 그들 중 소수는 섬에서 섬으로 이동하면서 카리브해를 가로질러 플로리다 키스를 통해 미국으로 들어갈 수도 있죠. 수컷들이 먼저 유카탄을 출발하고 약 10일 후 암컷들이 그 뒤를 따라갑니다. 이동은 3개월에 걸쳐 진행되는데, 이로써 악천후로 인해 종 전체가 사라지는 경우를 예방할 수 있어요. 일단 북아메리카에 들어오면, 벌새의 이동 속도는 하루 평균 약 32킬로의 속도가 되는데, 보통 이는 벌새가 좋아하는, 가장 먼저 개화하는 꽃들의 속도에 맞춰진 것이에요.

벌새들은 정말로 엄청난 거리를 이동해요. 예를 들어 캐나다까지 이동하기도 하는데, 캐나다에서는 알버타 중남부에서부터 노바 스코샤까지 벌새들이 고르게 관찰됩니다. 이들은 5월이나 6월 초에 도착을 해서 8월이나 9월 초에 떠납니다. 또한 이동하는 붉은가슴벌새는 북아메리카의 동부 지역에서 번식하는 유일한 벌새예요. 이에 대해서는, 음, 우리가 벌새의 이동에 관한 답보다 질문이 더 많다는 점을 이야기함으로써 마무리하고자 합니다. 몸무게가 3그램인 작은 벌새들이 안전하게 지니고 다닐 수 있는 충분히 작은 무선 송신기가 개발될 때까지는 밴딩이 각각의 새들에 관한 자료를 수집할 수 있는 최선의 방법이에요.

[12-17]

Script 🎧 09-08

M1 Professor: Good day! I hope everyone is ready for today's discussion. I'd like to get into the specifics on the different kinds of attachments developed between babies and mothers. So if you're ready, let's begin. As has already been mentioned in this class, the maternal bond is typically the relationship between a mother and her child. There are hundreds of factors, both physical and emotional, which influence the mother–infant bonding process. Bonding is a gradual experience that can take hours, days, weeks, or even months to evolve.

M2 Student: Um, Professor Snell, could you tell us when this relationship actually begins?

M1: Generally speaking, the maternal bond between a woman and her biological child usually begins to develop during pregnancy. From around, umm, eighteen weeks, the mother can begin to feel the fetus, or unborn child, moving, which can enhance bonding. The bond also strengthens when the mother can see her baby during an ultrasound scan. The developing fetus, um, hears the mother's heartbeat and voice and may respond to touch or movement. By the seventh month of pregnancy, two-thirds of women report a strong, maternal bond.

W Student: So, ah, you are saying that childbirth is the main positive bond between mother and child?

M1: Well, the process of childbirth greatly adds to this bond, but that is not always the case, as we all know that every birth and every mother is unique. For example, um, situational factors may include a traumatic birth, the pregnant woman's own mother's parenting style, experienced stress, social support, and the influence of the partner. It is also thought that babies and children emit a scent which makes many adults want to take care of them on instinct.

M2: Well, what other kinds of things cause the baby and mother to bond?

M1: Here's what we know. Newborns can feel many different sensations, but they respond most enthusiastically to soft stroking, cuddling, and caressing. For example, gentle rocking back and forth will oftentimes calm a crying baby as will massages and warm baths. Newborns may comfort themselves by sucking their thumb or a pacifier. The need to suckle is instinctive and allows newborns to feed.

W: Are there any other ways babies identify with their mothers?

M1: Well, newborn infants have pretty bad vision, being able to focus on objects only about, um, about eighteen inches directly in front of their face. While this may not be much, it is all that is needed for the infant to look at the mother's face when breastfeeding. A newborn has a developed sense of smell at birth, and within the first week of life can already distinguish the differences between the mother's own breast milk and the breast milk of another female.

M2: Excuse me. What about breastfeeding? I would have thought that it is the major way that babies and mothers bond.

M1: I was just getting to that. Um, breastfeeding is also strongly believed to foster the early maternal bond, via touch, response, and mutual gazing. However, this is not always the case, especially if the mother is experiencing some common problem of breastfeeding. Many believe that early bonding, like touching, ideally increases the response and sensitivity to the child's needs, further cementing the quality of the mother-baby relationship.

W: Are there any instances when the baby-mother bond is weak or nonexistent?

M1: Of course! Do you remember the emotional Velcro bonding theory that we discussed last class? Well, when it first appeared in the mid-1970s, the bonding process was analyzed to the point of creating another term: poor bonding. Now, this can occur because of a couple of well-known reasons. As we all know, childbirth can be a stressful event. Some women report symptoms compatible with post-traumatic stress disorder after birth. Between seventy and eighty percent of mothers in the United States report some feelings of sadness or "baby blues" after childbirth. This can last quite a long time.

W: You said there were other reasons?

M1: Yes, there are others, but the most important one is colic. Colic, which is a terrible pain many babies feel in their bowels, can place an enormous strain on parents and other family members. The feeling that, um, they are not providing something their child desperately wants or needs can induce stress, depression, feelings of helplessness, and low self-esteem. If crying is prevalent during nighttime hours, then these problems can be aggravated by sleep loss. Exhaustion may also result. **Many first-time mothers experience this, and it can lead to a long-term dysfunctional relationship between certain mothers and their children.**

해석

M1 Professor: 안녕하세요! 오늘 수업에 대한 준비가 모두들 다 잘 되어 있기를 바랍니다. 아기와 엄마 사이에서 형성되는 다양한 종류의 애정에 대해 구체적으로 살펴보고자 해요. 준비가 되었으면 시작해 보죠. 이번 수업에서 이미 언급했던 것처럼, 모성 유대는 일반적으로 엄마와 아기 사이의 관계입니다. 엄마와 유아와의 유대감 형성 과정에 영향을 미치는 육체적 및 감정적 요인들은 수백 개에 달하죠. 유대감 형성은 수 시간, 수 일, 수 주, 혹은 심지어 수 개월에 걸쳐 일어날 수 있는 점진적인 경험이에요.

M2 Student: 음, Snell 교수님, 그러한 관계가 실제로 언제 시작되는지 말씀해 주시겠어요?

M1: 일반적으로 말하면, 엄마와 생물학적 자식 사이의 모성 유대는 보통 임신 기간 중에 형성되기 시작해요. 대략, 음, 18주부터 엄마는 태아, 즉 아직 태어나지 않은 자식이 움직이는 것을 느낄 수 있는데, 이로써 유대감이 강화될 수 있습니다. 또한 초음파 검사를 통해 아기의 모습을 들을 때에도 유대감이 강화되고요. 발달 중인 태아는, 음, 엄마의 심장 박동 소리와 목소리를 들으면서 손길이나 움직임에 반응을 보일 수도 있어요. 임신 7개월이 되면 여성의 3분의 2가 강한 모성 유대를 느낀다고 합니다.

W Student: 그러니까, 어, 출산으로 인해 주로 엄마와 자식 간에 긍정적인 유대감이 생긴다는 말씀이시죠?

M1: 음, 출산 과정이 이러한 유대감을 증가시키기는 하지만, 모든 출산과 모든 엄마가 유일하다는 점을 우리 모두 알고 있기 때문에, 항상 그런 것은 아니에요. 예를 들어, 음, 상황적 요인으로 정신적인 충격을 동반한 출산, 산모 어머니의 양육 방식, 스트레스 경험, 사회적 지원, 그리고 배우자의 영향이 포함될 수 있습니다. 또한 아기들과 아이들은 본능적으로 여러 성인들이 자기들을 돌보고 싶게 만드는 냄새를 발산한다고도 생각되고 있어요.

M2: 음, 아기와 엄마 사이의 유대감을 형성시키는 또 다른 요인들은 무엇인가요?

M1: 알려진 바를 말씀드리죠. 신생아는 여러 다양한 감각을 느낄 수 있지만, 부

드럽게 쓰다듬고, 껴안고, 그리고 쓰다듬는 것에 가장 적극적으로 반응합니다. 예를 들어 부드럽게 아이를 앞뒤로 흔들어 주면 울던 아이도 울음을 그치는 경우가 많은데, 마사지나 온수 목욕을 해 주는 경우도 마찬가지입니다. 신생아들은 손가락이나 고무 젖꼭지를 빨면서 편안함을 느낄 수도 있어요. 입으로 빠는 욕구는 본능적인 것으로, 신생아들이 음식을 먹도록 만들죠.

W: 아기가 엄마를 알아보는 다른 방법들도 있나요?

M1: 음, 신생아들은 시력이 나빠서 얼굴 바로 앞의, 음, 약 18인치 앞에 있는 물체에만 초점을 맞출 수 있어요. 얼마 안 되는 거리지만, 수유 시 아기가 엄마를 쳐다보기에는 충분한 거리입니다. 신생아는 출생 시 후각이 발달해 있어서 생후 1주일 내에 벌써 엄마의 젖과 다른 여성의 젖을 구별할 수 있어요.

M2: 죄송합니다. 수유는 어떤가요? 수유가 아기와 엄마 사이의 유대감을 형성시키는 주된 방법이라고 생각했거든요.

M1: 그 얘기를 하려던 참이었어요. 음, 손길, 반응, 그리고 상호 응시를 통해 수유하는 과정에서도 초기의 모성 유대가 형성된다고 널리 알려져 있습니다. 하지만 꼭 그런 것은 아닌데, 특히 엄마가 수유와 관련된 일반적인 문제를 겪고 있는 경우에는 그렇지가 않죠. 많은 사람들은 터치와 같은 초기의 유대감 형성 행위로 인해 아이에 욕구에 대한 반응성과 민감도가 이상적으로 증가해서 엄마와 아기 사이의 관계가 공고해진다고 생각합니다.

W: 엄마와 아기 사이의 유대감이 약하거나 아예 존재하지 않는 경우도 있나요?

M1: 물론이죠! 지난 시간에 논의했던 정서적 벨크로 유대 이론을 기억하세요. 음, 1970년대 중반 이 이론이 처음 등장했을 때, 유대 과정에 대한 분석이 이루어졌고, 그 결과 유대감 부족이라는 용어가 만들어지기도 했죠. 자, 이러한 일은 두 가지 잘 알려진 이유로 일어날 수 있어요. 다들 아시다시피 출산으로 인해 많은 스트레스를 받을 수 있습니다. 일부 여성들은 출산 이후에 외상 후 스트레스 장애와 비슷한 증상을 겪는다고 보고되고 있어요. 미국 내 산모의 70%에서 80%가 출산 후 슬픔 감정이나 "산후 우울증"을 경험하는 것으로 보고되고 있죠. 이는 꽤 오랫동안 지속될 수 있어요.

W: 다른 이유도 있다고 하지 않으셨나요?

M1: 네, 다른 이유들도 있지만 가장 중요한 것은 배앓이입니다. 배앓이는 많은 아기들이 경험하는 장의 극심한 통증을 말하는데, 이는 부모 및 기타 가족들을 크게 긴장시킬 수 있습니다. 자신들이, 음, 아이가 절실히 원하는 것, 혹은 필요로 하는 것을 제공해 주지 못한다는 생각에서 스트레스, 우울함, 무기력감, 그리고 자책감을 느낄 수가 있어요. 밤에 아기가 우는 경우가 잦으면 수면 부족으로 인해서 그러한 문제들이 악화될 수 있습니다. 그 결과 극심한 피로가 찾아올 수도 있고요. 첫 아이를 출산한 많은 엄마들이 이를 경험하고 있고, 이로 인해 특정 엄마들과 아기 사이의 장기적인 관계에 문제가 생길 수도 있습니다.

How to
Master Skills for the

TOEFL® iBT
LISTENING   Basic